Second Edition

INFORMATION SYSTEMS SERIES

Consulting Editors

D. E. Avison BA, Msc, PhD, FBCS
Professor of Information Systems
Department of Accounting
and Management Science,
Southampton University, UK

G. Fitzgerald BA, Msc, MBCS
Cable & Wireless Professor of
Business Information Systems,
Department of Computer Science,
Birkbeck College, University of London, UK

This series of student and postgraduate texts covers a wide variety of topics relating to information systems. It is designed to fulfil the needs of the growing number of courses on, and interest in, computing and information systems which do not focus on the purely technological aspects, but seek to relate these to business and organisational context.

Second Edition

David Benyon
Professor of Human–Computer Systems
Napier University
Edinburgh
UK

The McGraw-Hill Companies

London · New York · St Louis · San Francisco · Auckland · Bogotá ·
Caracas ·Lisbon · Madrid · Milan · Montreal · New Delhi · Panama · Paris ·
San Juan · São Paulo · Singapore · Sydney · Tokyo · Toronto

Published by
McGraw-Hill Publishing Company
Shoppenhangers Road, Maidenhead, Berkshire, SL6 2QL, England
Telephone 01682 23432
Facsimile 01628 770224

British Library Cataloguing in Publication Data
The CIP data of this title is available from the British Library, UK

Library of Congress Cataloging-in-Publication Data
The CIP data of this title is available from the Library of Congress,
Washington DC, USA

ISBN 0–07–709241–4

McGraw-Hill

A Division of The McGraw-Hill Companies

1234 BL 9876

Typeset by David Benyon and printed and bound by Biddles Ltd,
Guildford, Surrey.

Printed on permanent paper in compliance with ISO Standard 9706

For my Mother

and

in memory of my Father

... . of information systems at universities. The two major changes which have occurred in information systems are (i) the emergence of SQL as the standard relational database language and (ii) the development of object-oriented techniques for information system analysis and design. Accordingly, this edition includes a new chapter on each of these. The changes in the teaching of information systems has encouraged me to completely reorganise the book, taking it from the nine chapters of the first edition to the sixteen chapters of the current edition. This reorganisation has been prompted in part by the movement towards semester based courses lasting between twelve and fifteen weeks, but it also helps to bring the main principles to the foreground. The material is now organised so that one chapter should take about one week, or five to six hours, to study. Each chapter includes clear objectives, a summary of the key points and an annotated section of further reading.

Whilst making these changes, I have been careful not to lose sight of the unique contribution which this text makes to information systems and database design. Most books on database systems still focus on the implementation of databases. This text focuses on design and on understanding the key theoretical underpinnings of information systems. It therefore complements other texts, perhaps forming the basis of a half year second or third year undergraduate course, which would be followed by a half year on implementation. It could be used on a conversion MSc course, or on an information systems MBA and is suitable for students of computing, business or management.

The non-technical orientation of the text proved popular with the first edition and has been retained in this edition. Readers require no previous knowledge of computers and there is little reference to programming or to the internal workings of computers. The text deals with the fundamental issues of how to organise data so that it can be used to produce reliable and accurate information. These issues are as relevant for an individual developing a database for personal use as they are for a large corporation developing a complete management information system. It is all too easy to sit down with a modern database system and create a database. But unless the design of the database is properly formulated, it will soon become inaccurate and inconsistent.

Understanding the requirements for information and the structure of the data in an application can prevent the spiral into chaos which is all too familiar in poorly designed database systems.

Information and Data Modelling begins by considering the nature of information and how it can be produced from data. Information and data are valuable resources for any organisation and therefore need to be managed effectively. In chapters 3 and 4, the main issues concerned with managing the information resource are considered. Chapter 5 is a pivotal chapter in the book. In order to understand and design any complex system, we develop models — simplified representations of the system which highlight the important aspects for the purpose at hand. The main models and modelling methods for information systems are introduced and discussed. These include all the main representations used in the structured methods of analysis and design and places these alongside the models used in object-oriented systems. The basic computer structures which need to be understood are presented in chapter 6.

The next five chapters deal with the relational model and the process of normalisation. The importance of the relational model cannot be over emphasised and it is quite appropriate to spend five chapters dealing with it. Even with the advent of object-oriented approaches to information systems development, normalisation of data is critical. Relational databases still represent the prevailing technology for implementing information systems. However, normalisation is important not just because it leads to the design of relational databases; it is vital to understanding the meaning of data.

SQL is covered in chapter 8 where it is used to illustrate how relational databases can be manipulated. Chapters 12 to 14 deal with the entity-relationship (E-R) model — a graphically based technique for database design which complements the relational model, and which is more appropriate for the design of whole databases. Chapter 15 shows how the various models can be used together to represent the information requirements of an organisation. The final chapter, chapter 16, looks at object-oriented information systems and at how the relational and object-oriented can be brought together.

Some people reading the above description of this book will be thinking that the content looks old fashioned. Why doesn't he talk about object-oriented design methods more? Why doesn't he mention graphical user interfaces or client–server architectures? Surely relational databases are on their way out? The answer to these questions is that the content of this book is far more fundamental than these passing flavours of the computer industry. The purpose of this book is to show that, far from being out of date, the need to understand data and information is even

... geographical information systems. Others say that the process of normalising the model is too complex or not relevant, or complain that the theory underlying of relational database design is too obscure. Others argue that the design does not adequately reflect the concerns of the users of the database. As a result relational database systems have developed, and information system design methods have been produced, which try to simplify things and try to make relational products more amenable to developers and users alike. This unfortunate state of affairs means that the benefits of relational theory are still not available to system developers.

Many of these criticisms have arisen because researchers and practitioners have failed to understand the difference between the conceptual issues concerned with understanding the relationships between data and the implementation issues concerned with organising data on a computer and presenting data to people. In this text, the focus is on the conceptual issues. How the database is implemented is an important aspect of database development. But how it is designed is, in the first part, independent of the implementation. The relational model helps us to understand the meaning of data. Once the designer understands what people mean by some data and what they want to do with that data then decisions can be taken as to how to implement the system. The techniques presented in these chapters are as relevant for a system which is to be implemented in a purely paper-based system as they are for implementations using object-oriented systems or one of the modern database systems.

Indeed understanding data is essential for any systems development. These days, it is somewhat disturbing to see many of the pitfalls being repeated which the relational model sought to overcome. The rise of object-oriented methods of analysis and design encourages developers to look for objects in the 'real world' which users are interested in and to develop systems which reflect those objects. Methods arising from the human-computer interaction (HCI) community encourage developers to focus on the tasks which users perform and to base their designs on these tasks. Both of these approaches are flawed if they fail to understand and consider the nature of the data in a system. The data-centred emphasis of the methods developed in the late 1970s — which include the relational model, the entity-relationship model and dataflow modelling — arose because of the frustrations caused by computer systems which reflected the objects and processes in the existing world. Developing computer systems allows us to escape the restrictions of current systems. We do not want to instantiate current methods of working in future systems. We need to have methods which allow us to abstract from current activities and which provide the freedom to explore the possibilities offered by carefully structured, data-centred representation of the organisation and its information requirements. The relational model allows us to do just that.

It is certainly true that a system designer cannot sit down with the users or owners of a system and show them a relational model to check that the information requirements have been correctly understood. This is why we need a more user-oriented model, the entity-relationship (E-R) model. The E-R model is just as important as the relational model. Indeed the two need to developed together. However, because it is a graphical model, the E-R model encourages the designer to think about the inherent structure of an information system and to explore various alternative representations. E-R modelling is central to all structured methods of information systems development and is used in many object-oriented methods. It can also be used to look at how information is displayed to users. E-R models provide a map of the information system. In this book we examine only the map provided by a database design. However, Thomas Green of the Medical Research Council's Applied Psychology Unit in Cambridge, suggested that E-R models could prove effective at dealing with how information is displayed as well as how it is structured in a database. The resulting extension to the E-R model, known as Entity-Relationship Modelling of Information Artefacts (ERMIA; see Green and Benyon, 1996 or Bental, Benyon and Green, 1997) allows designers to focus on user-centred design issues and the fundamental concerns of how people navigate their way through information structures and the difficulties which they may experience in trying to work out what they can do and how they should do it. Related to this is an approach to developing user-centred systems which adopts a data-centred approach (see Benyon, 1995, 1996).

Another important aspect of the debate about the utility of entity-relationship models is whether they should be considered from an objectivist position — that entities exist in the world to be discovered by analysts — or from a subjectivist position — that entity-relationship models are a subjective representation of a perceived situation. The books by Lewis (1994) and by Hirschheim, Klein and Lyytinen (1995) bring these issues to the fore. My view is certainly subjectivist; information system designers need to work with the users of systems in order to understand *their* needs and the things which *they* perceive to be important. The entity-relationship model and the subsequent database

... this book to deal with all the issues concerned with data-centred design and with the wider concerns of data modelling, I hope that the book can be read by students and researchers coming from other communities — such as the HCI community. A detailed treatment of the philosophy and impact of data-centred design will have to wait for another book. In the meantime *Information and Data Modelling* provides an accessible introduction to the importance of data to organisations and how that data can be understood.

David Benyon

Napier University, Edinburgh

on information systems and computing which do not focus on purely technical aspects but which seek to relate information systems to their commercial and organisational context.

The term 'information systems' has been defined as the effective design, delivery, use and impact of information technology in organisations and society. Utilising this broad definition it is clear that the subject is interdisciplinary. Thus the series seeks to integrate technological disciplines with management and other disciplines, for example, psychology and sociology. These areas do not have a natural home and were until comparatively recently, rarely represented by single departments in universities and colleges. To put such books in a purely computer science or management series restricts potential readership and the benefits that such texts can provide. The series on information systems provides such a home.

Although mainly for student use, certain topics are more research oriented for postgraduate study. The series includes: information systems development methodologies, office information systems, management information systems, decision–support systems, information modelling and databases, systems theory, human aspects and the human–computer interface, application systems, technology strategy, planning and control, expert systems, knowledge acquisition and its representation.

A mention of the books so far published in the series gives a 'flavour' of the richness of the information systems world. *Information Systems Development: Methodologies, Techniques and Tools, second edition* (David Avison and Guy Fitzgerald) provides a comprehensive coverage of the different elements of information systems development. *Information Systems Development: A Database Approach, second edition* (David Avison) provides a coherent methodology which has been widely used to develop adaptable computer systems using databases; *Structured Systems Analysis and Design Methodology, second edition* (Geoff Cutts) looks at one particular information systems development methodology in detail; *Software Engineering for Information Systems* (Donald McDermid) discusses software engineering in the context of information systems; *Information Systems Research: Issues, Techniques and Practical Guidelines*

(Robert Galliers - Editor) provides a collection of papers on key information systems issues which will be of special interest to researchers; *Multiview: An Exploration in Information Systems Development* (David Avison and Trevor Wood-Harper) looks at an approach to information systems development which combines human and technical considerations; *Relational Database Design* (Paul Beynon-Davies) offers a practical discussion of relational database design. Other recent titles include *Business Management and Systems Analysis* (Eddie Moynihan), *Systems Analysis, Systems Design* (David Mason and Leslie Willcocks), *Decision Support Systems* (Paul Rhodes), *Why Information Systems Fail* (Chris Sauer).

This is a new edition of a successful text. It builds on the strengths of the previous edition and adds a number of important new dimensions, including SQL, the standard relational database language, and the object-oriented model. Although the book has been substantially revised, the elements that made the original edition successful are retained, many of these elements being perhaps even more relevant today than previously.

Unlike many books in the area, which concentrate on database systems and internal database organisation, this book starts at a much earlier stage and focuses on the underlying fundamentals relating to the nature of information and its importance to organisations. Databases are, after all, only a means to an end, that end being more efficient and effective storage and retrieval of information to support the objectives of the organisation. Thus it is not the database itself which is so important but the underlying fundaments of information and data that are necessary pre-requisites to understanding this field. The book concentrates on these aspects and the relationship between them rather than the more transient details of particular database implementations. These fundamentals are taken forward to in-depth treatments of information representations and data modelling and into database design. This enables the reader to appreciate and understand the reasoning and rationales underlying good design at each step. The book is easy to digest, it contains plenty of examples and illustrations and it poses, and answers, those questions that are most frequently asked.

Although it is primarily designed for the computing and information systems student the book can be equally well recommended to the professional systems developer. Indeed, if more practitioners adhered to the principles expounded in this book we might have significantly better and more robust systems than many of those we currently encounter in everyday life!

David Avison and Guy Fitzgerald

of information to the organisation of the late 20th century. It is 'essential to render human activity effective' or 'the life blood of organisation'. The problem is that information does not simply fall out of the sky. Information — particularly information which is going to be useful for the control and management of an organisation — has to be carefully considered. The developers of systems designed to produce information need to be aware of just what information is and how it can be made available to the people who need it.

After studying this chapter you should be able to:

- describe why information is important for management

- describe the structure of information and how information is produced

- describe the difference between data and information

- understand what an information system is and what is does

- understand the term 'database'.

1.1   The need for information

We use information throughout our daily tasks to enable us to deal with the world. Without accurate, up-to-date information, we make mistakes and misjudgements. For example, you arrive at the bank after it has closed because you did not know the correct time, or arrive at the station as the train disappears because you had an old train timetable. Information is such a familiar concept that, as users of information, we rarely think about it. For designers and developers of information systems, some understanding of information is vital.

Of course there are many types of information. If you watch a wildlife programme on television you may gain some information about the flora and fauna of the world. If you read a novel you will obtain information about fictional characters or about life in previous eras. If you read a newspaper you can find information on political arguments

1

or foreign affairs. If you talk to your friend you may discover information about mutual acquaintances.

In this text, our main consideration is with information which will assist people in managing some enterprise. The enterprise which they wish to manage may be as simple as catching a train, going to the bank or choosing a summer holiday. At the other extreme the enterprise may be as complex as running a multi-national business, administrating a large school or directing a feature film. Whatever the size or complexity of the enterprise, it cannot be managed without information.

Information is required to plan operations, to monitor the progress of activities and to control what happens. The film director needs information about suitable locations, actors, lighting, scripts, etc. The school administrator needs information about budgets, expenditure, classes, numbers of pupils, teachers and so on. The person catching a train needs information about destinations, train times and the location of the station.

At a very general level we can think about the need for information as illustrated in Figure 1.1. This shows that people have a desire to manage some enterprise. In order to do this they will use some way of obtaining information — an information system. In its turn the information system represents the enterprise. Data is gathered on the structure and operation of the enterprise. The information system organises data into information relevant to the needs of the people wishing to manage the enterprise. This information system can be formal or informal, large or small, computer-based or not. A train timetable is a formal information system; often paper-based rather than computer-based. Discussing alternative locations for a summer holiday with your friend is an example of an informal information system. A database of screen actors used by a film director is a formal, computer-based information system.

The focus of this text is on how to design the structure of the information system; how to determine what data is required and how that data should be organised. More particularly we are concerned with developing computer-based information systems. There are many features of information systems which this book does not touch upon in any great detail but which are ultimately vital to the successful development of an information system. Such aspects as the informal uses of information, the best way to present information to people and how people interact with information systems are left aside so that we can focus on the structure of information systems.

1.2   What is information?

The concept of 'information' is generally associated with the idea of
'surprise value'. Something is information if it enables the recipient to
know something which they did not know before. Information is 'an
increment of knowledge' (Tsichritzis and Lochovsky, 1982). However,
care must be taken when talking about information as there are a
number of different perspectives which can be taken on information.
Stamper (1985) draws an analogy with the concept of 'size' in physics.
Size can mean length, weight, volume or mass depending on which
aspect of the object an observer is interested in. Similarly information
has various different meanings depending on how it is measured. At
one level it is a measure of the relative frequencies of signals coming
from a source. The area of study known as information theory deals
with this view (Shannon and Weaver, 1949). An alternative view — and
the one which interests us — deals with the meaning which information
is able to convey; the usefulness of information to people in some
situation.

This view of information is concerned with semantics — the idea of
meaning — and it derives from work in semiotics; the theory of signs.
This is an area of study which dates back over a century. Semiotics deals
with all types of signs, how they are used in various subjects such as
literature, communication theory, anthropology and so on and how
people are able to obtain meaning from these different signs. One aspect
of semiotics which is particularly relevant to information system
designers is the recognition that signs can be examined at three levels.
Signs have syntax which is concerned with structure and rules. The
syntax of natural and formal languages (for example mathematics or
computer programming languages) is an example. Signs have semantics
which govern the relationships between what they are and what they
signify. Thirdly, signs have pragmatics which is concerned with the use
of signs by people. How convenient they are to use, how people
perceive them, and so on.

This analysis is important because it reminds us that we cannot simply concentrate on the rules and structure of the systems which we develop. Information is concerned with the meaning which is conveyed and must be seen in the context of the recipient of that information. The same signs may be interpreted by different people in different ways depending on their existing knowledge and their ability to interpret the signs. Designers must constantly bear in mind the information receiver (which in our case is usually a computer user) when designing information systems. Through convention many signs have some meaning ascribed to them. '1' means one, '100' means a hundred and 'a' is the letter a. Such signs are called symbols. In this text, we will have little to say about how signs should be expressed — the pragmatics of signs — we will concentrate on the underlying content and structure of signs. It is the content which we call 'data'.

1.3   The structure of information

Information is the increment in knowledge which a person is able to derive from the receipt of some data. But data is more than just numbers, letters or other symbols. Consider the symbols below.

a)   128

b)   folio number 013458

c)   at lunch they were 3 for 1

d) $13.35

e)   Bu4NPh4B

Most readers will already be asking 128 what? What is a folio? Many people will have recognised the third example as a cricket score. (However, British readers will have interpreted it completely differently from Australian readers because of the different conventions — the different syntax — for expressing cricket scores in those two countries.) Example d) looks like a price (of what?) and example e) will mean little to anyone except a chemist or pharmacist.

The problem is that symbols are of no use until they are described or interpreted in some way. The examples above are able to provide information only when the following descriptions and interrelationships are added.

a)   128 is the quantity in the ···

b)   'folio' is ·

··· uninteresting or irrelevant to many ··· not provide information at all.

The preceding examples suggest that a single piece of data — a data element — must be more than just symbols. In fact a data element consists of three parts:

- the symbols
- the description of the symbols (often simply a name)
- the context.

Consider the bus timetable in Figure 1.2. Here the three parts of the data are clearly shown. Without the context, this could be interpreted as a timetable for (probably) buses, but the reader would have no idea whether it was the current timetable, or whether it was a Sunday, Saturday or weekday service. Without the data descriptions, there is no indication where the bus is going and without the context or description, the symbols are open to so many interpretations as to render them useless. Moreover, the timetable only provides information because the pieces of data are related together in a tabular form and the intended recipient is expected to assume that the symbols in each row refer to the same route number, and that the symbols in each column refer to the description given at the top of the column. Information is only made available when these pieces of data and their associated descriptions are related together in a manner relevant to the receiver of the information. Bill Kent puts it succinctly 'Relationships are the stuff of which information is made' (Kent, 1978 p. 63).

As an aside it is interesting to notice that the context itself consists of data and descriptions and relationships. Indeed, the descriptions are data! Such data, (that is, data about data), is known as 'metadata' (see chapter 4).

When people talk about a piece of data (or data element), they generally mean that the context is known or assumed. In most information systems, the context is not stored or stated explicitly, but it is the humans who interpret the data who provide the context. This can and does cause problems both in the definition and interpretation of the data.

| TIMETABLE N8 effective June 30 1995 Leicester Hi-Frequency to and from Harborough Weekdays from Leicester | | | } Context |

Route number	Leicester depart	Kibworth depart	Harborough arrive	} Data description
348	6.45	6.55	7.07	
351	7.00	7.10	7.22	} Symbols
348	7.25	7.25	7.37	
351	7.40	7.40	7.52	

Figure 1.2   *Bus timetable*

Data needs to be described and it is the description and context of the data which allows it to have meaning. Symbols or values alone (e.g. '6.45') do not have any meaning, but described symbols (e.g. 'Leicester depart 6.45') can have meaning. This as the 'semantic contents', or the semantics of data (Sundgren, 1975). However, semantic contents does not map simply onto a set of symbols. For example, the symbols 'Dog', 'Chien', 'Hund' all have the same semantic contents (provided you, the recipient, understand some rudimentary English, French and German). They mean the same thing. Although they have the same semantic contents, they are composed of different arrangements of symbols. So different symbols may have the same semantic contents.

However, just because some words, or some data has some semantic content, it does not mean that they have any information content, '...the meanings of individual words do not, by themselves, convey information: this is obtained by suitable combinations of, and relations between, individual word meanings' (Langefors and Sumuleson, 1976 p. 4). Similarly we have shown that individual pieces of data do not provide information, it is data described and related to other data (which we call a data 'message') which enables information to be produced.

Although a message can have meaning (but does not have to), it is only when the message is received that information becomes available. Data conveys a message to the recipient of the data, but the meaning of that message depends ~~ '

~~ data did
~~ ~~activated some process which
~~ to recall previous knowledge).

Information is produced, then, by structuring and relating data elements into messages. These messages are interpreted by the receiver (to derive the semantic contents) and subsequently integrated with existing knowledge to derive the information contents. As we will see later, the importance of knowing this is that the information system designer has to represent the enterprise in such a way that the meaning of the data is accurately recorded and conveyed to the recipient.

1.4   Information systems

Our purpose — as information system designers — is to design and develop structures and procedures which will make information available to people. Moreover we want to make information available which will help people to manage their activities. Management is concerned with the planning, controlling and monitoring of some enterprise. In order to manage any undertaking, information is required. This statement is as true for an individual managing the household accounts to a group of people planning a trip around Europe to the board of a multi-national company. It may be possible to undertake some activity without having information, but that activity cannot be managed.

The term 'enterprise' is used to mean any purposeful activity which requires managing. A typical enterprise consists of people, activities, artefacts and events. People undertake some activities using some artefact(s). Activities are processes which make use of artefacts within the system and are triggered by some events. The enterprise has a boundary, outside of which the enterprise can be considered to have little or no influence. Events may arise from inside the enterprise or from outside.   The concept of an enterprise can be illustrated as shown in Figure 1.3.

The concept of an enterprise as used here is very similar to the concept of a system (Checkland, 1981). An enterprise is a coherent set of interdependent components which exists for some purpose, has some stability and can usefully be viewed as a whole. As illustrated above, such systems consist of people, artefacts, processes and the resultant activities which are undertaken as a result of events. In this sense we can consider the National Health Service is a system, a football match is a system, Marks & Spencer is a system, my family is a system.

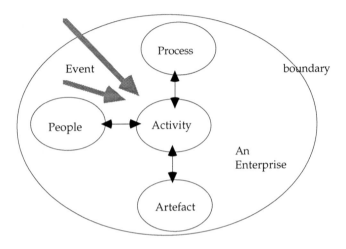

Figure 1.3   *Illustration of the components of an enterprise*

Each of these also has an information system, the purpose of which is to help manage (that is, plan, control, monitor and maintain) the enterprise. The information system may be informal (for example, casual conversation), or it may be formalised to a greater or lesser extent. For example, the information system for my family is almost totally informal. We do attempt to record activities using diaries and a calendar, but this formal part of our information system is somewhat unreliable! In the football match some of the information system is formalised through the use of flags and whistles, but much remains informal as the referee has a 'quiet word' with an offending player, rather than formally recording the offence. The National Health Service and Marks & Spencer also use informal information systems, but much more of their information comes from formal information systems which use computers.

The information system is a system which has a similar structure to the enterprise. The important difference is that it uses data to represent relevant features of the enterprise. Users of the information system engage in various activities by performing various processes on the data — such as selecting items of interest, calculating totals, comparing

.... been anticipated during the design of the database. The database must support these unanticipated, *ad hoc* inquiries. The database must be able to deal with the different levels and types of information required by different levels of management. Strategic information is needed to make long-term plans. Summary information is required to monitor and control the enterprise to see that it is consistent with those plans. Detailed information is needed to deal with the day-to-day transactions, problems and inquiries.

Databases for (management) information systems have to support multiple users and unanticipated use. The integrated database provides the opportunity to share data between different people and functions in the enterprise. Other sorts of database exist which do not place the same emphasis on structure or multiple use. Some databases (for example, bibliographic databases) are oriented to a single type of inquiry. The multiple-use criterion is not relevant. Others, such as text databases for use in word processing, do not have the data elements structured, or categorised, in the same way that they are databases for management information. In others (such as those employed in computer aided design and manufacture) there are a relatively small number of quite complex objects. These databases may have quite different considerations from database for management information systems; the databases which are discussed here.

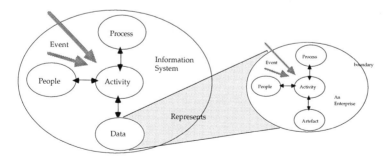

Figure 1.4   *The information system*

The design of a database must recognise that information needs change as the enterprise and its management changes. There must be flexibility in the design to accommodate the evolution of requirements and a long-term view must be taken. Indeed, one of the arguments in favour of looking at information systems from the data point of view is that this view offers a more long-term and permanent perspective. However, changes will occur, so it is important not to be tied totally to the current perceptions of information needs.

It is the structures which are imposed on the data which are so important in producing information. There needs to be selectivity in the data which is gathered and the information which is produced. Also the recipient of the data message must be borne in mind if the message is to provide appropriate information. If that person does not understand the syntax of the message or the semantics of the data, or if the pragmatics are inappropriate, the intended information will not be produced. In a commercial information system the recipient will frequently be unknown to the system designer. The designer is forced to have an 'average user' in mind and make certain assumptions about the recipient's frame of reference and their ability to interpret data. These characteristics may be drastically different, though, for a senior manager, an accounts clerk, a member of the general public, a computer specialist or a machine operative, who may all be using the same information system. Different users of the system will have different information requirements, different backgrounds and abilities and will be sensitive to different methods of presentation. The design of appropriate displays and input methods is an important aspect of information system design, known as human-computer interaction (HCI). The computer is a useful tool to assist with the production of information as it provides an efficient medium for storing, describing, structuring and manipulating data.

1.5   Key points

This chapter has introduced the concept of information and how information systems can be developed to produce it.

- Information comes from the relationships between pieces of data.

- Information is a valuable resource without which management cannot function.

- An information system provides information about some enterprise using data to represent the enterprise.

Further reading

Hirschheim, R., Klein, H. K. and Lyytinen, K. (1995) *Information Systems Development and Data Modelling: conceptual and philosophical foundations* Cambridge University Press, Cambridge, UK

> An excellent, but very detailed treatment of the philosophy of data modelling. Chapter 2 provides definitions of data, information and information systems.

Computer Journal vol. 28 no. 3 July 1985. pp 193–216

> A debate about the nature of data and information is provided in this special issue of the journal. It contains 5 papers on the topic 'towards a theory of information'. See the articles by Stamper, Rzevski, Scarrott, Tully and Land.

Sundgren, B. (1975) *The Theory of Database* Mason/Charter

> Sundgren provides a detailed discussion of the concept of information and its relationship to data.

Kent, W. (1978) *Data and Reality* North-Holland, Amsterdam

> This is a classic book and an excellent text for everyone interested in the problems of capturing real world semantics in a database. He does not offer many solutions, but he raises a lot of problems which the database designer would do well to bear in mind. (Particularly relevant to this chapter are the preface and chapter 2.)

Stamper, R. (1985) *Information* B. T. Batsford Publishers, London

Eco, U. (1976) *A Theory of Semiotics* Indiana University Press, Bloomington IN

> Eco's theory of semiotics provides a detailed account of how information is derived from signs and how we need to consider the production of signs in order to convey information. Stamper relates semiotics more closely to the needs of information system designers.

..., items of data. It is vital, therefore to understand data before trying to produce information. The information system designer needs to understand the relationships between data and information and the characteristics of data itself. Where and how to find data are also important skills.

After studying this chapter you should be able to:

- describe the processes involved in producing information
- identify and describe the characteristics of data
- undertake an analysis of the data in a simple enterprise.

2.1   Producing information

Information cannot really be created in the same way as some physical artefact can. Information can be made available to the recipients of messages, but it is the people who must *derive* the information from the messages provided. Notwithstanding this difference between information and other products, we can understand the process of producing information by drawing an analogy with the development of any product. Just as cloth is made from cotton and supermarket trolleys are made from steel, so information is made from data. Data is our raw material and this can be structured and joined together in a variety of ways to form different information products.

In the production of any artefact, it is important to concentrate both on the process of producing that thing and on the various representations which are produced along the way to a finished article. In later chapters we consider a number of representations which help in database design. This chapter concentrates on the process of producing an information system.

Consider manufacturing a product such as a supermarket trolley from steel. The manufacturer needs to do the following.

1.   Research the purpose of the product

It is important to determine the needs of any product and to identify the requirements of that product so that it can meet those needs. This will involve considerations as to whether it has to be waterproof, to be able to move, to be able to carry heavy weights, etc. These considerations constrain possible designs.

2.   Design the product

The design of any product involves developing various representations, or models, of the product. These evolve into a specification of the product and a list of the raw materials which are required to manufacture the product. For example, a supermarket trolley may be described by its structure — a base, four wheels, a handle, four sides — and hence the raw materials, wheels, steel wire, handles and so on can be identified. In addition to understanding the structure it is important to consider the processes involved in producing the sub-assemblies and how the sub-assemblies will be connected together. The designer also uses knowledge of the limitations, or constraints which are imposed by the nature of the various materials and structures. In the case of steel manufacturing, the designer must

(a)   understand the different types of steel (the raw material) that are available, their characteristics (e.g. mild steel, tungsten steel, stainless steel) and the basic structures which are available (e.g. plate, tubing, wire, etc.)

(b)   understand the ways in which these structures can be joined and manipulated (e.g. welding, bending, bolting, etc.) and the sequence in which these tasks must be carried out

(c)   understand the constraints imposed by the materials and by the requirements of the product (e.g. mild steel rusts, the base must be solid, etc.).

3.   Obtain the raw materials

The developers must then identify where they can obtain suitable raw materials. Indeed designers must consider whether the raw materials which they require are available at all or whether they must change the design to fit the materials which are available.

4.   Store the raw materials and be able to locate appropriate materials when required

The developer will need to identify where suitable raw materials can be obtained and gather appropriate amounts of the material. These will be stored for future use, but the developer must then keep a record of where the materials are.

In short, in any manufacturing environment, the raw materials must be understood, the basic structures designed and built and the final product tested and produced. The production of information can be viewed in much the same way.

1.   *Research the purpose of the product*

Designing an information systems means that the designer must consider the information requirements. This is essentially a management task which arises from consideration of the aims of the enterprise, the need for information and the constraints on that information. There are many different approaches and techniques to help with this systems analysis or requirements capture activity which are beyond the scope of this text. It is also important for the information systems developer to realise that the introduction of a computer-based information system may change the type and amount of information which management require.

2.   *Design the product*

Information systems development is concerned with many things; one of the most important being database design. The process of design is known as 'data modelling' and is extremely important if the product is to be useful. Later chapters are concerned with developing appropriate and accurate data models. The data model must be developed so that it can be implemented on a computer and so that it can be understood by the people who will use it. In the manufacture of anything — from a mousetrap to a suspension bridge — it is the design process and the construction of suitable models which is critical. The same is true of developing an information system. Designers must

(a)   understand the different types of raw material — data. What are its characteristics and basic structures. This chapter is devoted to this topic.

(b)   understand how the data structures can be joined and manipulated into larger and more useful structures. This text is concerned with the logical structures which enable information to be produced. The most important of these is the tabular representation, such as in the bus timetable in Figure 1.2. This may seem a very simple structure, but it is a very powerful one. Chapters 7–11 are concerned with understanding tables as a data structure.

(c)   understand the constraints which are imposed by the data, the basic structures and by the nature of the information required.

3.   *Obtain the raw material*

This process is concerned with identifying where data comes from, how data can be collected and input without error into the computer and how that resource can itself be controlled. Once again, these questions are dealt with in this chapter.

4.   *Store the raw material and be able to locate it*

The database is where the material is stored. The main concern here is how to describe the data to the computer system. This proves to be comparatively simple if the design has been successfully completed. The data dictionary system is the system for controlling and locating data. Chapter 4 deals with the idea of a data dictionary and chapter 3 with data management issues.

5.   *Produce the product*

To produce information the database has to be implemented on a computer. Hardware and software is required and computer languages are needed to retrieve and structure the data. The subject of implementing databases is a book in itself and we do not consider it in detail in this text. However, chapter 8 introduces the basic ways of setting up a database and looks at how data can be manipulated once the database has been designed.

6.   *Use the product*

In this case we want to derive information from the structured data messages which are produced by manipulating the data.

This brief outline shows how information can be produced from data and how similar it is to the manufacture of any product. However, an interesting difference between information and other products is that it does not use up its raw material. If the database is well-designed, the same data can be used to produce all sorts of information.

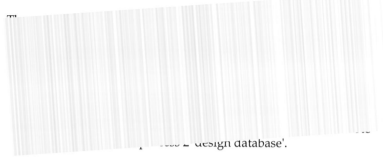

... ... design database'.

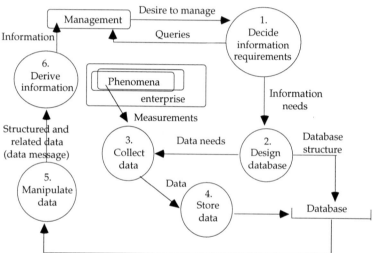

Figure 2.1   *Producing information*

2.2   Characteristics of data

To produce an information system we need data. It is vital, therefore, to understand the data — the data elements, the relationships between data elements and the constraints on the data — before trying to produce a database. Understanding data is an important part of the discipline of data analysis.

The basic component of a database is a data element. A data element is any piece of data which is of interest to the application. Things such as *CustomerName, Address, TelephoneNumber, QuantityInStock, Colour, Height, ArrivalTime,* and so on. There is no firm or fixed definition of a data element. It is simply any aspect of a phenomenon which the organisation in question wishes to know about.

In chapter 1, we stressed that data elements consist of three components: the symbols, the description (or name of the data element) and the context. The distinction between the name of the data element (such as *LeicesterDepart*) and the symbols, or values (such as 6.45, 7.00 and so on) is vital as it is this distinction enables us to deal with a whole class of things which share common characteristics. We distinguish between a data element type, the general category, and a data element value ('instance' or 'occurrence' are synonyms). *CustomerName, Address, TelephoneNumber*, and so on are data element types. Types describe categories, the different kinds of data which are of interest in the application and we use an italicised type face for data element types to clarify when we are talking about types. The names of data element types are chosen to be as meaningful as possible and, where a name would naturally consist of more than one word, the name concatenates the words using a capital letter in place of a space. A data element type can have different values, for example *CustomerName* may take the value 'D.R. Jones', 'Steptoe and Son' or 'Woolworth PLC', while *QuantityInStock* may take the value 262, 4986 or 180. The values which a data element can take are known as its value set.

The value set is the set of allowable values for a data element and therefore expresses certain constraints on that data element. The designer must consider the nature of the data and the required information and ensure that the value set is neither too broad nor too restrictive. Sometimes the value set is as broad as 'any number of alphabetical characters' or 'any whole number', but on other occasions a value set can be more closely defined. It may be possible to specify the value set as 'a numeric item in the range '01 – 12' or a code might be defined as 'a letter, B, D or K followed by 4 digits'.

Another important characteristic of data is its accuracy. Data is always only an approximation of the situation which the information system is helping to control. It is often more difficult and costly to collect precise measurements and in many instances such precision is not required. The designer must consider how accurate the data should be. For example data for the production of invoices must be accurate to 2 decimal places, but monthly sales figures are adequate to the nearest £100. Sometimes it may be infeasible to collect the data to the level of accuracy desired.

Also important is the reliability of data. Maintaining reliability demands unambiguous and stable methods of collecting data. Similarly, the data must be reliably transferred and thoroughly checked before being stored in the database. It is important to ensure that data ıne use of coded data can be very useful in information systems design. Sequence codes provide a unique identification which can be used to check the integrity of data and ensure that confusion does not occur. Perhaps the most common sequence code is the number found on bank cheques. When a statement is received, the account owner can verify that all cheques have been cashed by looking for gaps in the sequence numbers and can cross reference each to their own records of what each cheque was for. In computer systems, it can be useful to create sequence codes to ensure that each instance of a record can be uniquely identified and to verify that all instances have been processed. A sequence code can also be used to show the order in which things have happened or are allowed to happen. Semantic codes contain meaning and structure. A good semantic code can be very useful, but is unsatisfactory when the structure of the code is broken. For example, in the UK the licence plate number of a car contains a letter to indicate the year in which it was registered (it contains other information as well, but we shall ignore that). The number had the form abc 123X where X indicated the year of manufacture. Inevitably, the coding system could only last for a maximum of 26 years and after that the structure had to be changed (it became X123 abc). This was a minor irritation for most people, but would have caused severe problems for anyone who used that structure for the provision of information. Semantic codes are a powerful and useful technique of capturing the meaning and structure of data, but there is always danger in encoding too much meaning (what happens when the characteristics of the phenomenon no longer fit the code?). In computer systems data elements, typically one or two characters long, called 'flags', are often created. These code important information. For example, a customer may have status 'L' = live, 'D' = deleted, 'H' = held a library book may be 'B' = borrowed, 'S' = shelf, 'D' = disappeared.

These characteristics of data are important because they will help to inform the designer on the best way to obtain data in the context of the information system being developed. Understanding the nature and characteristics of data may in fact change the requirements of the information system if that data cannot be gathered accurately, reliably and within an appropriate timescale.

2.3   Obtaining data

It is not possible, or desirable to collect all data which exists in an
enterprise and store it in the database. Collection of data requires
accurate and reliable measurements, storage of data incurs expense and
output of data requires time. The processes involved in obtaining data
are outlined in Figure 2.2. This diagram shows the 'inside' of process 3 in
Figure 2.1. Whilst some of these problems are outside the scope of this
text, it is important to realise just how much is involved in obtaining
data before it is used for anything!

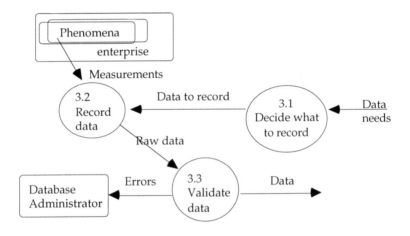

Figure 2.2   *Obtaining data*

Consider the following observations on the processes in Figure 2.1 (the
numbers refer to the numbers on the diagram).

3.1.Decide what to record

In this process the designer must establish the aspects of a phenomenon
which are to be recorded. This involves high level management
decisions about what things the enterprise is interested in and which
aspects are to be recorded.

3.2.Record data

This process involves several related activities. The designer must
consider the measurements which are to be taken, how accurate must
they be and how often should they be taken. How are the measurements
to be transmitted to the recording position and what error is this likely

... cases, it
... measurements.

Finally the data has to be safely transmitted to the central database. The designer must consider how quickly the data has to be entered onto the computer. In many systems (for example making payments to a book club) it is quite acceptable to transmit data using the postal system. Other systems require the data to be input immediately so that the computer system is as up-to-date as possible. The method of data transmission also effects the type of controls that can be enforced to ensure that data does not get lost or corrupted *en route* to the computer.

3.3 Validate data

The data, once received must be checked for accuracy and completeness, errors reported and the valid data sent to be stored in the database. Data validation is concerned with checking that the data is consistent with data already on the database as well as checking that the data message is internally consistent. For example, when an order is received from a customer, it is usual to check that the products ordered are consistent with the description of products stored in the database and that the order total equals the sum of the order items. Any errors in the data must be reported to the database administrator or one of the data administration staff (see chapter 3) and the system should ensure that all error data is corrected and re-input to the computer.

2.4   Finding and describing data

Data exists and is structured in any system and where a computer is to replace an existing system the analyst must examine and analyse all current uses and structures of data elements. An analysis of the documents currently in use is a good place to start looking for data elements, but it may not reveal all the data. Other data elements may be implicitly represented in the way that documents are stored or structured, for example, or in the way that people deal with the data. For example, in a university application, enrolment forms may be stored in a certain sequence and this may provide important data such as the order in which they were received. The data analyst needs to be aware of such possibilities.

For example, colour coding, wall charts or other perceptual devices may be used in a manual system which the computer has to represent by a data element. Sometimes important data is passed informally between people, perhaps by phone, casual conversation, observation or gestures. This too must be represented by a data element if it is to become part of the formal computer system. This can be virtually impossible to achieve sometimes and may be far less effective even if it is possible. Consider how to start a running race without the use of a starting pistol!

The initial stages of identifying data requirements are concerned with identifying the data elements. Each data element will need to be given a name, a short description of its meaning within the application and a description of its value set. The analyst should be careful to distinguish data element types from data element values. It is also important to distinguish data element values which can be calculated from other data elements from those which cannot. In database design we are primarily concerned with structure, not with the details of calculations.

In order to illustrate these points consider the document and enterprise description in Figure 2.3. This application concerns a manufacturing company, CND (engineering). Many of the data elements are clearly identified; *Day,* (name of the day) *Date,* (the calendar date) *JobNo* (the job number), and so on.

Some of the data is simply descriptive headings or text (such as 'C.N.D. (engineering) Job Sheet'). Since this data has no value *set*, it will not be part of the database. 'For office use only' is another example. Some data elements are calculated from other data elements. For example, *TotalHours* (with a value of 41.5 in the example document) will not be represented in the data model of this application. Rather it will be represented, ultimately, as a calculation in an application program, or other user process as *TotalHours = HoursDay1 + HoursDay2 + HoursDay3* ... etc. *GrossWage* is the sum of the individual payments.

Payment is also calculated (the description tells us that an amount is associated with a data element *HourlyRate* which is multiplied by the value of the data element *HoursWorked* to give *Payment*). Although the data elements which are calculated from other data elements will not appear in the database, at this point in understanding the data in an enterprise it is important to register that such data exists and how it is obtained. It is also important to notice that some data elements do not directly appear on the document. For example, the existence of the data element *Grade* is described in the application description and, as we will see later, there are data elements which are only implicitly represented in the documents.

		Job no.	Job Description	No. of hours	Task	Hourly rate	Payment (£)
Mon	23/3	0123	Supermarket trolley	6	Smoothing	A	42.00
				2	Welding	K	20.00
Tues	24/3	0066	Computer table	3	Scraping	A	21.00
				1	Painting	A	7.00
				2	Finishing	A	14.00
		0067	Hospital trolley	1	Loading	B	6.50
				2	Welding	K	10.00
Wed	25/3	0123	Supermarket trolley	8.5	Bending & Joining	C	85.00
Thurs	26/3	0067	Hospital trolley	6	Painting	A	42.00
				2	Loading	B	14.00
Fri	27/3	0066	Computer table	5	Welding	K	50.00
				3	Finishing	A	21.00
			Total hours	41.5		Gross wage	332.50

CND (engineering) is a small firm based in Derby. It manufactures a variety of products in its factory, processing bought in steel bars, tube, wire, etc. and finishing the processes off by painting the completed articles. Each job is for one customer and is given a unique job number. Every week, all employees complete a job sheet which records the work which they have done during that week. Employees work for a single department and their gross wage is calculated using the figures on the job sheet multiplied by an hourly rate which varies with the grade of the employee and the task. For each job there are a set number of tasks which must be completed in sequence. However, an employee does not necessarily work on all tasks associated with a job.

Figure 2.3   *CND (engineering) application*

There are other data requirements which appear in the application description but which do not immediately affect the individual data elements. Rather they deal with relationships amongst the data elements. For example there are constraints on the data. We are told that each job is for one customer and that employees work for a single department. As we will see later in the book, representing such constraints are vital to the success of the information system. However, at this juncture we simply note their existence.

A complete list of all the data elements in the CND (engineering) enterprise is shown in Figure 2.4. Each data element has a name, a value set and a short description of its meaning.

Data element Name	Value Set	Description
Name	any characters	Employee's name
DepartmentNo	numeric (integer)	Department number
WeekNo	numeric (integer)	Payroll week number
EmployeeNo	numeric (integer)	Works payroll number
DayName	any characters	Abbreviated day name
Date	DD/MM/YY	English date including year
JobNo	numeric	Number as issued by job controller
JobDescription	any characters	General purpose job title
HoursWorked	numeric (decimal)	Hours worked on a task (allow for half hours only)
TaskName	any characters	Name of task
HourlyRate	Any single letter	Code for hourly rate
Payment	numeric (decimal)	Amount paid for an hourly rate
TotalHours	numeric (decimal)	Total hours worked this week
GrossWage	numeric (decimal)	Total payment for this week

Figure 2.4   *Data element list for CND (engineering) application*

..........useful

.... must be collected, transmitted, validated and stored before it can be structured into a form from which the user can extract information. Each of these stages needs consideration and careful design.

- Data has important characteristics such as accuracy, reliability and timeliness.

- The environment of the enterprise and the purpose of the data will affect what data is required and how that data can be collected.

- Data can be found through discussions with users and through an analysis of the documents which exist in the current system.

Further reading

Yourdon, E. (1989) *Modern Structured Analysis* Prentice-Hall, Englewood Cliffs, NJ

Senn, J. (1986) *Analysis and Design of Information Systems* McGraw-Hill International, Maidenhead

Few texts provide a concise discussion of the nature of data and where to find it. Any general text on systems analysis and design (such as Yourdon (1989) on structured methods) will cover some of the issues and will deal with the wider issues which are outside the scope of this text.

...—...ws of an enterprise.
...—..ore require careful and thoughtful control. The purpose
of data administration is to manage the information system, its
data and its associated database. This chapter looks at a number of
the issues of data administration.

After studying this chapter you should be able to:

- understand the importance of context in information systems development

- describe the benefits and costs associated with adopting a database approach to information systems development

- compare the database approach with an application approach to information systems development

- identify and describe the need for three views of data, the user views, the conceptual view and the internal view

- understand the importance of the concept of program/data independence

- describe the responsibilities of the data administrator.

3.1   Understanding context

In chapter 1 we saw that a data element consisted of three aspects:

- the symbols (i.e. the value of the data element)

- a description of the symbols (often the name of the data element type)

- the context.

The context in which data is defined and used has an important bearing on both the meaning and the use of that data. One of the goals of an information system is to allow for unanticipated (or *ad hoc*) usage of data and it is therefore important that the information system designer is aware of the wider context and on how the data may subsequently be interpreted. Consider a simple system.

The enterprise in question wishes to use a computer to produce mailing lists so that advertising material can be quickly sent to all customers. An analysis of the requirements has concluded that the following data element (types) are required.

CustomerNumber
CustomerName
CustomerAddress
CustomerType.

Suppose the enterprise now wishes to implement a credit checking system on the computer. An analysis of requirements for this system reveals that the following data elements are required

CustomerNumber
CustomerName
CreditLimit
AmountOwing.

It would appear sensible to share the data between the two applications since the data elements *CustomerNumber* and *CustomerName* are common to the two applications. However, if the database is designed to hold the data elements

CustomerNumber
CustomerName
CustomerAddress
CustomerType
CreditLimit
AmountOwing

then some problems arise. Is it the mailing list application or the credit checking application which has the authority to change the customer's name and address? (the problem of maintaining data). Is the data held in customer number sequence, customer name sequence, or some other sequence? (the problem of structuring data). Should the mailing department be able to gain access to the customer's credit limit. If not, how can this be prevented? (the problem of security of data).

Although this is a trivial example (and those readers familiar with computer programming will be able to see several ways around the problems stated), it highlights some significant problems. In larger systems, these problems can become severe. The problems arise because the different applications of the computer — the different contexts in which the data is to be used — have different requirements of the data.

...........ss, which

However, it is not just the processing of data which can produce problems. The description of data is also difficult when it is to be used in more than one context. For example, a local authority in London wanted to use data on addresses of properties for rating purposes and planning purposes. They found it very difficult to agree on a definition of 'address' because the rating department was concerned with the use of that address for the purpose of assessing and collecting rates and for this application there could be more than one ratepayer at one address. The planners used addresses for planning applications, dealing with addresses which did not exist for rating purposes and only being concerned with the person applying for planning permission.

As another example, consider a person's name. It should be simple enough to agree on such a widely used data element. But what is my name? Mr D.R. Benyon BA, MSc, PhD.? or Dr David R. Benyon? or D. Benyon? People sometimes change their name during their life, for example when they get married. Which is their name? Are they allowed two names? Only two or several? In which case how many?

The final example of the difficulty of defining data is taken from Bill Kent's book (Kent, 1978, pp 3-4):

"Consider 'book'. If an author has written two books, a bibliographic database will have two representatives. (You may temporarily think of a representative as being a record.) If a lending library has five circulating copies of each, it will have ten representatives in its files. After we recognise the ambiguity we try to carefully adopt a convention using the words 'book' and 'copy'. But it is not natural usage. Would you understand the question 'How many copies are there in the library?' when I really want to know how many physical books the library has altogether?

There are other connotations of the word 'book' that could interfere with the smooth integration of data bases. A 'book' may denote something with hard covers, as distinguished from things with soft covers like manuals, periodicals, etc. Thus a manual may be classified as a 'book' in one library but not in another. I don't always know whether conference proceedings constitute a 'book'.

A 'book' may denote something bound together as one physical unit. Thus a single long novel may be printed in two physical parts. When we recognise the ambiguity, we sometimes try to avoid it by agreeing to use the term 'volume' in a certain way, but we are not always consistent. Sometimes several 'volumes' are bound into one physical 'book'. We now have as plausible perceptions: the <u>one</u> book written by an author, the <u>two</u> books in the library's title files (volume 1 and volume 2), and the <u>ten</u> books on the shelf of the library which has five copies of everything.

Incidentally, the converse sometimes happens, as when several novels are published as one physical book (e.g. collected works).

So, once again, if we are going to have a data base about books, before we can know what one representative stands for, we had better have a consensus among all users as to what 'one book' is."

These examples illustrate some of the problems of defining data. Data which is to be used in different contexts may have different meanings in those contexts. Furthermore, the problems of maintaining, securing and structuring data which is to be shared between contexts have to be dealt with and decisions have to be made as to how the data will be defined and controlled. The person or team of people responsible for making these decisions is know by the term data administrator.

3.2   The database approach to systems development

The simple example provided above demonstrates that the data administrator has to make a choice; to store data across applications (the database approach) or to provide each application with its own database (the application approach). Even the micro-computer user who has only a small database must consider how it will be administered. For example, if I produce a document on my word processor which deals with the human issues of database systems should I file it with my other work on databases or with my other work on human factors? If I file it in one place I may forget where it is. If I duplicate it in both locations I must remember to update both copies if I change the text. Even if the computer will only be used by one person, it will still be used for more than one use and it is this multiple use — sharing data between different contexts — which causes many problems.

The application approach has the advantage that control of the database rests with the department or person responsible for the system. The data and data structures can be tailored for that application and can be maintained (i.e. data can be added, changed or deleted) when required. However, because the same data element will then exit in more than one application inconsistencies are likely to occur. There is unnecessary

... . nave the surname
, ...-, ...ue value 'Jones' would be duplicated because it would
appear in both their records. In some systems it will be desirable to
duplicate values in order to provide quick access to the data, or to assist
with the security of the data. Whether or not data is duplicated
unnecessarily depends on the requirements of the system and the way
that system is implemented on the computer.

The problems of redundancy only really become apparent in larger
systems, when inconsistencies 'creep up' on the organisation. It is
frequently only late in the day that it is recognised that the database
contains inconsistent values, and then it can be extremely costly to
rectify the situation. Redundancy can at best be *controlled* through the
facilities of data management software and good database design. In
small systems redundancy can be controlled to some extent through
good administration, but in large systems this is not possible and
software assistance for the control of redundancy is essential. However,
whether the system is large or small, there can be no substitute for
careful and considered design of the database.

Sharing data between applications is the hallmark of the database
approach and ideally each data element value is stored in only one
place. This overcomes the problem of redundancy but introduces its
own problems of security (who can gain access to that data),
maintenance (who is in control of the data, when is it updated) and
access to the data (how should the data be structured to allow a variety
of accesses by different users?).

The problems are summarised in Figure 3.1. This shows that the
database approach avoids redundancy by storing each data element
value once only. The application approach avoids security, maintenance
and data structuring problems by only allowing each application to
access the data which it requires.

Clearly, it would be nice to combine the features of the database
approach with those of the application approach to gain the benefits of
each. That is, to have a system which had none of the problems of
redundancy, security, maintenance or access. The problems of data
definition can only be overcome by good data administration (see
section 3.5). Ideally, there should be a single definition and description

of each data element and to store each data element value only once. Then a view of the database for each application can be provided so that each application imagines that the data is in whatever sequence is most appropriate and further that responsibility for maintenance of that data rests with the appropriate application. Finally, if each application is unaware that it sees only a portion of the database, than security can be maintained. The idea of a 'view' of data is an important concept. 'View' is used in its English language sense of a 'way of looking at'. In terms of this discussion, it is a way of looking at data.

Problems of Sharing data	Database approach	Application approach
Redundancy	no	yes
Security	yes	no
Maintenance	yes	no
Structuring	yes	no
Definition	yes	yes

Figure 3.1   *Problems of sharing data*

3.3   Three views of data

When data is shared between applications, or by different users, it will be viewed in different ways. In section 1.2 the timetable was a view of data suitable for many users. My view of that data, however, is shown in Figure 3.2. It is a subset of the timetable because I am uninterested in what time the bus gets to Kibworth.

In fact there are likely to be many views of timetables: by arrival time, by elapsed time, by departure time, and so on. These various views of the same data are termed external, local or user views. Whereas in the manual system such as the bus timetable, all the user views have to be shown together, this is not the case in computer systems. User views can be presented as if they were the whole view.

User views are important for a number of reasons. Firstly, they can restrict the user to seeing only a part of the global view (the whole database). This may be desirable to avoid cluttering up an individual's view by showing them the whole picture or to enforce security of data by making it impossible for an individual to see sensitive data. Secondly, it allows the data to be presented in any sequence which is desirable. For example, in a computer-based telephone book, the subscriber data could be sequenced: by name (alphabetically or reverse-alphabetically), by name and restricted to only those names beginning

.... is used because this global view does not define how
the data is physically stored on the computer; it is concerned with how
the designer thinks about, or conceptualises, the enterprise. It is
tempting to see the conceptual view as simply the union of all the user
views. But there is (or should be) more to it than this. The conceptual
view should contain detailed validation checks to ensure the accuracy of
data, security controls to protect the privacy of the system, constraints
on the data and other details about the database.

TIMETABLE N8 effective June 30 1995
Leicester Hi-Frequency to and from Harborough
Weekdays from Leicester

Route number	Leicester depart	Harborough arrive
348	6.45	7.07
351	7.00	7.22
348	7.25	7.37
351	7.40	7.52

Figure 3.2   *Restricted view of timetable*

The conceptual view is independent of the method of implementation,
that is, the type of computer hardware and software which is to be used
to run the database. However, the computer system must know where
the data is stored and how it is structured, so there is a need for another
view of data — the internal or physical view. The internal view is
concerned with the type of representation used for data elements, the
methods of grouping the data elements into records and the low-level
structures such as indexes and pointers which the computer must
maintain in order to access the data in the required sequences and
within the specified response time.

These three views of data are summarised in Figure 3.3. They provide
the basis for the three-level database 'architecture' first developed in the
early 1970s and still in use today (ANSI, 1975).

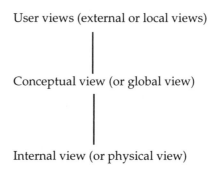

User views (external or local views)

Conceptual view (or global view)

Internal view (or physical view)

Figure 3.3   *Architecture of a database*

3.4   Data independence

The three views of data have always existed in computer systems, but until the 1980s it was not possible to separate one from another. The traditional computer program needed to define the files which it required and could only access whole records. It had to specify the sequence in which those records were stored and the way in which each field (a data element is called a field when it is stored in a record) was physically stored. This meant that any change to the file, record or field resulted in a change to every program which used it. Such programs are said to be data dependent and it is this dependence which results in much of the 'program maintenance' in many computer installations. Throughout the life of any information system, there are bound to be small changes which are required in the definition of data. With data dependent programs, every change results in a significant amount of program alterations and subsequent testing. This program maintenance can occupy up to 70% or 80% of available programmer time in some installations, leaving little time for new applications to be developed.

As a result of these problems, the idea of separating the definition of data from the specification of procedures (the programs) grew. This is program/data independence or, more simply, data independence. Separating programs from the data which they use means that a single definition of the data can be provided for the whole enterprise, but individual programs can be restricted to using a sub-set of this data. The database can thus be produced, maintained and defined independently (relatively speaking) from how it will be processed. This

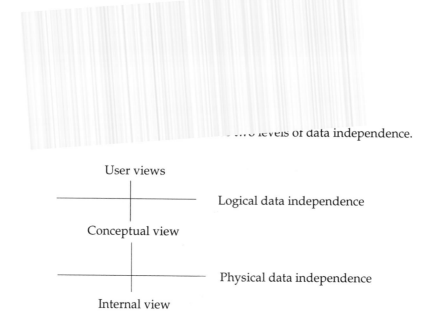

... levels of data independence.

User views

Logical data independence

Conceptual view

Physical data independence

Internal view

Figure 3.4   *Data independence*

In order to provide these levels of data independence, a database management system (DBMS) is needed. This is a software package which provides facilities for data independence and provides the translation (or mappings) between different levels of the database architecture. The data is described to the DBMS using a special language known as a data definition language (DDL). These data descriptions are often called 'schemas'. This is a rather awkward word which suggests that it is something special. In most modern DBMS defining schemas (i.e. describing the data to the system) is a fairly straightforward activity at the user and conceptual levels. The internal schema can often be 'tuned up' by a professional programmer, but increasingly this is a task best performed by the computer itself. The translations (or mappings) between the levels are usually handled by the DBMS.

The three levels provided by a DBMS overcome the problems of both the application and database approaches. The conceptual view provides a single definition of all the data in the system and, with careful design, can be free from redundancy. The user views provide the secure and tailored views of the data required by different users, or different uses. The internal view allows data to be changed without having to maintain any programs which do not use that data.

Another outcome of data independence is that programming becomes much more straightforward. Since all the definition and much validation of data is covered by the conceptual view, the programmer simply has to state what he or she *wants* to happen, rather than worry about *how* it happens. This has resulted in the definition of very high level programming languages usually termed query languages. The most important query language, called SQL, is discussed in chapter 8. Our principal concern in this text is with the conceptual view.

3.5 The data administrator

The data administrator is the person, or team of people, responsible for dealing with issues of data administration. We use the abbreviation DA to mean both the person or team of people responsible for data administration and the management function of data administration.

The main responsibilities of DA include data definition and description, the control of redundancy, the establishment of user, internal and conceptual schemas and matters of data security, privacy and integrity. As can be imagined from this list of activities, it is a demanding role which requires a variety of skills, not least of which is political skill. This is required to deal with uniting the often conflicting requirements of the variety of users into a shared database.

Data administration does not make direct use of the formal information system for controlling the enterprise. The function of data administration is to manage this information system for use by others. However, we have seen in chapter 1 that in order to be effective in any management activity an information system is needed. The data administrator requires information about the information system. The data administrator needs to know how data is defined, where and how it is stored, who can gain access to which data elements and what those users will be able to do with the data. The information system for the data administrator is discussed in the next chapter.

Data administration includes both technical and management roles: what should happen in the area of the enterprise's data and how these things can be accomplished. It is an important function within the enterprise, and for that reason should be at a level of management high in the information systems area. Like any management function, the DA must be involved in the planning, design, operation and control of the resource.

In planning for database development, the DA has an advisory function. The DA must examine and assess priorities for business system development, establish the information requirements for the

organisation and create a framew… …
information system… …
for d…

…. ine DA has a
…, security and standards for
…ation and in the design of the internal
…ia. During the operation of the database, the DA is
supporting technical staff in their monitoring of access to different parts of the database so that performance can be evaluated and optimised. In addition, the DA has to support the training and use of query languages. Finally the DA also plays a supporting role in ensuring the integrity and security of the data and in handling changes to the user, conceptual and internal schemas.

The DA thus needs to have, or to direct, a variety of skills. The skills of the systems analyst are required to establish user requirements, design the human-computer interfaces and to provide information as appropriate. This involves discussions with individual users to establish what data is important and the characteristics of that data. Hence the DA must define the data and the rules which govern the relationships between the data. This is not a passive task of documenting the users definitions. The DA must play an active part in deciding how to define data and in resolving inter-departmental conflicts. Additionally, the DA needs to define security and validation procedures to ensure the integrity of the data, and most importantly, establish the ownership of data — who has responsibility for adding, amending or deleting that data.

The DA is in a unique position within the organisation because he or she has to bring together into a single conceptual model, the different definitions and desires of many individual departments. Data crosses the organisational boundaries, and yet may be seen as 'private' data by any single department. The DA must be a diplomat and co-ordinator if these political problems are to be overcome and the database is to serve the needs of the organisation as a whole.

Data administration is an important function because the database represents a valuable asset. Once the decision has been taken to use a computer for data processing, the enterprise administration must make a conscious decision on its approach to data management: the application approach or the database approach. In fact, the answer is likely to be a hybrid of these two extremes and some data will have to be duplicated. The best approach is probably to define logical 'information areas' and have one database for each of these.

The DA has to oversee the design and implementation of the database. The goal of data administration is primarily to establish and control the definition of data within the enterprise. The DA needs to have substantial authority and political strength if this goal is to be achieved. The political problems of departments regarding data as their own need to be overcome. No single department is responsible for data and no data is completely local. Data can only be used for multiple purposes if it is defined and designed appropriately and the only way for good data definition is through good data administration. Ross (1981) has produced the Data Administrator's Charter which he describes as 'a political document' and those intending to introduce the DA function would do well to read his book.

3.6   Key points

In this chapter we have looked briefly at some important aspects of data administration.

- The issues of data administration arise from the need to share data in different contexts in an enterprise.

- The major problem of not sharing data is redundancy which can cause severe problems and should be avoided where possible and carefully controlled where it is necessary.

- The three major problems of sharing data — security, maintenance and structure — have to be dealt with. They are overcome by establishing an amount of data independence.

- Logical data independence facilitates the sharing of data and the provision of tailored views of that shared data.

- Physical data independence allows designers to concentrate on the essential logical, or conceptual, structure of the data without being concerned with details of implementation.

- Data independence can only ever be a relative concept because at some point the separate components must be brought together.

- User views must be mapped onto the conceptual view and the conceptual view must be mapped onto the physical view. These mappings can be provided by some database management software.

, ...glewood-Cliffs, NJ

Chapters 1 and 2 provide a good introduction to the issues of database systems and chapter 15 covers data administration

Weldon J-L. (1981) *Data Base Administration* Plenum, New York

Ross, R. (1981) *Data Administration and Data Dictionaries* AMACOM

Two good books on data administration and data dictionaries. Although they may appear dated, they still provide some relevant and detailed discussion.

Date, C. J. (1995) *An Introduction to Database Systems* 6th Edition Addison-Wesley, Wokingham

Chapters 1–2 describe the significance of data independence and the database architecture

Rothwell, D. M. (1993) *Databases: an introduction* McGraw-Hill, Maidenhead

Chapter 15 covers data administration

...ormation

...inistrator, therefore,

... the things in the information system. The term

... dictionary' is used to describe the data which the data
administrator is interested in.

After studying this chapter you should be able to:

- understand the term 'metadata'

- describe the contents of a data dictionary

- distinguish between an active and a passive data dictionary

- understand the importance of a data dictionary to data administration

- understand how the data dictionary is used throughout the development of an information system.

4.1 An information system for data administration

The 'enterprise' with which the data administrator is concerned, and about which information is required, is the information system. We saw in chapter 1 that information is made available through data. The data administrator, therefore, requires data about the things in the information system. That is, the data administrator needs data about the people who will use the information system and when and where they use it. The data administrator needs to know about the procedures which are used and about the data and how it is structured into a database which is central to the information system.

The term 'data dictionary' is used to describe the data which the data administrator is interested in. Until recently, a data dictionary was frequently defined as containing metadata — data about data — but it is increasingly realised that the data administrator is interested in much more than just the data in the information system. The data administrator needs data about when, where, who, what and how the information system is used. The data dictionary is the data administrator's database — the kernel of the data administration's information system.

In chapter 1 we saw that an enterprise consists of people undertaking activities by processing artefacts. We also saw (Figure 1.4) that an information system had a similar structure to any other enterprise, but used data to represent the enterprise. The data dictionary is a database containing data about the information system and the data dictionary system is an information system used by the data administrator to manage the users' information system. A data dictionary system accordingly has a similar structure to an enterprise or information system. The relationship between these systems is illustrated in Figure 4.1.

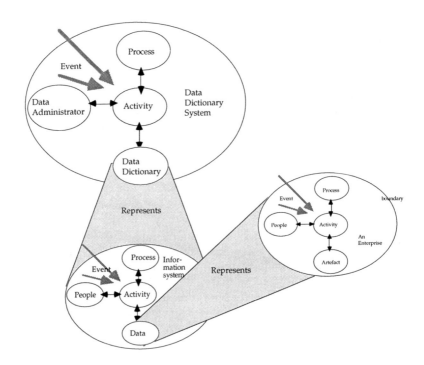

Figure 4.1   *The data dictionary system considered as an information system*

4.2   Content of the

...must,
...these things. So, for example,
...ator wants to manage the definition of a data
element such as *ProductCode*, information is required about the
cconceptual view of *ProductCode* — its meaning, the data elements
which it is related to, the programs and procedures which use it or
change it, and so on. The data administrator is also interested in the user
views of *ProductCodes* such as any homonyms (where the name
ProductCode may have different meanings for different users) or
synonyms (where different users may use another term, e.g. *PartNumber*
for the same data element) used. The data administrator is concerned
with the different sequencing required by different users and the types
of access which are appropriate. The data administrator is also
concerned with the internal view of *ProductCode* such as its stored
format on the disk, its location, the physical record of which it is part
and so on. These three views of data are required about every object in
the information system.

Since the information system is a system consisting of people, activities,
processes and data, the data administrator needs information about all
these different types of objects in the information system. There are data
objects such as files, records, fields, indexes, data elements, groupings of
data elements, etc. There are process objects such as programs and
procedures. There are user objects such as individual people, user
groups and departments. There are activity objects such as which user
ran which program from which computer terminal or which users are
able to access which (parts of) databases. There are event objects such as
when certain data was input into the information system, when reports
were produced or when the database structure was changed. The need
to accommodate the three views of a variety of objects makes the data
dictionary a complex and sizeable database.

4.3   Data dictionaries in information systems development

The data dictionary is a comprehensive database. However, it is not a
static documentation of a completed information system. On the

contrary the data dictionary is useful throughout the development of an information system.

During the early stages of development the data dictionary is used to document and understand the results of the systems analysis. As data elements are identified they will be entered into the data dictionary and described in as much detail as possible. For example, the value set for a data element will be identified along with its name, a more complete description and its relationship to other data elements. Any constraints which are relevant will be recorded. Documents and other data objects such as ledgers, price lists and so on will be recorded in a similar way. The analysis process continues by identifying users and their activities. The tasks which users have to carry out as part of their work will need to be identified and recorded.

During design the data administrator will be concerned with identifying and recording how the data elements in the new system are to be structured and how these structures are associated with one another. In addition to specifying the data model for the information system — the conceptual schema — the data administrator will design and record details of any required user views; how the data should be structured, ordered and summarised for different users. Processes will need to be defined and these should be recorded along with details of the activities which are being designed. Not all of the information system will be confined to the computer and the data administrator will use the data dictionary in order to document clerical procedures in addition to computer-based programs and user schemas. If the data dictionary is linked with other tools such as screen and report generators, there are greater opportunities to use the data dictionary as a part of a prototyping approach to systems development. The definitions in the data dictionary can be used to generate screen displays and these can be tested by the users. Changes can be quickly effected by changing characteristics of the definition in the data dictionary.

As the development of an information system moves into the implementation stage, the data dictionary can be used to generate internal schemas. Details of programs can be recorded and different versions of programs can be controlled. There may be details of physical storage to maintain in the data dictionary such as how the database is partitioned, or how physical records which the computer accesses relate to the conceptual model of the information system. Various indexes will be set up to increase the speed at which data can be retrieved and displayed. Authorisation mechanisms will be defined and implemented.

After the information system has been fully implemented the data dictionary can be used to monitor its usage and can form an important part for any changes which are needed. The data definition in the data dictionary can be used ·

...order to provide the facilities
...environment in which many different users are sharing
data, so the data dictionary as an information system requires software
to support the DA's activities. Such systems are known as data
dictionary management systems or just data dictionary systems. It is
easy enough for a data administrator to construct a simple data
dictionary system, by using the existing DBMS. However, such systems
are inevitably only *passive* aids to controlling the information system. A
passive data dictionary can be useful in recording data about the
information system objects, but it cannot be used to enforce the
characteristics of those objects.

In contrast an active data dictionary system is employed during the
operation of the information system helping to control the data.

Currently there are several data dictionary systems — software
packages oriented to the control of data about the information system —
which provide some, but usually not all, of this data. Some pieces of
data management software have an integrated data dictionary which
forces all users of the database to use the same data definitions
However, there are still many organisations where there is little or no
control over the information system.

The data dictionary is not simply a passive documentation of the
information system. It is a powerful tool of data administration and
should be used throughout the development of an information system.
It assists during the analysis and design stages of the information
system with the definition of data elements and the relationships which
exist between all the objects in the information system. It is useful in
planning changes to the database to gauge the effect that any alteration
may have. It is particularly useful in helping in the rapid production of
working information systems as, with all the objects defined, the system
can be quickly and automatically generated.

The data dictionary is a subject which will grow in importance as the
value of data as a major resource of organisations is increasingly
recognised. Indeed some recent authors on the subject prefer the term
'information resource management' to data administration to emphasise
this and 'system encyclopaedia' is preferred to 'data dictionary' in order

to stress the variety of functions and data which is now considered integral to effective data management.

For the purposes of this volume, the data dictionary is treated in a much simplified fashion. We have argued earlier that giving something a name is an important step to understanding that thing and giving it meaning. If the full benefits of the data dictionary are not to be utilised then at the very least each data element must be defined and described, and the relationships between data elements must also be understood. This is the main use which we make of the data dictionary. We use it to define the data elements and the basic characteristics of those elements, the data element type — its name — and the set of allowable values for the data element — its value set. Additionally we require data about the movement of data elements — data flows — and the logical structuring of data elements. The data element list for the work sheet (Figure 2.4) is a primitive, but useful, data dictionary.

4.5   Key points

- The data administrator needs an information system to manage the information system.

- Such a system is known as a data dictionary.

- The data dictionary contains data about all the things of interest in the information system — data, processes, users and activities.

- The data dictionary is useful throughout the development of an information system.

- Data dictionaries which are used during the operation of the information system may be active data dictionaries.

- Even a simple data dictionary — such as used in this book — can be extremely useful in ensuring consistency in data definitions.

Further reading

Yourdon, E. (1989) *Modern Structured Analysis* Prentice-Hall, Englewood Cliffs, NJ

> Chapter 10 discusses data dictionaries. For a detailed, but dated treatment see Weldon (1981), Ross (1981) or Van Duyn (1982).

— —.—υαϑϵ is

... . iiiuiiiiation system and its design crucial to the efficacy of that system. In order to design the database it is necessary to understand the requirements of the system users and the nature of the information required. The data dictionary offers a useful tool for analysing and defining data elements. The next stage in the process of database design is to group the data elements in such a way that redundancy (unnecessary duplication of data) is minimised and all user views are accommodated. To do this a number of models are constructed which represent an appropriate structure for the data and help the system analysts and designers think about the meaning of the data. These models form the basis of the final, implemented database.

After studying this chapter you should be able to:

- understand the purposes and styles of models

- describe the various categories of models which are needed to represent the information system

- identify the components of the information model

- describe the three main record models

- draw simple dataflow diagrams (the process model)

- draw simple entity-life histories (the data processing model).

5.1   What is a model?

A model is a representation of something constructed and used for a particular purpose. We use models constantly in all walks of life because they present a simplified view of the world which highlights the parts which interest us. In particular, any design work involves the production of models, e.g. an architect's drawings, an artist's sketches, a knitting pattern, a street map, and so on.

Models are vital to the success of the designer. They can be used for exploration, communication, testing and making predictions. Different models are suitable for different purposes. A good model is accurate enough to reflect the important detail, but simple enough to avoid confusion. We use models because they remove some of the complexity of reality so that the aspects which interest us will stand out.

An example will clarify.

> A car designer has been commissioned to produce a new luxury sports car. He or she doodles a few designs on paper and shows them to the other designers. They make certain comments and criticisms and as a result changes are made in the designs. Finally the designer is satisfied with three of the designs and draws up detailed blue-prints which are given to the firm's model maker. Scale models of the design are produced and are sent to marketing and sales for customer reaction. The models are also subjected to wind tunnel experiments to investigate the aerodynamics of the design and the results of these tests are used in a computer program which will calculate the car's speed and fuel efficiency.

The designer is using four different models in at least four different ways.

1. The original models represent a clearing of the mind. In this case they are 'doodles' and sketches which are used to generate new ideas, examine possibilities and prompt for questions. Here the model is being used primarily for exploration of the problem.

2. The blue-prints given to the model maker and the scale model given to the marketing and sales departments are suitable models for accurately expressing ideas to others. These models are used for communication.

3. The wind tunnel experiments show models being used to test ideas.

4. The computer system is a model which is used to make predictions.

This example shows that different models are suitable for different purposes. Notice that the blue-print and the scale model are both used for communication, but the blue-print is inappropriate for communicating with marketing. Marketing are interested in the physical shape of the design, but the model maker requires a more precise description of the designer's ideas in the form of a blue-print. Also notice that the model must be accurate enough for its purpose, highlighting the

ore concrete (or
to provide the detail needed to complete
task. There may be several intermediate models required to provide
a smooth transition between these two extremes. Consider a very
familiar model, a book of road maps.

The first page contains a picture of the whole of the country with only
the major roads shown and divided into a number of sections each of
which references a particular page or pages on which further detail can
be found. These pages show all the major towns, cities and the main
connecting routes. However, details about roads within the towns can
only be discovered by turning to a town street map given at the end of
the road atlas. This approach permits the navigator to plan the strategy
of the journey in general and then to investigate detailed alternatives by
examining the characteristics of more detailed maps. We need all those
maps, but not at the same time. If you are out walking, you will need a
map of the scale 1:50000 or 1:25000, but to try and travel long distances
using such maps is extremely difficult. The level of accuracy must be
appropriate for the purpose. Pause for a moment and consider the
range of maps which we use, the purpose of those maps and their level
of detail. In addition to road maps, street maps and walking maps,
there are relief maps, weather maps, contour maps, physical maps and
many more.

Raphael (1976) gives some good examples of the appropriateness of
different models. For example a scale model is suitable for wind tunnel
experiments, but it is quite inappropriate for dealing with a problem
such as calculating how long it would take for a cannonball dropped
from the top of the leaning tower of Pisa to hit the ground. The height
of the tower is an essential feature of the problem which would be lost if
a scale model were produced. In this case the mathematical model

$$time = \sqrt{(distance)}/4$$

is suitable. We simply have to determine the height of the tower of Pisa
and put it into the formula. Notice in this problem that the cannonball is
irrelevant and hence a model which avoids reference to it assists the
usefulness of the model. Raphael also emphasises the use of diagrams

which focus attention on relationships which might otherwise have been missed. Many people find it useful to sketch a picture of a problem to help them think about it. Diagrams are particularly useful in database design as we shall see in chapters 9 to 15.

It is important to recognise that the construction of models is just as important as the finished representation. A good model effectively provides a language for exploring and experimenting with ideas and an appropriate language allows far more subtle expression than an unsuitable one.

Other models are more effective for communicating ideas. Consider the stylised notation used for writing music or choreographing a dance, the symbols used in circuit diagrams or chemistry. These are all specialised models which have been designed, or which have evolved, to assist in the precise expression of ideas.

Often a series of models is required in order to reflect the different levels of detail required for different purposes. This is called 'hierarchical modelling'. The book of road maps demonstrates the idea of a hierarchy. When constructing a hierarchical set of models, it is desirable to have a consistent and rigorous way of translating between the different levels. For example, in the book of road maps, if you see on the front page that the A34, M4 and A303 leave the bottom of the area indicating page 28, you would expect to see them shown on page 28 and leaving the bottom of the page. If they were not shown, the models would lack consistency and hence be less credible. Some models (such as the map example) have the desirable characteristics of ensuring that a model at a finer level of detail is a true explosion of the model one level up, others ensure that one form of representation suitable for one purpose can be accurately translated into another representation.

The choice of a model can be critical to its success for the purpose at hand. For example, a circle can be described as a picture, as a formula or as a computer program in the language 'Logo', as shown in Figure 5.1. Clearly these are different representations of essentially the entity (a circle) which can be used for different purposes as is appropriate. The desirability of the different representations is not an issue here — that depends on the purpose to which the model is to be put.

Three different models of a circle

5.2   Modelling methods

Models can be constructed in three main ways. One approach is to begin with the general concepts (the coarse grained model) and gradually fill in the details. This is 'top-down' modelling. Another is to begin with the detailed, fine grained, model and collect details together into larger units. This is 'bottom-up' modelling. Both these approaches have things to recommend them, and adopting one approach does not preclude using the other. In practice the designer will typically iterate between the two extremes depending on the problem at hand. He or she may start in the middle and then jump from middle to top to bottom. This is 'middle-out' modelling. The method is not that important. The significant feature is that an appropriate model is used for the purpose at hand and that the final model (or series of models) is appropriate in accuracy and representation for its purpose and can provide the various types and levels of interpretation which are required.

In database design we need to use a number of models; to capture the different levels of representation required, to offer alternative perspectives and to use for different purposes. The translation between these different models must be consistent to ensure that the models represent the same things. The question then rises as to what models are required and what should they be like.

The definition of a model given above is that it is an abstract representation of something which suppresses unnecessary detail. This suppression of unnecessary detail can be achieved in two ways. Firstly a model can group related things together and represent just the aggregate object, thus suppressing details. Another technique is to represent a whole class of objects as a single object, thus suppressing details of the individual objects. The first of these techniques is known as *aggregation* and the second as *classification*. Together they produce abstractions.

Aggregation is the process of collecting together a number of characteristics of something and treating it as a single thing. For example, when I talk about my car, I do not need to explain that it has wheels, a body, an engine and so on. By 'car' I mean the aggregate of all these various properties. By 'house' I mean the aggregate of the properties doors, windows, rooms and so on. By 'customer order' I mean the aggregate of customer name and address, items ordered, quantities required and so on.

Classification is the process of recognising that various objects share certain characteristics and can therefore be treated as a single thing. For example, I might classify cars, lorries, buses and tractors as vehicles. I might classify houses, libraries, factories and barns as buildings. I might classify Dipak Patel, David Benyon and Manuel Imaz as people. We are able to classify things in this way because we recognise that they have certain shared characteristics (restricting the characteristics to those things which are of interest for the purpose at hand). For example, I am able to classify houses and barns as buildings because I am not considering the use of the building as part of the classification scheme.

Classification of objects means that we can represent and discuss a complex situation in simpler terms. From the examples above it should be apparent that there are many levels of classification. As we deal with the more abstract concepts, we make *generalisations* about things and as we move towards the more concrete objects we make *specialisations*. So car is a generalisation of Fords, Nissans, Vauxhalls and so on. Ford is a specialisation of car. Ford Mondeo is a further specialisation of Ford and the Ford Mondeo parked outside my house is a specialisation of Ford Mondeo. Moving in the opposite direction — towards the more abstract classification — vehicle is a generalisation of car.

Selecting appropriate classes or categories and identifying the defining properties which determine whether or not something belongs to a class is an area which has been studied by philosophers over many years. One of the most famous examples is Wittgenstein's (1953) discussion of the class of games — see if you can find the defining properties which allow us to treat football, chess, card games, board games, ring-a-ring-a-roses as a single class; games. You will find many overlapping properties, but not a single property which connects them all. A related issue is concerned with individuals — at what point do you stop specialising? For example, which is the individual amongst the following: The *Daily Telegraph*, The *Daily Telegraph* on 17th January 1996, The *Daily Telegraph* delivered to me on 17th January 1996, The *Daily Telegraph* delivered to me on 17th January 1996 which I used to light the fire on the 18th January 1996?

...erprise.

... ...ition to using abstraction, models may focus on different aspects of the object being modelled. The modeller can look at the structure of the object, the functioning of the object or at the way the object changes over time. Once again there is a large amount of interplay between these views and the level of abstraction which is used to represent the object will affect the view which is relevant.

A *structural* view of some system focuses on the main objects which are in the system and how those objects are related. For example, the structural view of a car would describe a car in terms of the main components — engine, gearbox, drive shaft, brakes and so on. A *functional* view focuses on how some substance, or some object moves through the system; it describes the dynamics of the system. In the example of a car, we could look at how fuel flows though from the fuel tank to the engine, how it transformed into exhaust gases and flows out through the exhaust system. Another functional view might focus on the braking system and the flow of hydraulic fluids. The third view of a system is how it changes state — how the structure and dynamics are related and the behaviour which results. Thus a car has an initial state of 'engine off', following an event of 'ignition' the car is 'running' and following and event of 'put in gear' and 'release brake' then the car will be 'moving'.

These three views are complementary and interrelated. The appropriate view and the appropriate level of abstraction at which to describe a system will depend on the purpose of the modeller. In the case of information systems we have seen that what the information system developer needs to concentrate on is the structure and flow of data. The developer constructs models, made of data, to represent the enterprise.

5.3   Modelling the enterprise

The components of an enterprise are people, artefacts, events and processes. Since an enterprise is a complex system, we need to model it so that the important aspects stand out and the less important are ignored. Our purpose in modelling the enterprise is to develop an information system.

A single model will not suffice for this purpose. Just as in the design of the sports car, a series of models are needed to reflect the different perspectives required. For example, a model is required by the users of the proposed system so that they can understand and verify it. Another is needed which is suitable for the design of the database. In information systems design it turns out that at least four models are necessary to cover all the required perspectives and ensure accuracy and consistency. Two of these are models of the structure of the enterprise, one is a model of the dynamics, or processing, in the system and one a model of the behaviour of the system; the relationship between structure and dynamics. Collectively, these constitute the 'information model'. The structure model is called the 'data model', the dynamics model is called the 'process model' and the model of the relationship between structure and dynamics is the 'data processing model'. They are shown schematically in Figure 5.2

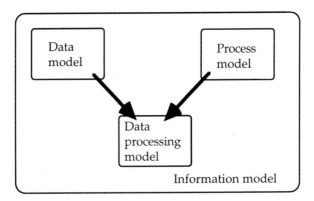

Figure 5.2   *Content of the information model*

The data model represents the enterprise structure in terms of the things of interest to the enterprise, their characteristics and the relationships between those things. The process model focuses on the transformations which take place in the system, highlighting how data is changed by the processes which act upon the data. The data processing model checks that sufficient data is available in the data model to support the processes and that enough processes have been identified to produce and manipulate the data.

It is an unfortunate historical accident that the term 'data model' equates with a model of structure. In fact all three models could be called data models as they are all models *made from* data. An information system

....om data, so we produce data *models* of the enterprise in order to abstract the features which interest us. The three data models constitute the information model — the main artefact processed by an information system. However, we also know that an information system can be seen as consisting of three separate views; the user, conceptual and internal views. Accordingly, we could develop a conceptual and an internal information model and a number of user information models. However, it is the conceptual view which represents the information content of the information system as it must accommodate all the user views. Accordingly we concentrate on developing the conceptual information model. It is important to remember, however, that the conceptual view takes no account of how the system will be implemented. Indeed, there is no requirement that the conceptual information model be implemented on a computer at all. The tools and techniques described for information modelling can be mapped onto a whole range of manual, mechanical or electronic internal models, but this decision can be postponed until the conceptual model is complete.

Within the conceptual information model, we will concentrate on the conceptual data model. It is this part which deals with the inherent structure of the data. Most database research effort has gone into developing conceptual data models, and there is a wealth of literature on the subject. However, increasingly database theorists are realising that the data model on its own is insufficient as an information model — there must be some account taken of the processes which are to transform the data. We consider briefly the process model, data model and data processing model before devoting our energies and several chapters to developing the data model in detail.

5.4   Process models

Process models have been encountered several times already in this text. Figure 2.1 showed the processes involved in producing information and Figure 2.2 showed the processes for obtaining data. Processes are triggered by events. The result of a process may become an event which triggers other processes. Events can come from outside the system or arise from inside the system. In fact, at one level of description, a system can be viewed as a process. An information system takes measurements of some phenomenon as its input and produces data messages (that is, data elements more usefully structured, and related to other data elements) as its output. The arrival of the measurements is the event which triggers the information system process. The arrival of the data message at a manager's computer is the event which triggers some decision making process.

Processes take data as input and produce (different, hopefully more useful) data as output. Conceptually speaking, if a process is to be at all significant, every process must transform the data in some way. In the physical world, many processes to not transform the data. Many manual systems are plagued by 'paper pushing' where processes consist simply of copying data from one form to another. At the conceptual level we would not consider these to be a processes, because the semantic content of the data is unchanged. The processes which concern us must transform the data through some manipulation, re-structure it more usefully, or relate it to other data. In order to do this, the process may need to reference a more permanent store of data.

For example, the process 'Calculate Total Price' takes as its input the data elements *PartNumber* and *Quantity*, produces as its output a value in pounds and pence (*TotalPrice*) and uses a data store of *PartNumbers* and *PricePerPart*. The process can then be checked for completeness. It must have access to enough data — either as input or from a data store — to be in a position to produce the required output.

The basic requirements of the process model are, thus, inputs, outputs, processes and stores of data. Since the output from one process may be the input to another, it is better to view all data which travels between processes as a single concept: a dataflow. These ideas are based on the ideas of the 'structured approach' to systems analysis, which developed during the late 1970s, principally due to the work of people such as DeMarco (1981) and Yourdon (1989). Here we use the diagrammatic technique of DeMarco to represent the process model. The symbols used are shown in Figure 5.3.

These concepts are illustrated with a short example (Figures 5.4 and 5.5). Inevitably there is some overlap between the concepts. When is a dataflow a datastore or when is a source or destination a process? These questions can only be answered in consultation with the users of the system and so we need not worry about getting the dataflow diagrams 'right' first time. The model is useful as a means of exploring ideas as well as documenting them.

The final feature of dataflow diagrams is that they can maintain a consistency when used at different levels. A process can usually be split dictionary in Figure 5.5. Notice in Figure 5.4 that process 1 is split at Level 1 into process 1.1, 1.2, 1.3 but that the total inputs and outputs are consistent with process 1 at level 1. Also that all data is described in the data dictionary (Figure 5.5). All dataflows are named except those flowing into or out of datastores. These are left unnamed because, at this stage, we are just saying that we want to access these stores, not exactly what data will be transferred.

The Sales system consists of two events 'Order (received)' and 'Order checked' which trigger the processes 'Check order' and 'Produce receipt', respectively. These are also recorded in the data dictionary process model (Figure 5.5(d)). The diagram will take several attempts before it accurately reflects the processes involved. Where possible, the events should appear on the level 1 diagram.

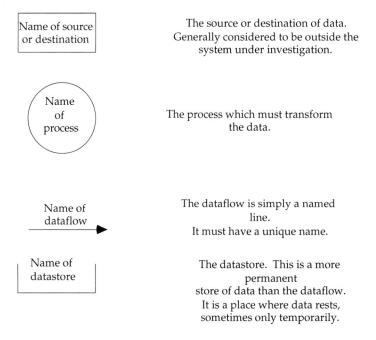

Name of source or destination	The source or destination of data. Generally considered to be outside the system under investigation.
Name of process	The process which must transform the data.
Name of dataflow	The dataflow is simply a named line. It must have a unique name.
Name of datastore	The datastore. This is a more permanent store of data than the dataflow. It is a place where data rests, sometimes only temporarily.

Figure 5.3   *Symbols for the dataflow diagram*

DFD level 0

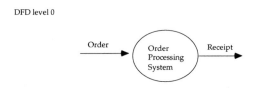

DFD level 1

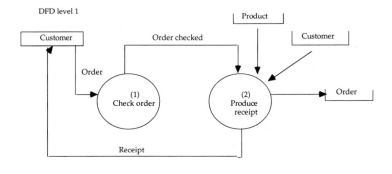

DFD level 2 for process 1

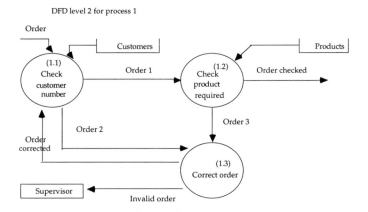

Figure 5.4   Levelled dataflow diagram for orders system

invalid order = Order + *ProductCheck* + *CreditCheck* + Corrected = n

Order corrected = Order + *ProductCheck* + *CreditCheck* + *Corrected* = y

Receipt = *CustomerNumber* + *CustomerName* + *CustomerAddress* + *{ProductNumber, Price, QuantityOrdered, Total}* + *OrderTotal*

(b) Data elements

Name	Value set	Description
OrderDate	DD/MM/YY	date order received
CustomerNumber	numeric	our unique identifier
ProductNumber	numeric	unique product identification
QuantityOrdered	numeric	quantity ordered
CreditCheck	{yes, no}	yes = customer credit OK, no = customer credit not OK
ProductCheck	{yes, no}	yes = product identification OK, no = product identification invalid
CustomerName	any characters	customer's initials and surname
CustomerAddress	any characters	customer's home address
Price	numeric	price of one product
Total	numeric	*Price* × *QuantityOrdered*
OrderTotal	numeric	sum of *{Total}*
Corrected	{y, n}	y = order corrected, n = order not corrected

Figure 5.5   *Data dictionary for Sales system*

(c) Data stores

Customer   (*CustomerNumber, CustomerName, CustomerAddress, CreditCheck*)

Product   (*ProductNumber, Price*)

Orders file   (*CustomerNumber, OrderDate, OrderTotal*)

(d) Processes

1. Check order	triggered by event Order (received)	consists of:
		1.1 Check customer number 1.2 Check product required 1.3 Correct order

2. Produce receipt	triggered by event Order checked	consists of:
		for each product
		    retrieve *Price* each
		    calculate *Total*
		calculate *OrderTotal*
		retrieve *CustomerName* and *CustomerAddress*
		print Receipt
		write to Orders file

1.1 Check customer number	access Customer by *CustomerNumber*	if *CreditCheck* = yes then Order1, else Order2
1.2 Check product required	access Product by *ProductNumber*	if *ProductNumber* on file then Order checked, else Order3
1.3 Correct order	check Customer and/or Product details	if solvable then correct order and Order corrected else Invalid order

Figure 5.5   continued

5.5   Data model

When the term 'data model' is used, it always means a conceptual data model unless otherwise qualified. There have been many conferences, much argument and considerable research into data models, and we cannot hope to cover all the subtleties and nuances in this text. In this section a brief introduction to data models is provided before devoting later chapters to examining specific models.

For those wishing to pursue the various models in depth, the book by Tsrichritzis and Lochovsky (1982), entitled *Data Models* still provides an excellent summary. Data models are models of structure made of data.

...p.... rules are

...... by nature and hence the static model of data relationships (the data model) is a suitable model. Some enterprise rules can best be represented by processes (a process or functional model). Sometimes there is a choice of suitable representations as in Figure 5.1 with the different models of a circle. In such cases the decision will be based on other factors such as ease of realisation of the model and the purpose for which the model is to be used.

Although we are concerned with developing a conceptual data model, we must not lose sight of the fact that the system has to be used by people and has to be implemented on a computer. The conceptual model must, therefore, capture the information which people require (and the different views required by different users) and the data definition must be precise enough to be implemented by computer professionals. In addition, the conceptual model is used by designers to help them understand the data, its interrelationships, characteristics and context so that they can explore different possibilities.

Some authors have suggested that a natural language such as English is the only appropriate model for representing information, but because of its vagaries and verbosity, this is not suitable. Returning briefly to the example of maps as models, a map contains far more information, far more concisely than an English narrative could do. Furthermore, users cannot ignore the limitations of computer and must be aware of the physical restrictions of implementing a database, just as they are of the physical limitation of a road system when interpreting a map.

In order to accommodate these two perspectives on the conceptual data model — the physical perspective concerned with implementing a database and the external perspective concerned with ensuring that user requirements are accommodated — the conceptual data model actually needs to consist of two models. One is concerned with producing a model of the areas of the enterprise which users are interested in; what data should be collected, how the users view that data and the semantic relationships which exist in the enterprise. The other is concerned with designing the database so that it can be implemented.

Diagrams are the most appropriate tool for modelling the user-oriented realm because a concise pictorial representation can be quickly understood, and does not rely on computer jargon for its interpretation. They are also useful for assisting the designer. The computer-oriented view employs 'record models' because they map easily onto the needs of relational and other database implementations.

As a final observation on data models, it is important to notice that the database itself is a data model (a physical data model). The database consists of data values, data structures and data descriptions. If we inquire of the database about the quantity in stock of product X and get the result 143, that is not reality! The actual quantity in stock of product X can only be found by inspecting the warehouse and counting the physical items. Hopefully there will be 143 there, but that depends on the accuracy of the database. The database is, thus, just another model. But it is a model of values or instances rather than a model of types. The database values are constantly changing — they are 'time variable' — because stock quantities are amended, customers are added and orders are despatched and deleted. The conceptual data model aims to express the (relatively) 'time-invariant' structure of the database, i.e. data element and table types. The database values, then, constitute only a snapshot model of the enterprise, which, as explained in chapter 2, is only as accurate as the response time, data collection methods, validation rules and integrity constraints allow it to be.

5.6   Data processing models

The process model defines the events and operations which must take place in the information system. The data model defines the structure of the data which must be stored so that the required information can be made available. These two models express the dynamic and static features of the information model. The purpose of this section is to examine how these two models can be linked together. The term 'data processing model' is used to describe this connection.

Data processing models are used to check that the data and process models are consistent and also to provide an alternative perspective on the enterprise. The simplest of these is the data/processing matrix which simply cross references the processing model with the data model. This is a tabular model which shows the entities needed for any particular process. The table has rows corresponding to processes and the entities as columns. The process may need to retrieve details (R), add (A), delete (D) or update (U) particular attributes. A sequence number indicates the order in which the operations are performed. In more detailed versions of the transaction/process matrix, each attribute can be shown. The order systems example is shown in Figure 5.6.

An altern...

...ents which have a
...ted on the level below, in sequence from left
to right starting with the 'birth' (creation) of an entity occurrence and
moving through the life of the entity to finish with the 'death' (deletion)
of an entity occurrence. The effects which these events have (such as
'create occurrence', 'amend attribute x', etc.) are listed on subsequent
levels, with no sequencing from left to right, and using the symbols '*' to
mean that the effect is iterative or 'o' to mean that either one or another
effect results from the event. Provision can be made for a null effect (i.e.
no effect). Almost all entities will have an event corresponding to 'add
an occurrence', 'amend details' and 'delete an occurrence'. An example is
shown in Figure 5.7.

The power of ELHs is really apparent when an entity changes state
frequently. For example in a library system a book will change its status
when affected by events such as acquisition, borrowed, overdue etc., or
in an educational system when an applicant may be provisionally
accepted, finally accepted, enrolled, etc.

The data processing model provides a test for completeness and
consistency between the process model and the data model and offers
an alternative perspective — focusing on behaviour — of the system. A
popular model for this perspective is the state transition diagram (STD).
Sully (1993) introduces a version of the STD known as the entity STD
(eSTD) which performs a similar function as the ELH described here. An
STD for the orders system is shown in Figure 5.8. The eSTD has the
added advantage of showing pre-conditions and subsequent actions
associated with an event. The STD can be used for a number of purposes
in order to show a change in state and various versions of this technique
exist.

Process/Entity	Orders file	Product	Customer
1.1 Check customer name			Retrieve
1.1 Check product required		Retrieve	
2. Produce receipt	Add (3)	Retrieve (1)*	Retrieve (2)

Figure 5.6   *Transaction/entity matrix*

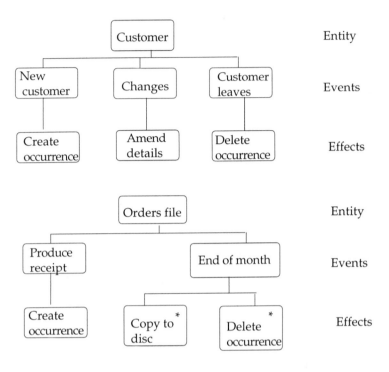

Figure 5.7   *Entity life history*

Yourdon (1989) points out that STDs are most applicable to systems which have to react to external stimuli and where the main concern is what happens when. For example, a computer may patiently wait for a user to log on. When a user does log on the system moves to its next state, 'select service' say and waits there until the user selects a service or until a certain time has elapsed and the user is logged off automatically.

5.7   Summary

This chapter has explored the notion of a model. It is important to be quite at home with this concept, as all the 'tools of the trade' in information system design are models. Models are used for different purposes and different models are effective for different problems. Choosing an appropriate model is an important skill of the designer, though one that is often overlooked.

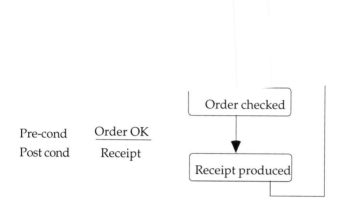

Pre-cond   Order OK

Post cond   Receipt

Figure 5.8   *State transition diagram*

Throughout this chapter the focus has been on conceptual models; models of abstract relationships which do not anticipate the method of implementing or realising those models. In terms of the information system there is a need for a data model (representing the structural view of the enterprise) and a process model (representing a dynamic view). Both of these models are implementation independent and may be realised with or without a computer as is appropriate in a particular enterprise. However, since this text is concerned with using the computer as the central part of the information system, the models must be relevant and accurate enough to be used for that purpose. In addition the models must be understandable to users of the information system so that they can verify that the system meets their needs, i.e. there is a requirement for both user-oriented and computer-oriented models.

The forms of the three models which have been demonstrated here are not the only forms available and different practitioners will have their own preference for notation of the models. The argument presented there is a need for a data model, a process model and a data processing model and that it is necessary to model the information system at the user and computer levels. Individuals can express their own preference for the style of the model providing it meets the criteria of appropriate accuracy and representation.

Another important aspect of information systems which has not been discussed is what the users have to do to use the system. In order to represent these aspects, information system designers will develop task models — representations of the actions which users have to take in order to achieve some goal. These may focus on the logic of the task and how this helps (or hinders) users to achieve their goals, the knowledge and thought processes which people have to use in order to use the system or how users learn about a system. Considerations about the usability of systems is outside the scope of this text but are presented in detail in Preece*et al.* (1994).

Finally it is important to mention object-oriented models (see also chapter 16). The object-oriented approach seeks to *combine* the data and processes rather than separate them. In fact, although there is much debate about object-oriented design, the models developed in this chapter are just as applicable to an object-oriented *implementation* as they are to an implementation as a database.

A comprehensive account of different models and different notations can be found in the book by Martin and McClure (1985). This gives clear descriptions of the options available and should be read by anyone considering adopting enterprise standards for information systems modelling. He spends considerable effort in describing consistent notation so that the various models can be used together. He describes many models which go beyond the conceptual level and which are more oriented towards the detail of implementation. His list of features of a good model are worth repeating here.

A good model should:

- be an aid to clear thinking

- be capable of manipulation on a computer

- be readable by end users

- provide a good basis for communication

- be able to be drawn on ordinary paper

- be capable of subdivision (i.e. hierarchical models)

- have a consistent notation.

5.8   Key points

This chapter has been concerned with looking at various aspects of models and modelling in information systems.

- Developing models is a vital part of successful information system development.

appropriate for users and accurate enough for the computer system.

- The data model we shall use consists of diagrams for the user side and records for the computer side.

- Consistency between the process model and the data model is maintained by the data processing model.

- Together these three models constitute the model of the enterprise appropriate for the information system — the information model.

Further reading

Veryard, R. (1992) *Information Modelling: practical guidance* Prentice-Hall International, London

A clear introduction to modelling with some nice philosophical touches.

Tsrichritzis, D. and Lochovsky, F. (1982) *Data Models* Prentice-Hall, Englewood Cliffs, NJ

Excellent discussion of data models (chapters 1–3) also see chapter 11 on Infological Models.

DeMarco, T. (1981) *Structured Analysis. Structured Specification* Yourdon, Englewood Cliffs, NJ

Yourdon, E. (1989) *Modern Structured Analysis* Prentice-Hall, Englewood Cliffs, NJ

Two influential texts on dataflow diagrams. Generally both are good at dealing with the process model but I prefer DeMarco owing to its clear style. Yourdon covers state-transition diagrams well.

Martin, J. and McClure, C. (1985) *Diagramming Techniques for Analysts and Programmers* Prentice-Hall, Englewood Cliffs, NJ

Chapters 1–4 on models in general. Chapters 23 and 24 on data models.

Halpin, T. (1995) *Conceptual Schema and Relational Database Design* 2nd Edition Prentice-Hall, Sydney, Australia

This text deals with many important issues concerned with semantic models in describing a modelling method called NIAM.

... ... enterprise which ... ... structure of the data. It consists of two complementary views a user-oriented model of the information system and a computer-oriented model. The computer-oriented model needs to be relatively independent of computer implementation. The ideal computer-oriented model is not a physical (internal) model, but represents an implementation independent, yet computer-relevant view of the data to be stored. The computer-oriented model is thus part of the conceptual model (since it is not a model of the way data is physically stored) in the information system architecture. In this chapter we examine three common structures.

After studying this chapter you should be able to:

- identify and describe the record model
- distinguish record types from record occurrences
- describe the characteristics of the hierarchical model
- describe the characteristics of the network model
- describe the characteristics of the relational model.

6.1   The record model

Until the early 1970s, little thought had been given to the classification of data models. The various structures involving files, records and access methods had developed in response to changes in technology and requirements for more sophisticated manipulations of data. The original computers used tape as the method of mass storage of data, which only facilitated sequential processing (analogous to searching for a particular track on an audio tape). The emergence of disk storage allowed direct access to a given record (analogous to selecting a track on an audio disc), but forced designers to structure the data so that the required data could be speedily located. The original structures were hierarchical, reflecting the nature of typical applications (such as accounting systems and payroll systems). Subsequently the single hierarchy was replaced by multiple hierarchies resulting in a network structure, which facilitated a variety of alternative accesses.

This piecemeal development gave rise to some perfectly adequate systems, but as the size of those systems developed so the problems of dealing with increasing complexity became significant. It was E. F. Codd who stood back from the tangle of data structures and provided a framework for considering the computer-oriented view of data models. By way of illustration, we use a simple example database (from Date, 1995a).

In this database, data is to be stored about parts which the enterprise may wish to purchase and the suppliers who can supply them. For each part the information required is the *PartNumber* and *Description* and for each supplier, *SupplierNumber*, *Name* and *Address*. In addition data is required concerning which parts are supplied by which suppliers (not all parts are available from each supplier and not all supplier's can supply all parts) and the *Quantity* which each supplier can supply for each part.

Underlying the various data models is the view of data called a 'record'. A record is an aggregation of data elements; a collection of data elements which we decide to keep together for some reason. For example, in a telephone system, it is sensible to keep the subscriber's name, address and telephone number together. We all use records whenever we want to keep related data elements together. I keep a record of my friends' telephone numbers in a little book. I keep a record of appointments in my diary. The bank sends me a record of my income and expenditure.

Unfortunately the term 'record' is used in a number of different ways in common parlance. In terms of computer-oriented data models, a record is a record occurrence —e.g. one entry in my personal telephone book, one appointment in my diary or one line on my bank statement. The collection of such records is called a file. (This particular use of the terms 'record' and 'file' is important to note as in casual usage they often get confused. In a school the pupil's file should properly be called the pupil's record, the term customer file in an office should be the customer's record.) There is more confusion in computer jargon. In particular, it is necessary to distinguish a *logical* record from a *physical* record (sometimes referred to as a stored record or an internal record). A logical record is a collection of data elements which the designer wants to keep together. This may, or may not, be the same as a physical record which refers to the amount of data physically transferred to or from the computer's secondary storage. The considerations of what to put in a physical record are related to the method that the computer transfers data, matters of efficiency of processing and so on. This is

...suppliers or parts list. We distinguish between the general category — the record type and the specific instance — the record occurrence. At present our database appears as Figure 6.1.

Part Number	Description	Supplier Number	Name	Address	} Record types
P1	Nut	S1	Jones	London	
P2	Bolt	S2	Jones	Paris	} Record occurrences
P3	Nut	S3	Smith	London	

| Part | | Supplier |

Figure 6.1   *Logical records for suppliers-parts database*

There are two record types, Part and Supplier. Each of these has three record occurrences. These record types represent the relationships between the data elements *PartNumber* and *Description* on the one hand and *SupplierNumber*, *Name* and *Address* on the other. The record occurrences of the Part record type represents the facts that

- part number P1 has a description of Nut
- part number P2 has a description of Bolt
- part number P3 has a description of Nut.

The record occurrences of the Supplier record type record the facts that

- supplier number S1 has the name Jones and an address of London,
- supplier number S2 also has the name Jones and has an address of Paris
- supplier number S3 has the name Smith and the address London.

The question which now faces the designer is how to represent the relationship between suppliers, parts and the quantity supplied. In the following examples we wish to model the information that

- part P1 is supplied by supplier S1 in quantities of 500

- part P1 is supplied by supplier S2 in quantities of 300

- part P2 is supplied by supplier S1 in quantities of 200

- part P2 is supplied by supplier S3 in quantities of 100.

6.2   The hierarchical model

Hierarchical models represent the relationships between things by (logically and/or physically) showing that one thing is 'above' or 'below' another. A hierarchical model is often referred to as a tree structure; indeed the terms 'hierarchy' and 'tree' can be used interchangeably. The analogy which springs to mind when using the term 'tree', gives a reasonable picture of the structure, but care must be taken with this metaphor. A hierarchy is an upside-down tree! It has a single root at the top, various branches in the middle, each of which terminates with one or more leaves at the bottom. This is illustrated in Figure 6.2.

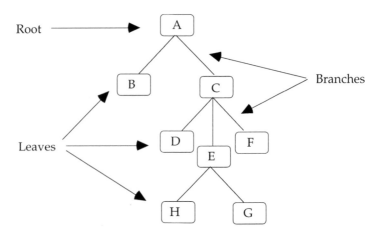

Figure 6.2   *Hierarchical structure*

.... node A is also said to be the
parent of nodes B and C. These in turn are said to be the 'children' of
A. In turn, D, E and F are the children of C, whereas B has no children.
Thus any parent node without children is a leaf node. A child must
have a parent and can have only one parent. Branches are sometimes
called links.

As usual, there is the distinction between node types and node
occurrences. So far we have been discussing node types. Occurrences
from an occurrence tree, hence a hierarchical database consists of
multiple occurrences of occurrence trees. Hierarchies occur often in life.
For example, animals are classified hierarchically in terms of: class,
subclass, order and family. The 'spiny anteater' occurrence of this
hierarchy is: mammal, egg-laying mammal, monotremes, spiny
anteaters. Occurrences of the class category are: mammals, birds,
reptiles, amphibians, fish. Each of these has its own occurrence of the
hierarchy.

Figure 6.3 shows a hierarchical model of the example database. Notice
the distinction between the type hierarchy and the occurrences of the
hierarchy. It is also important to remember that we are still discussing
this structure in primarily logical terms. The links can be implemented
in any of a number of different ways. Notice that supplier S1 has its
details (name and address) redundantly duplicated in the second
occurrence tree. However, this does not mean that the data is
necessarily physically duplicated (although in some implementations it
might be).

Whatever the physical realisation of the model, the hierarchical model
demonstrates some undesirable characteristics. First, a child node
cannot exist without a parent (though a parent does not have to have
children). Hence there are problems with inserting new record
occurrences. In the case of the hierarchy in Figure 6.3 it is not possible to
store details of a supplier unless that supplier supplies at least one part.
Similarly there are problems with deleting occurrences. If part P2 is
removed details of supplier S3 would be lost. Secondly there are
problems with redundancy. All supplier details occur for every part
which they supply. Data is thus unnecessarily duplicated. This leads to
problems of updates — changing a supplier's name or address requires

changing every occurrence of that supplier's details. Thirdly, there is the problem of asymmetry. Information on which parts are supplied by which supplier is only implicitly represented. To represent this explicitly (i.e. with a Supplier parent and Parts as children) causes further redundancy.

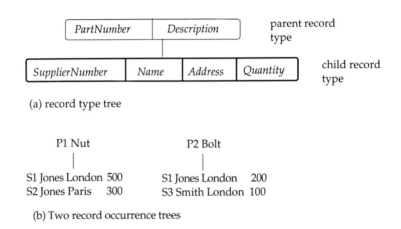

(a) record type tree

P1 Nut   P2 Bolt

S1 Jones London 500   S1 Jones London   200
S2 Jones Paris   300   S3 Smith London 100

(b) Two record occurrence trees

Figure 6.3   *Hierarchical structure for Suppliers and Parts database*

Another problem is the unnecessary complexity. Although the model is suitable for some applications which demonstrate a 'natural' hierarchy (e.g. a company consists of divisions each of which has departments which have employees), most applications are not as straightforward. If the data is not naturally hierarchical then various devices have to be employed in order to fit data from one structure into a hierarchy. These devices include having one physical and several 'logical' databases, using secondary indexes to facilitate sequencing other than through the hierarchical structure or duplicating data redundantly. However, even tactics such as these cannot overcome all the problems inherent in trying to provide symmetric access to the asymmetric representation of a hierarchy. In addition, users need to be aware of the hierarchical structure and the parents, children and links which exist in order to navigate through the structure.

The hierarchical model is not flexible enough to deal with the huge number of database applications. That is not to say that it is not a good model in some circumstances nor that it is not an effective and efficient method of implementation. But for the purposes of conceptual data modelling, a more flexible structure is required.

... representation of the ... database is shown in Figure 6.4.

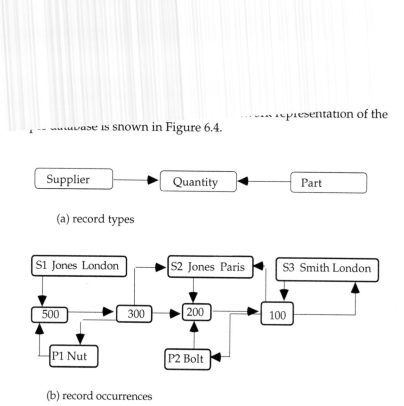

(a) record types

(b) record occurrences

Figure 6.4   *Network model*

The network model overcomes many of the problems of the hierarchical model because it does not have the restriction of a single parent for each child, but even in the tiny example above, it can be seen that it becomes very complex very quickly. In the network model, a distinction is drawn between records which are 'owners' and those which are 'members'. However, since an owner in one set can be a member of another, this is an overly complicated distinction. Notice that the term 'owner' is identical to the term 'parent' in the hierarchical model and that the term 'member' is identical to 'child'. The use of the term 'set' is equivalent to 'link' in the hierarchical model.

The main criticism of the network model is complexity. The existence of different types of records requires the existence of different operators which are required to manipulate them. The children of a parent are also ordered and hence there is a notion of first, second, third and so on in a chain. Adding links and members to sets is non-trivial. In short, the network model is complex — too complex for a logical model. However, as with the hierarchical model, it may be a perfectly good method of implementation and may give very good physical performance. Since the concern here is with a conceptual model, the network model seems unsuitable.

6.4   The relational model

Both the hierarchical and network models use two distinct concepts to represent relationships: 'record' and 'link'. In the relational model, there is no distinction between these as all links are formed using records. The entire model is thus describable in terms of records. The example database is shown in Figure 6.5. Where the Supplies relation represents the quantity of each part which is supplied.

The relational model is conceptually simple because all relationships are represented using a single structure. It is also a very flexible model. Insertions (adding new rows to the table) and deletions (removing rows) can be made without any complex manipulations of the existing data element values. Finally, there is no recourse to a sense of ordering, no information is represented in the order of the records.

One criticism of the relational model is that it requires an excessive amount of duplicated (though not redundant) data. *SupplierNumber*s and *PartNumber*s have to be duplicated in order to establish the links between supplier and part records. However there is no requirement that the model has to be physically implemented in this way. In fact if logical pointers are used instead of the data elements *SupplierNumber* and *PartNumber*, then the model becomes similar to the network model (though without the significance of the ordering). Another criticism is that users need to be aware of the relational structure in order to navigate through the system. For example, users need to know that it is *SupplierNumber* and *PartNumber* which provides links into the Supplies relation and, indeed, that the Supplies relation exists at all.

However, in the relational model there are no confusing terms or arbitrary distinctions such as 'owners', 'parents', 'members' or 'children'. The model uses just one construct — the relation — in order to represent the relationships between data elements. In short, the relational model offers a conceptually simple model, and we devote the next chapter to examining it in depth.

....	SupplierNumber	Quantity
P1	S1	500
P1	S2	300
P2	S1	200
P2	S3	100

Supplies

Figure 6.5   *The relational model for the example database*

6.5   Key points

This chapter has examined the four basic structures which can be used for representing the relationships between data elements.

*   Records represent aggregations of data elements.
*   Records can be related through a hierarchy.
*   Records can be related through a network.
*   Records can be related through other records.

Further reading

Most general database books provide brief discussion of the three main structures, though often from the perspective of database systems rather than general structural models.

Rothwell, D. M. (1993) *Databases: an introduction* McGraw-Hill International, Maidenhead

See Chapters 8 and 9.

Date, C. J. (1995) *An Introduction to Database Systems* 6th Edition Addison Wesley, Reading, MA

Elmasri, R. and Navathe, S. B. (1994) *Fundamentals of Database Systems* 2nd Edition Benjamin/Cummings, Redwood City, CA

Kroenke, D. M. (1995) *Database Processing: fundamentals, design and implementation* Prentice-Hall, Englewood Cliffs, NJ

_____ ..... uiai ine most useful and_ ..exibie computer-oriented data model in our enterprise is the relational model. It is important to remember that, in common with all models, the relational model is a subjective representation. It will represent the view of the enterprise which the model builder is interested in, and not some universally applicable representation of reality. The relational model consists of a number of relations, which link together to give a useful and consistent view of the information content of the relevant information system. This chapter is concerned with establishing the definition and theory behind the relational model.

After studying this chapter you should be able to:

- understand the basic structure of the relational model

- define the terms 'relation' and 'domain'

- recognise the similarities and differences between tables and relations

- describe the four properties of relations

- discuss the significance of null values

- identify and describe the two integrity rules in the relational model.

7.1 Foundations

The term 'relation' stems from a branch of mathematics called set theory, and the relational model is mathematically well-founded. We will not consider the mathematical foundations for relational theory in detail here as such a treatment is unnecessary for our purpose. Those interested in the detailed axioms and proofs should read Ullman (1982) or Maier (1983). However, a brief introduction to sets and set theory will help to establish the logic and significance of the model.

In mathematics, a 'set' is a collection of things — any things — which we wish to group together. Typically, the members of a set will have some shared characteristics. We might think of the set of all people, the set of integers, the set of trees and so on. In terms of the database, we have defined the value set of a data element as the set of values from which the actual values of the data element are drawn. The things which constitute a set are called its elements or members.

Sets are described in terms of their elements and hence have no ordering. For example, the set of numbers {1, 3, 2} is equivalent to the set of numbers {2, 3, 1}. Also, sets cannot have duplicated values, hence the set {1, 3, 2, 1} has an illegal entry (the second value '1'). The number of elements of a set is called the cardinality of the set. Thus, the set {1, 3, 2} has a cardinality of 3. The elements of a set may themselves be sets.

Sets can be manipulated by set operators, and an algebra of sets can be constructed. The usual set operators are union, intersection, difference, product and division. The union of two sets A and B (written A ∪ B) is a set consisting of all the elements of A and all the elements of B. The intersection of two sets A and B (written A ∩ B) is the set of elements which are members of A and also members of B. The difference of two sets A and B, in that order (written A − B), is the set of elements which are in A but not in B. The product of sets A and B (written A × B) is a set of *pairs of elements* constructed by taking the first element of A and pairing it with each element of B, then taking the second element of A with each element of B, and so on. Division is the reverse of product. A set of pairs of elements, P, can be divided by a set of elements, E. The resulting set, R, is the set of elements of P which match all the elements of E. These operations are shown diagrammatically in Figure 7.1.

It is possible to take the product of any number of sets. The product of 2 sets is a set of pairs. The product of 3 sets is a set of triples (or '3-tuples'), of 4 sets a set of quadruples (or '4-tuples') up to the general case of 'n' sets which is a set of 'n-tuples'. (The word 'tuple' is pronounced to rhyme with 'couple'.) Division can similarly be extended. In addition to the set operations (which always produce another set as their output), we can examine the associations or mappings between elements of two or more (not necessarily distinct) sets. This is also called a function.

These few basic concepts have lead to many important developments in Mathematics. It was Dr E. F. Codd who applied them to database design and who developed the relational model.

7.2   Basic structure

The relational model consists of two basic concepts: domains and relations. Other concepts emerge as a result of these basic concepts and the relationships between them. Domains are sets of values from which

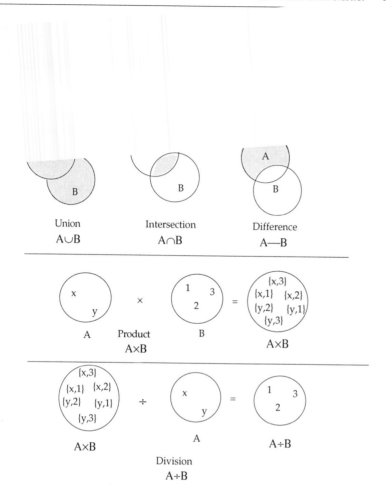

Figure 7.1   *Basic set operations*

The term 'relation' has been defined in various slightly different ways since it was first used by Codd (1970). It is not intended to pursue these subtleties in this text. Interested readers are referred to Date (1995a). For most purposes a relation can be thought of as a table and the terms 'relation' and 'table' are almost interchangeable. Most authors treat the terms as synonyms and in this text we follow that lead. Although we try and avoid the term 'table' during definitions, in subsequent discussions the terms get used more loosely and interchangeably. The reason for being careful during definitions is that whilst a table is a suitable *physical* model of a relation, it is important to remember that a relation is a mathematical concept. The significance of the definitions and properties described in this and the following section should not be overlooked.

Previous chapters have stressed the distinction between a data element
type and data element values. For example, the data element (type)
OrderNumber may have the value 14387. In the relational model, data
elements in relations are called 'attributes'. 'Attribute' can be thought of
in its usual English language sense of characteristic. Thus a relation
holding details about individuals would have attributes of height,
weight, etc. As with data elements, we talk of attribute types and
attribute values. *Height* and *Weight* are examples of attribute types. The
set of possible values which an attribute can take is called its domain.
For example, in a relation Order, the domain of *OrderNumber* may be the
set of all 5-digit integers excluding 0. In another enterprise the attribute
(type) *OrderNumber* may have a domain of all 4-digit integers, or
perhaps all 4-digit integers in the range 2001–9999, and so on.

A relation is defined on a number of domains and consists of two parts.
The header part is a (mathematical) set of attribute types such that each
attribute type corresponds to one of the underlying domains (though the
domains on which attributes are defined do not have to be distinct — in
a relation there may be more than one attribute defined on the same
domain). The body is a set of tuples. (More precisely, 'n-tuples', where n
is the number of attributes in the relation; the degree of the relation.
However, the 'n' prefix is usually dropped.) Each tuple is a set of values.
A tuple has one value, taken from the relevant domain, for each
attribute in the relation header.

In fact, a tuple is a set of pairs of attribute type and value. However, it
would be very long winded if we had to write the relation as pairs such
as (*OrderNumber*, 2005), (*OrderNumber*, 2013), (*OrderNumber*, 2135) and
so on. Accordingly, the attribute type is usually inferred from the
relation header. Notice the distinction between the physical model (the
table) which links the column heading with the values in that column
and the mathematical model which has no notion of a column.

Each domain is a set of values. Whereas the tuples represent the current
values of the attributes, the domains represent the possible values. The
tuples will almost certainly change over time ('time-varying') whereas
the domains, attribute types and relation headers are relatively time-
invariant. (To be pedantic, we could consider any change to the
structure of the data — i.e. the relation headers — to be the destruction
of the old relation and the creation of a new one. Hence relation headers
can be considered completely time invariant.)

A relation may have any number of tuples and attribute types. If a
relation has only one attribute it is called a 'unary' relation, if it has two
it is a 'binary' relation, 3, 'ternary', etc. up to n an 'n-ary' relation. The
number of attributes is called the degree of the relation. The number of
tuples is called the cardinality of the relation. Although not usual it is

_ ...uvanaDle in
..., uie terms tend to get muddled and used
...eicnangeably. The purpose of highlighting the differences here is so
that the interested reader can examine the literature without being
bewildered by the terminology. In this text, the terms are used
interchangeably and in an informal manner.

Tuples of the relation show particular occurrences or instances of the
relation. The columns show the values of particular attributes. The
column heading is the attribute type and corresponds to a domain
(though the column heading may have a different name from its
corresponding domain). The terms 'value' and 'type' are used when
talking about attributes, (thus giving attribute value and attribute type),
the terms 'row' or 'occurrence' and 'type' are used when referring to a
table (giving table row or table occurrence and table type). Some authors
use the term 'instance' instead of occurrence or value.

Hence, in the above example, *PartNumber* is an attribute type, and P3 is
an attribute value. The triple (or 3-tuple) {*PartNumber, Description,
QuantityInStock*} is a table type whereas {P3, Washer, 3500} is a table
occurrence or a table row. When just using the term 'relation', we mean
both the type and the occurrences. The term 'tuple' is equivalent to a
table row (i.e. an occurrence) and 'relation header' is equivalent to table
type. Elsewhere in the system are the domains. In the example in Figure
7.2, there would be domains corresponding to each attribute:
PartNumber, Description and *QuantityInStock*.

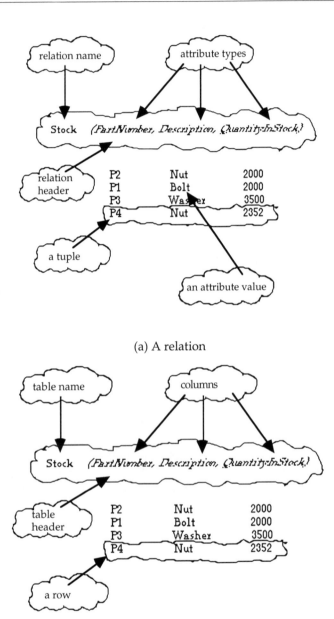

(a) A relation

(b) A table

Figure 7.2   *Terminology for tables and relations*

Column ordering

The attributes of a relation are considered to be unordered. This property follows from the definition of the relation header part. Since this is a (mathematical) set of attribute types, and sets do not have any ordering, it follows that the columns should not have any ordering. In addition, there is a loss of data independence because we may wish to alter the column order for some reason. If information is contained in the ordering of columns it would be changed if the order were changed. Finally, it is an unnecessary burden for users to have to remember the significance of the position of an attribute.

Person	(*Name*	*Name*	*Name*)
	Steven	Trevor	John
	Arnold	Arnold	Peter
	Masako	Ogami	Masako

Figure 7.3   *Column order significant table*

Consider the table occurrences in Figure 7.3. The table is ambiguous because we do not know which is the person's forename, which their family name and which is their second forename. If we switch the columns round then we change the information in the table whatever assumptions we have made. The situation can be overcome by insisting that each column in a table should have a unique name. Notice, however, that the attributes are still taken from the same domain — Names, say. The data from Figure 7.3 is shown in Figure 7.4, but is no longer ambiguous.

Person	(*FamilyName*	*FirstForeName*	*SecondForeName*)
	Steven	Trevor	John
	Arnold	Arnold	Peter
	Masako	Ogami	Masako

Figure 7.4   *Column order not significant*

It is desirable to make clear when attributes are taken from the same domain so that comparisons can be made which are semantically sensible. For example, it would normally be unhelpful to compare values from the domain of people names with values from the domain of city names. Various naming conventions have been proposed, but we prefer to store such information in the data dictionary. The relationship between attributes and domains is metadata and should be stored with other metadata.

Row ordering

A more common problem is when information is dependent on the ordering of the rows in a table. This must be avoided because we may want to resequence the rows of a table or to add or delete rows. We also want to avoid any reference to the way data is physically stored. The relational model is a conceptual model. If information is contained in the ordering of rows, some physical data independence is lost. Furthermore, since the body of the relation is itself a set (a set of tuples), the unordered nature of sets once again demands that rows should be unordered. Consider Figure 7.5, a table holding information about product manufacturing.

Manufacture	(ProductNumber,	TaskDescription)
	P1	sawing
	P1	bending
	P1	welding
	P1	painting

Figure 7.5   *Row order significant table*

In this case the sequence of the rows contains information as to the sequence in which the tasks have to be carried out. Re-ordering the rows changes the information. If a new task, e.g. drilling is to be added then it must be put into its correct place.

This problem can be more difficult to overcome than column order significance, but the addition of another attribute *SequenceNumber* is a common way of alleviating it. In fact the *SequenceNumber* is an example of an implicit data element. Recall the warnings given in chapter 2, that the analyst must be aware of *all* data. *SequenceNumber* was not so much invented to overcome a problem as it was discovered. The use of the sequence number is shown in Figure 7.6.

The table in Figure 7.6 can be sorted into any sequence without changing the information contained in the table. However, adding a new task is still not easy, as several of the sequence numbers may have to be changed. In chapter 2 we mentioned the use of sequence numbering and its importance to database design. If it is anticipated that additions will have to be made to a sequence, then the sequence numbers can be incremented in tens rather than units, or the attribute *SequenceNumber* can be taken from the domain of real numbers rather than integers. The additional operation 'drilling' can now be added in between operations 2 and 3 without causing any disruption to the existing table as shown in Figure 7.7.

Manufacture	(ProductNumber,	TaskDescription,	SequenceNumber)
	P1	sawing	1
	P1	bending	2
	P1	welding	3
	P1	painting	4
	P1	drilling	2.5

Figure 7.7   *Adding a new operation to the Manufacture relation*

These first two properties of relations emphasise the problems of representing relations as tables and serve as a reminder that they are not exactly the same. The physical representation of a relation as a table suggests an ordering of left to right and top to bottom. It is one of the most significant features of the relational model that no information is contained in the ordering of the rows and columns. In terms of the discussion in the previous chapter, we must remember that tables and relations are different data models, the difference being that tables appear to have an ordering. In using tables as the realisation of the relational model, this unfortunate feature must be constantly borne in mind.

Distinct rows

In order to avoid ambiguity and redundant data, the restriction that no two rows can contain exactly the same values throughout is imposed on tables. Once again this follows from the definition of the relation body as a set of tuples. Sets do not have duplicated values. In many cases it is easy to ensure that there are no duplicate rows by designating one or more attributes as a row identifier, or primary key (see below). This is the case in Figure 7.2 when any value of *PartNumber* will only appear once in the table occurrences. However it can prove more difficult in a table such as in Figure 7.5 when the product many undergo the same task more than once during manufacture. Again it can be alleviated by inventing a sequence number and hence the identifier of the tables in Figures 7.6 and 7.7 is the composite attribute formed by the concatenation of *ProductNumber* and *SequenceNumber* usually written {*ProductNumber, SequenceNumber*}.

This rule is very important as it means that any row in a table can be identified by specifying a combination of attributes. The row identifier ('identifier', 'primary key' or simply 'key' are often used as synonyms) is the least number of attributes needed to distinguish one row from another. It may be a single attribute or a composite attribute. Often there is more than one possible identifier for a table. In this case each is known as a candidate identifier, or candidate key. The final decision of which data element(s) to choose as the identifier can be quite complex. Whichever candidate identifier is chosen becomes known as the 'primary key' or 'identifier'. Recall from the introduction to the relational model given in chapter 6 that links between tables are maintained by the existence of a (possibly composite) data element. The 'distinct rows' rule means that every table has an identifier. It is the identifier which is used to form links because it unambiguously identifies a row of the table which it is linked to. When an identifier is used to link tables together in this way it is called a 'posted identifier' or 'foreign key'.

For example, we want to store details of employees and the departments which they work for. Employees have attributes such as *EmployeeNumber, Name, Age* and *DepartmentNumber* and departments have the attributes *DepartmentNumber, Name* and *Budget*. Some table occurrences are shown in Figure 7.8.

In the Employee table the primary key is the *EmployeeNumber*. This is sufficient to uniquely identify table occurrences and does not contain any superfluous attributes (it cannot because it is a single attribute). There are no other candidate keys. The only possibility is *Name* and in this case *Name* equates with surname, and, as can be seen from the sample data, surname can take duplicate values, i.e. more than one person can have the same surname.

‖

Figure 7.8   *Employees and departments —sample data*

In the Department table, *DepartmentNumber* and *Name* are candidate keys (if we accept that no two departments will have the same name — a reasonable assumption). *DepartmentNumber* is chosen as the primary key simply because it is felt to be more convenient. (Any candidate key which is not chosen to be the primary key is an 'alternate key'.) In the Employee table, *DepartmentNumber* is a foreign key (or posted identifier) because it is an attribute of one table (i.e. Employee) and a primary key of another (i.e. Department). It is the existence of a foreign key which enables us to link the tables together. And without the links there would be no structural relationship between the relations. In some cases the foreign key may be a part of the primary key.

Thus there are four roles which a data element can play: primary key, foreign key, alternate key or non-key attribute.

Repeated attributes

It is quite common for designers to create tables which have a repeated attribute, often called a repeating group. For example, the information about how a product is manufactured (see Figure 7.5) could be represented by the table in Figure 7.9.

Manufacture	(*ProductNumber*,	*Tasks*)
	P1	sawing, bending, welding, painting
	P2	sawing, drilling, welding
	P3	welding, painting

Figure 7.9   *Table with repeating group*

This structure occurs frequently when storing information about days of the week or months of the year, or when dealing with anything that occurs several times; the books which a student has on loan from the library; the products which a supplier can supply; the employees who are attached to a department.

A repeating group is unsatisfactory for modelling data. This is because it introduces a level of complexity which is undesirable. Effectively it is a table within a table. It is a hierarchical structure. Often repeating groups consist of more than one attribute (for example, on an order there is a repeating group (*PartNumber, QuantityOrdered*) for each part ordered). This introduces a further level of complexity. Instead of an attribute containing a single value in each tuple, it now contains a whole relation!

Repeating groups come in two forms:

- where the maximum number of attributes is known, for example, a customer's monthly sales figures are kept for 12 months only;

- where the maximum size of the repeating group is indeterminate, for example, the number of products on an order.

The latter can only be dealt with adequately by eliminating the repeating group whereas the former can be represented by giving each element of the group a unique attribute name. For example sales figures kept for a year could be held as *SalesJan, SalesFeb, SalesMar*, etc.

Although the requirement that relations cannot have repeated attributes is not a feature of a relation being a mathematical set, it is a feature of the relational model. This property of relations follows from our definition of a domain as a set of simple (often called atomic) values. A complex domain is one in which the elements each consist of more than one value. In terms of the relational model such a domain is a domain of tuples and is to be avoided if the simple structure of the model is to be maintained.

Any table obeying this last rule is said to be 'normalised' (or in first normal form , written 1NF). Hence all *relations* are in first normal form (though tables might not be). Although an unnormalised table (i.e. a table in which there are repeating groups) is an unsuitable structure for the data model, it is a structure which often arises in the user's world. Users frequently think of data as having repeating groups. Fortunately it is a simple task to transform any unnormalised table into an equivalent (normalised) relation. The process is to write out the repeated attribute(s) in a vertical fashion and then duplicate all other attributes for each of the newly created occurrences. The new table can then be

~~~~~~~~ ~~ ~~~~~~~~~~ ~~~~ ~~~ ~~~~~~~ or ensuring that the data model accurately reflects the enterprise. In chapter 2 we mentioned some of the problems of collecting and transmitting data. These data collection procedures must be designed to minimise erroneous data being entered onto the computer. Given that the data is accurate when it arrives, it must then be validated before it is accepted by the database. The data dictionary can be very useful in this respect by checking data for format, range, etc. and programs can be written to check intra-transaction calculations. However, there is also a need for inter-database validation, checking for such things as the role which a data element plays in a relation. Two integrity rules form an integral part of the relational model.

Each relation must have a unique identifier or primary key (by virtue of the distinct rows rule). This key is used to form links between tables by including it as an attribute of the other relation. When an attribute which is the primary key of one relation exists as an attribute in another relation, then it plays the role of a foreign key in the other relation. Problems can occur in our data model, if we do not know the value of a data element.

Null values

When a designer produces a relational data model of an enterprise, he or she specifies what the attribute types are, how they are grouped into relations and the domains of values which are allowable. Some of these domains will permit the values zeros for numeric data elements and blanks for alphabetic data elements, but some will not. For example, the domain of product numbers or order numbers would probably not include zeros or blanks.

A problem arises when the database is operational if the value of an attribute is unknown. If the price of a product has not been fixed before details of the product are entered onto the database, then that price cannot be said to be zero, or any other figure The price is unknown. Unknown values in the relational model are called 'null' values.

A null value is not zero or spaces (although it is often physically represented as such). Null values are unknown values — unknown at an instant in time, but presumably will be known later, and can then be inserted into the database. (There is another sort of null value that can occur, this is when an attribute value is not applicable in a certain occurrence. These sorts of null can be eradicated through careful database design.)

The unknown type of null causes problems. For example if a value is unknown, it cannot be compared with a known value. In general we cannot overcome this problem by forbidding null values, sometimes the value of an attribute is unknown — hence null. However, we can ensure that certain important values are not null.

Integrity rules

In order to ensure that the data is consistent the relational model includes the rule that the primary key cannot be null. This is necessary to avoid duplication (at most we could only have one such occurrence) and because it defeats the idea of an identifier. By definition, a null value (i.e. an unknown value) cannot identify anything. This argument can be extended to cover all attributes in a composite identifier.

This is known as entity integrity. The entity integrity rule states that

Primary keys cannot be null, or contain any parts which are null.

Now, what about foreign keys? It may be the case that a foreign key could be null — e.g. the *DepartmentNumber* in a table Employee (*EmployeeNumber* Name, Address, DepartmentNumber) is a foreign key because it is an attribute of the Employee relation and a primary key of another relation (the Department relation). If it cannot be null, then details of an employee can only be stored on the database if he/she has been allocated to a department, that is if the value of *DepartmentNumber* is known. In some enterprises this may be exactly what is required , but it would be an overly restrictive rule to include in a general model. Whether or not the enterprise allows foreign keys to accept null values is a decision of that organization. The relational model must allow for foreign keys to be null. However, if the value of a foreign key is known, then it is reasonable to insist that that value is present in the relation of which it is the primary key. If this were not the case, there would be no way of knowing whether the value was a valid one or not. Hence in the relational model, foreign keys can be null. However, if a foreign key is not null, then the value which it has must exist in the relation of which it is the primary key.

This is known as referential integrity. Referential integrity states:

g ...ucuici the situation will improve
 over the next few years as new relational systems are developed is a
matter of debate. At present it is left up to the data administrators in
particular organisations to enforce the good practice of the integrity
rules if the full power of the relational model is to be utilised.

Other constraints

The two integrity rules should not be seen as the only measures to be
taken to ensure that the database retains its integrity. There are many
other aspects of integrity such as ensuring that related relations all get
updated at the same time and ensuring that certain constraints which
have been represented in the model are adhered to. The entity and
referential integrity rules do not tell the designer what to do if they are
violated. I have certainly had experience of integrity being waived aside
by the immediate demands of the business. (Try telling a sales
representative that the computer will not accept an order until an order
number has been issued!) With referential integrity, what should
happen if a relation occurrence is deleted, the primary key of which is a
foreign key in another relation? For example, what should the Suppliers
and Parts database do with the shipments for a supplier who is deleted?
Should all shipments be automatically deleted or should the attempted
deletion be forbidden?

There may be other constraints in the model such as domain constraints
which determine which values are allowable for a domain. Constraints
can be applied to whole relations, for example employees with a certain
status cannot have a salary over a particular value. Other constraints
may cross two or more relations. For example, in a room booking
application it may be necessary to check that the room has the necessary
facilities to hold a particular type of meeting. The expression of
constraints is an extremely important part of database design and
database management systems are increasingly providing facilities for
the data administrator to implement these in a declarative manner (i.e.
by declaring constraints as part of the data model, rather than
implementing them through programs or other user processes.

In his Turing lecture in 1981, E. F. Codd argues that the relational model
was motivated by three factors. The data independence objective (*cf.*
chapter 3), the communicability objective which intended to provide a

model so that all kinds of users and programmers could understand the data, and the self-procuring objective which was to provide data processing without the need for complex looping mechanisms found in most programming languages. The relational model achieves these objectives.

However, Date (1995a) warns us that the relational model is not a panacea, it is a beginning rather than an end and there will be plenty of developments over the years. One such development, the extended relational model, RM/T or the relational model version 2 (see Codd, 1990), has already come but has not been widely accepted and object-oriented systems represent another development (see chapter 16).

7.5   Key points

Our treatment of the relational model has necessarily been somewhat brief. However, the essence of the model has been established.

- Everything is defined in terms of relations which consist of attributes which take their values from simple domains which are sets of atomic values.

- The relational model consists of relation occurrences (tuples) which vary with time according to the values which they contain and relation headers which are relatively time invariant.

- Domains represent the possible values for data elements.

- A relation must obey four 'rules': no column ordering, no row ordering, no duplication of rows, no repeated attributes.

- A relation, since it consists of attributes which have simple domains is normalised, or in first normal form.

- The relational model includes rules governing entity and referential integrity.

- The relational model can represent other constraints.

Further reading

Codd, E. F. (1970) The Relational Model of Data for large shared Data Banks *Communications of the ACM* Vol 13 no. 6 June

The classic paper well worth reading.

...relational model is that
relations can be manipulated in a variety of ways which
always result in a new relation being produced. This can then be
manipulated in a similar fashion. The original language for
manipulating the data in relational models was the relational
algebra. For general use, this has now been superseded by a 'query
language' known as SQL ('ess - que - ell'). SQL is now the standard
relational query language and some knowledge of it is vital for
anyone working in the database area. This chapter provides a brief
overview of the main aspects of SQL.

At the end of this chapter you should be able to:

- understand the basic manipulation of relations through
  selecting rows, projecting columns and joining relations

- write simple queries in SQL

- understand the structure of the SQL language

- understand the importance of the 'join' operator in relational
  data manipulation

- be able to create a simple database in SQL.

8.1   The development of SQL

The normalised relation is the basic building block, the basic structure,
of the computer-oriented data model. In order to be able to produce
information, it must be possible to manipulate the basic structures in
ways that are consistent and unambiguous. The relational model allows
us to perform such operations at the conceptual level, i.e. no knowledge
is needed of how the data is physically stored.

The relational 'algebra' was an important part of Codd's original
definition of the relational model. This algebra consisted of a number of
operations which could be performed on relations and which would
always result in another relation which obeys the four rules established
in chapter 7 and which can itself be manipulated by the same operators.
The relational algebra was based closely on the various set operations

which provide the basis of set manipulation in mathematics plus a few other operations necessary for dealing with relations. The relational model of data is a 'closed' system; operations can be undertaken which produce an outcome consistent within the data model.

Another important concept underlying the relational algebra is the idea that manipulation is manipulation of a *whole relation*. Unlike more procedural programming languages in which the programmer has to tell the system which record (or table row) to get and what to do with it, the relational algebra does this for the programmer by operating on the whole relation. Relational data manipulation frees the programmer from details of control and means that programmers can concentrate on what is required rather than how to accomplish it. Although it was originally believed that SQL would provide a good language for users to express their own *ad hoc* queries in, SQL does not succeed at this. Even without the complications of more procedural languages, SQL remains complex and still requires careful thought as to how a particular query should be expressed.

SQL grew out of early versions of relational databases which were developed during the 1970s. The international standard was published in 1986. However, even as this standard was being published, work was beginning on the next version of the language, SQL2 (also known as SQL/92). The standard for this language was published in 1992 and remains the current standard. However, already plans are underway for a third version (SQL3) which is expected in the late 1990s.

Although SQL2 is an international standard, most database management systems do not implement it completely and many use a slightly different syntax from that presented here. In this book, we are not concerned about specific implementations, nor about all the details of SQL. We are concerned with the principles of data manipulation in the relational model and use SQL as a convenient and commercially important language in which to do that.

8.2   The basics of SQL

The basic idea of SQL is that users or programmers can:

* select rows from a table according to various criteria

* select columns from a table

* link or *join* tables together, based on the attribute(s) which they have in common

* compare, add, subtract, multiply and divide tables, attributes and values

keys), create and delete domains and control access to the data by
organising and maintaining authorisation mechanisms — allowing
different users to update the database, others just to see part of the
database and so on. Finally it is necessary to provide facilities so that
other constraints on the data can be specified.

In fact the variety of features which are necessary to deal with all these
things and to accommodate all the requirements of programmers, the
database administrator and the end-users means that SQL has become a
very large and complex language. A detailed treatment of SQL can be
found in Date with Darwen (1993). The purpose of this chapter is to
illustrate the power of the relational model by showing how relations
can be manipulated through the more basic functions of the language. It
is not intended to cover all aspects of the language in detail. Throughout
the following sections we use the tables and values shown in Figure 8.1;
a variation of the suppliers and parts database.

Part Number	Description	Colour		Supplier Number	Name	Address
P1	Nut	red		S1	Jones	London
P2	Bolt	blue		S2	Jones	Paris
P3	Nut	red		S3	Smith	London
P4	Bolt	red		S4	Smith	Basle

Part   Supplier

SupplierNumber	PartNumber	Quantity
S1	P1	500
S2	P2	300
S1	P3	200
S3	P1	100
S2	P4	400

Supplies

Figure 8.1   *The relational model for the example database*

8.3   Selecting rows and columns

Once a relational database has been created and populated with data (see section 8.7), users will want to retrieve various subsets of the data.

For example, a user who wants to find all the parts in the Part table which have a description of 'bolt' would enter

```
Select PartNumber, Description    (Query 1)
From Part
Where description = 'Bolt'
```

This would give the result

PartNumber	Description
P2	Bolt
P4	Bolt

Another user might want to know which suppliers can supply parts in quantities greater than 200. In which case, they would enter

```
Select *                          (Query 2)
From Supplies
Where Quantity > 200
```

This would give the result

SupplierNumber	PartNumber	Quantity
S1	P1	500
S2	P2	300
S2	P4	400

Several points are worth noting about Query 1 and Query 2. First the user has to specify which *columns* or attributes of the table that are required by issuing a 'Select' statement.

```
Select columnname1, columnname2, ...
```

Sometimes (where there may be ambiguity) it is necessary to qualify the column name by the table's name using the 'dot' notation; tablename.columnname means the attribute with columnname in the

```
..... tablename1, tablename2, ...
```

Third, the user specifies the conditions under which data should be retrieved by issuing the 'Where' statement such as 'where description = 'Bolt'' in Query 1 or 'where Quantity > 200' in Query 2

```
Where attribute <some condition> attribute
or value, ...
```

This is the basic structure of the language and is sometimes known as the 'Select-From-Where' structure.

In both Query 1 and Query 2 the user only needed to use one table as all the required attributes were contained in one table. However, if, for example, the user wanted the part description as well as the part number then it would be necessary to access both the Supplies and the Part relations. This would be accomplished by issuing a statement such as Query 3.

```
Select SupplierNumber,               (Query 3)
PartNumber, Description, Quantity
From Supplies, Part
Where PartNumber = PartNumber
and
Quantity > 200
```

Query 3 would result in the following table.

SupplierNumber	PartNumber	Description	Quantity
S1	P1	Nut	500
S1	P2	Bolt	300
S2	P4	Bolt	400

As you can see, Query 3 is quite a lot more complex than the previous queries. The user has to specify the tables required and the criteria which are required in order to match the rows in the two tables. The tables are *joi*ned together and queries such as this are often called Joins. In this case the match (or joining condition) is that the part numbers in Supplies and Part should be the same. We return to joins in section 8.5.

Finally it is important to notice that the user can specify various conditions under which rows are selected. These are expressed in the 'where' clause of the query. The conditions under which rows can be selected are many and vary between implementations of SQL. Some of the more common are shown in Figure 8.2. These conditions can be related together by using the 'Boolean' operators AND, OR and NOT as is illustrated in Query 3 and Query 4.

=	equal to	(not) Like	compares strings of characters
<>	not equal to	(not) Between	checks for values between other values
>	greater than	Is (not) null	checks for null values
>=	greater than or equal to	(not) In	checks if a value is in a set of other values
<	less than	(not) Exists	checks if a values exist
<=	less than or equal to	Unique	checks for uniqueness

Figure 8.2   *Common comparison operators*

For example, the following query (Query 4) answers the query 'find the part numbers which supplier S1 can supply in quantities greater than 200 or which supplier S2 can supply in quantities greater than 200'.

```
Select PartNumber, Quantity        (Query 4)
From Supplies
Where Quantity > 200 and SupplierNumber = S1
or Quantity > 200 and SupplierNumber = S2
```

One important point to notice about SQL is that the result of a query is *not* always another relation. For example, if a user issues the query shown in Query 5

```
Select Description              (Query 5)
From Part        ˙
```

then the result will be

Description

Nut
Bolt
Nut
Bolt

and this table contains duplicate rows — something strictly forbidden in the relational model. In order to express the query 'find out which part descriptions we have', the user only wants one occurrence of each and must, therefore, specify that only 'distinct' rows are required (see Query 6).

```
Select Distinct Description     (Query 6)
From Part
```

which gives the following relation

Description

Nut
Bolt

Another important feature of SQL is that queries can be embedded in other queries. This is particularly useful when using the search or comparison conditions. However, such queries can get quite complex. For example, Date gives the example (Query 7) in (Date with Darwen, 1993) which answers the query 'find the suppliers who are in the same city as supplier S1'.

The nesting of queries can continue as is illustrated in Query 8 which shows the use of the 'in' operator and answers the query 'find the supplier names for suppliers who supply at least one red part'.

```
Select SupplierNumber              (Query 7)
From Supplier
Where Address =
        (Select Address
        From Supplier
        Where SupplierNumber = 'S1')


Select Name, Address               (Query 8)
From Supplier
Where SupplierNumber in
        (Select SupplierNumber
        From Supplies
        Where PartNumber in
                (Select PartNumber
                From Part
                Where Colour = 'red'))
```

The result of Query 7 will be S3 since S3 has an address of London which matches the address of S1. The result of Query 8 is shown below. The logic of Query 8 is (i) find the red parts, i.e. {P1, P3, P4}, (ii) find who supplies those parts, i.e. {S1, S3, S2} and (iii) select the Name and Address of those suppliers

Name	*Address*
Jones	London
Jones	Paris
Smith	London

8.4   Group by and Having clauses

In addition to specifying the rows and columns which they want to see, users can specify other conditions such as how to group the results and the conditions under which to select those groups. For example, a user may want to know the total quantities for each part in the Supplies relation (see Query 9), or to count the number of suppliers at each address (Query 10). These are often called 'aggregate' functions as they perform some operation on whole groups of rows. The other aggregate functions which are typically available for use with the grouping operation are: MAX (find the maximum value), MIN (find the minimum value) and AVG (find average value). One important restriction which using a group by clause imposes is that the attributes

```
                                          (Query 10)
       count (SupplierNumber)
       From Supplier
       Group by Address
```

The Having clause is often associated with grouping operations. This clause specifies the conditions under which certain groups should be selected. The aggregate functions can be applied in the Having clause. For example, Query 11 would answer the query 'find the supplier numbers for suppliers, except S4, who supply parts in average quantities greater than or equal to 100'. Query 11 also specifies the order in which the result should be displayed. The order refers to the columns of the table resulting from the query. It is possible to specify a column number (so, for example, order by 3 in Query 11 would refer to the Avg (Quantity). Alternatively the user can specify a name for the attribute by specifying 'As <name>' following the attribute. This is the method used in Query 11.

```
       Select    SupplierNumber,           (Query 11)
       Avg (Quantity) As Qty,
       From Supplies
       Where SupplierNumber <> 'S4'
       Group by SupplierNumber
       Having Avg (Quantity) >= 100
       Order by Qty
```

The result of Query 11 is shown below. All Supplies quantities for supplier S3 are excluded through the 'where' clause. The average of the quantities is calculated for each supplier and any which have an average less than or equal to one hundred are excluded through the Having clause. The result is presented in Qty (i.e. the average of the quantities for each supplier) sequence.

SupplierNumber	Qty
S1	350
S2	350
S3	100

8.5   Joining tables

The ability to join tables in the relational model is one of its most important characteristics. Recall from chapters 6 and 7 that every relation has some attribute, or combination of attributes which uniquely distinguishes one row from another. This attribute or attributes is known as the primary key of the relation. When the primary key of one relation appears as an attribute of another relation it takes on the role of a foreign key. The existence of foreign keys means that relations can be linked though the values of this attribute. In the suppliers and parts database *SupplierNumber* is a foreign key in Supplies because it is the primary key of Supplier and hence allows us to obtain additional details of suppliers which are not kept in the Supplies relation. Similarly *PartNumber* is a foreign key in Supplies as it is the primary key of Part and allows us to retrieve details of parts not held in the Supplies relation. {*SupplierNumber, PartNumber*} is the primary key of Supplies.

The way in which attributes are assigned to relations is crucial to an effective database design; that is one which eliminates redundancy in the relational model. We devote the next three chapters to looking at how to design relations (i.e. how to decide which attributes should be in which relations). This is important because we do not want to lose any information in the way in which we design relations. Our concern here is how to retrieve, or make available, information which requires us to link tables together. We consider how foreign keys and primary keys are specified in section 8.7.

When two tables are joined, the result is a table in which all the each row of one table is put together with all the rows from the other table. (This can be extended to more than two tables.) This is also known as the Cartesian product of the two tables. Now it is possible to join any two tables together. For example, the Cartesian product of Supplier and Part is shown in Figure 8.3. However, there is usually not much point in doing this if the two tables do not have any meaningful relationship. This is the case in Figure 8.3 where the resulting table does not mean anything. It certainly does not mean that the various parts are supplied by the various suppliers as might be suggested by the table.

Although this operation is possible in SQL by issuing the statement

					London
			S1	Jones	London
1 4	Bolt	red	S1	Jones	London
P1	Nut	red	S2	Jones	Paris
P2	Bolt	blue	S2	Jones	Paris
P3	Nut	red	S2	Jones	Paris
P4	Bolt	red	S2	Jones	Paris
P1	Nut	red	S3	Smith	London
P2	Bolt	blue	S3	Smith	London
P3	Nut	red	S3	Smith	London
P4	Bolt	red	S3	Smith	London
P1	Nut	red	S4	Smith	Basle
P2	Bolt	blue	S4	Smith	Basle
P3	Nut	red	S4	Smith	Basle
P4	Bolt	red	S4	Smith	Basle

Figure 8.3   *Cartesian product of Supplier and Part*

It is more useful and more meaningful to join tables which have some attribute(s) in common. Moreover it is more useful to specify the conditions under which the join should be made. We have already seen that tables can be joined by specifying more than one table name in the From clause (Query 3) where the Supplies table was joined with the Part table so that the *Description* attribute could be retrieved for each part.

SQL provides a number of ways of specifying joins. For example both Query 12 and Query 13 produce similar information to that produced by Query 3 (except that certain quantities less than or equal to 200 are not excluded). The differences being that the ordering of columns may be different and the joining attribute will appear twice in the resulting table in Query 12 and only once in Query 13 (see Figure 8.4). However, these details (which again will vary from implementation to implementation) are not our major concern here. Query 13 is also know as the *natural join* of Part and Supplies. The natural join of two tables is a table which includes all the attributes of the two tables, excluding any duplicate attributes, where the values of all matching attributes are used as the joining condition. In the case of Query 13 the matching attribute is

PartNumber so the tables are joined where the *PartNumber* in Supplies equals the *PartNumber* in Part. All attributes of both tables are shown except that the PartNumber attribute (the joining attribute) appears only once. Query 14 shows an example where three tables are joined.

```
Part join Supplies              (Query 12)
on PartNumber = PartNumber
```

```
Part join Supplies              (Query 13)
using (PartNumber)
```

Supplier Number	PartNumber	PartNumber	Description	Quantity
S1	P1	P1	Nut	500
S2	P2	P2	Bolt	300
S1	P3	P3	Nut	200
S3	P1	P1	Bolt	100
S2	P4	P4	Nut	400

Join of Supplies and Part on *PartNumber*

SupplierNumber	PartNumber	Description	Quantity
S1	P1	Nut	500
S2	P2	Bolt	300
S1	P3	Nut	200
S3	P1	Bolt	100
S2	P4	Nut	400

Natural Join of Supplies and Part on *PartNumber*

Figure 8.4   *Join and Natural join of Supplies and Part*

```
Select Name,                    (Query 14)
Description, Quantity
From Part, Supplier, Supplies
Where PartNumber = PartNumber and
SupplierNumber = SupplierNumber
```

Query 14 gives the result below. This again is not very useful because the names and descriptions are not unique so we do not know which Jones or which Smith is being referred to, nor which Nut and which Bolt.

ˌ ˙˙˙ ˏ ᴡᴇ ᴜiscussed some of the problems which are caused by the existence of null values in tables. In particular, what should happen when we try to join tables which have nulls in the joining condition? All the examples given so far will only retrieve those with matching values and hence will not include nulls since a null value is not the same as a non-null value. Such joins are referred to as 'inner joins'. The other sorts of join which are possible are:

full outer join   includes rows from both tables where there are null values present

left outer join   includes rows from the first table specified where there are null values

right outer join includes rows from the second table where there are null values.

It is important to understand the basic join operation as it is one of the most powerful features of the relational model. The most common type of join is the natural join, i.e. the linking of tables based on the primary key/foreign key relationship which excludes rows containing null values and which removes the duplicated attributes.

8.6   Further features of SQL

There are many other features of SQL which it is not appropriate to deal with in depth in this text. These other features have to do with

Authorisation

Various options are available for granting access to data by other users — e.g. allowing users to update certain data, view the data or add or delete items.

Data types

SQL provides for a range of data types such as integers, dates, character strings and so on. Some implementation allow types such as money and time which make comparisons and calculations more flexible and semantically sensible.

Schemas

SQL provides detailed access to the schema definitions so that users can find out which columns are in which tables, which indexes exist and so on.

Transactions

SQL provides some support for transaction management — when several queries which update the database must be undertaken altogether.

Controls

SQL can be embedded in other programming languages, 'cursors' can be declared which allow the user to step through individual rows of tables as required.

Views

Views provide tailored and restricted access to the database. A view can be created in terms of a Select expression which results in a 'virtual table', i.e. it appears to the user as if it were a real (or 'base') table, but in fact is derived from the base table(s) by means of the Select expression. For example, an expression could be written which displayed only the portion of the Supplies table, along with the supplier's name and which related to suppliers based in London. This could be useful for a user who worked only in the London office of an organisation. This example is shown in Query 15.

```
Create View London                    (Query 15)
(SupplierNumber, Name, PartNumber, Quantity)
      As Select SupplierNumber, Name,
      PartNumber, Quantity
      From Supplier, Supplies
      Where SupplierNumber = SupplierNumber
      and Address = 'London'
```

Set operations

Since relations are sets in the mathematical sense, certain operations which are applicable to sets are applicable to relations. These are the operations Union, Intersection and Difference. There are a number of quite complex conditions for expressing these operations in SQL, but the basis of the set operations remain as described in section 7.1. The union of two tables produces a table consisting of the rows of both tables. The intersection of two tables produces a table consisting of the rows common to both tables and the difference of two tables produces a table

... ... uie query find
... ... currently being supplied' is shown in Query 16.

```
(Select PartNumber from Part)      (Query 16)
Intersect
(Select PartNumber from Supplies)
```

8.7   Creating a database

We saw in chapter 7 that the relational model consists of two
fundamental objects: domains and relations. These can be created,
altered and deleted (or 'dropped' in SQL terminology) in SQL databases.
Once again there are some subtle aspects of these commands which we
will not consider, but which readers can find explained in detail in Date
with Darwen (1993). Most notably, we will not consider the creation of
an entire database schema. Once again these details vary between
implementations.

Tables are created by means of a Create Table statement. This statement
defines the columns in the table, their characteristics and any table level
constraints. An example is shown in Query 17. This establishes the
Supplies table assuming that the Part and Supplier tables already exist.
The primary key and any foreign keys are specified in the table
definition.

The table once created does not have any data in it. Values for the
attributes are entered subsequently either through using an Insert
statement or by Importing values from elsewhere (which could, for
example, be the result of another query). Most database management
systems provide simple 'from filling' methods of entering data into
tables.

```
Create Table Supplies                (Query 17)
    (SupplierNumber Char,
    PartNumber Char,
    Quantity Decimal,
    Primary key (SupplierNumber, PartNumber)
    Foreign key (SupplierNumber references Supplier
    Foreign key (PartNumber references Part))
```

In Query 15, the characteristics of the columns are simply specified as a data type (Char meaning any string of characters and Decimal meaning any real number). However, a better alternative is to make use of the capability of SQL to specify domains. Domains are specified with a Create Domain statement such as the one below which creates a domain called Parts.

```
Create Domain Parts Char
```

One of the advantages of creating domains is that systematic and consistent constraints can be used in the database. The user can provide default values for domains and can specify constraints on the values which the system will allow users to enter. If no value is provided for a column in a table and a default value has been, then the system uses the default value. If the user tries to enter data which violates the constraint, SQL will not permit the data to be entered onto the database. Constraints such as the one in Query 18, which defines a domain called 'ECities' with a default value of 'Missing' and which checks that only the four cities specified can be entered, can be applied to column definitions within the table definition statement , as domains do not have to be used in SQL

```
Create Domain ECities char          (Query 18)
        Default 'Missing'
constraint Eurocities
check (value in ('London', 'Paris', 'Basle',
'Brussels'))
```

and the subsequent creation of Supplier would be

```
Create Table Supplier
        (SupplierNumber Char,
        Name Char,
        Address ECities,
        Primary key (SupplierNumber))
```

In addition to domain con~~t~~
We have ~~al~~

~~...~~cription <>

~~A~~ctually, other general constraints can be specified using a statement

```
create assertion <name> check (Select...
```

These general constraints can be as complex as is required. For example, we may have the constraint that no supplier based in Basle can supply any part in a quantity greater than 500. This would be expressed as shown in Query 20 which can be read as 'where there does not exist a supplier with an address of Basle who has an entry in the Supplies tables which has a quantity over 500'.

```
create assertion c2 check           (Query 20)
  (not exists
     (Select * From Supplier
     Where Address = 'Basle'
     And Exists
        (Select * From Supplies
        where Supplies.SupplierNumber =
        Supplier.SupplierNumber
        And Quantity > 500)))
```

8.8   Key points

In this chapter we have looked at the language SQL in terms of the facilities it provides for manipulation of relational databases. We have not attempted an exhaustive coverage of SQL. The most significant things about relational data manipulation and SQL from our perspective are:

- Relations can be manipulated by *projecting* columns, *selecting* rows and *joining* tables and by use of the set operators.

- The basic form of a query in SQL is Select <columns> From <tables> Where <conditions>.

- The Select statement also allows grouping of items, having some conditions and which can be ordered by some attributes.

- Tables can be joined in SQL in a number of ways. The Join operation (whether using a specific join statement or by listing the tables in a Select statement) is absolutely central to relational database manipulation.

- SQL provides many other features including the set operators.

- Tables and domains can be created (altered and dropped).

- Constraints can be specified including entity and referential integrity constraints (through the primary and foreign key declarations), domain constraints, table constraints and general constraints.

Further reading

Date, C. J. with Darwen, H. (1993) *A Guide to the SQL Standard* 3rd Edition Addison-Wesley, Reading, MA

A very comprehensive guide to the standard, but not easy reading for the novice. See also their Relational Database Writings, and, for an easier introduction,

Date, C. J. (1995) *An Introduction to Database Systems* 6th Edition Addison-Wesley, Reading, MA

...., ... can be created and manipulated. However, we have examined the principles of relations in some detail, but have yet to explain how to allocate attributes to relations, decide on relation identifiers or establish links between relations by means of foreign keys. This chapter begins to explore these issues by introducing the concept of a functional dependency. The following chapter examines the reasons behind the normalisation process. We introduce a useful tool — the dependency diagram — to assist in the understanding and use of dependencies between attributes.

After studying this chapter you should be able to:

- describe the three 'anomalies' which can occur in poorly designed relations

- define the term 'functional dependency'

- recognise the difference between full functional dependency and partial functional dependency

- draw dependency diagrams.

9.1   Three problems with relations

Our definition of a relation includes the requirement that attribute domains must be atomic (or simple). This ensures that there is only a single value at any row/column intersection and hence that the relations are 'normalised' or equivalently that they are in first normal form (1NF). Such relations are sufficient for use with relational operators, but still demonstrate some undesirable characteristics.

Consider the suppliers and parts database introduced in chapter 6. If it is designed as a single relation, it would appear as in Figure 9.1 (though we have added an extra row). The identifier of the relation (the minimum number of attributes necessary to distinguish one row from another) is {PartNumber, SupplierNumber}

PartNumber	Supplier Number	Description	Name	Address	Quantity
P1	S1	Nut	Jones	London	500
P1	S2	Nut	Jones	Paris	300
P2	S1	Bolt	Jones	London	200
P2	S3	Bolt	Smith	London	100
P3	S2	Nut	Jones	Paris	200

Figure 9.1   *Suppliers and Parts database designed as a single relation*

This relation contains the same information as the three relations used in chapters 6 (Figure 6.5). Which representation is preferable, and why?

The single relation seems to contain a lot of redundancy. It certainly contains a lot of duplication, but some of this is not redundant because it is unavoidable (for example, the fact that S1 and S2 are both called Jones has to be represented in the relational model by duplicating the data element value 'Jones'). Redundancy is unnecessary duplication.

In the example in Figure 9.1, it is unnecessary to duplicate the fact that supplier S1 is based in London whenever it is required to store the products which supplier S1 supplies. The meaning of the data is that S1 is always associated with London irrespective of the association with products. If redundancy is not eradicated, or at least carefully controlled, it produces some undesirable effects as follows.

Insertion

If a new supplier who does not yet supply any parts is to be added to the database, the relation will have to contain null values. As we saw in section 7.4 null values are awkward to deal with and should be avoided if possible. Adding supplier S4 called Sateesh who lives in Delhi produces

PartNumber	Supplier Number	Description	Name	Address	Quantity
????????	S4	????????	Sateesh	Delhi	????????

where '????????' indicates a null (unknown) value.

Updating

If a supplier changes address then we must ensure that every row of the relation concerning that supplier is updated correctly and accurately. For example if supplier S1 moves to Dublin, rows 1 and 3 have to be changed. In a large database there could be many such updates to be made.

Deletion

If we no lo~

~~ons rather than

~ ~esign.

...cs of relations mean that more care must be taken
...giung the relations. The first step in removing these problems is
to separate all attributes into a separate table which are not determined
by the whole key. 'Determined' is used in a specialised sense here and
the concept of a determinant is explored in detail below. Anticipating
ourselves somewhat, A is determined by B if, given a value of B, you can
always discover the corresponding value of A. For example *PartNumber*
P1 is always associated with 'Bolt', P2 with 'Nut', etc. Hence *PartNumber*
determines part *Description*. Since *PartNumber* is part of the key, but
Description is determined by *PartNumber* alone (rather than {*PartNumber*,
SupplierNumber}, we need to separate *PartNumber* and *Description* into a
separate table. Hence the two relations in Figure 9.2.

Part Number	Description	Part Number	Supplier Number	Name	Address	Quantity
P1	Nut	P1	S1	Jones	London	500
P2	Bolt	P1	S2	Jones	Paris	300
P3	Nut	P2	S1	Jones	London	200
		P2	S3	Smith	London	100
		P3	S2	Jones	Paris	200

Figure 9.2   *Suppliers and Parts database as two relations*

Clearly an analogous argument holds for *SupplierNumber, Name* and
Address. If these are removed to a separate table, we finish up with the
three tables for our original supplier and parts database (Figure 7.4).
Tables in which all the attributes are dependent on the whole key are in
second normal form (2NF).

It is still possible that 2NF relations contain redundancy. Let us
introduce some further attributes to the supplier table, *AreaCode* and
AreaName. The meaning of these attributes may be expressed as an
AreaCode identifies an area of Europe, and an area has a name. There
may be more than one area code with the same name (e.g. *AreaCode* 09 is
England and *AreaCode* 10 is England). Figure 9.3 shows what happens
when *AreaCode* and *AreaName* are added to the Supplies and Parts
database.

Supplier Number	Name	Address	AreaCode	AreaName
S1	Jones	London	10	England
S2	Jones	Paris	12	France
S3	Smith	London	10	England

Figure 9.3   *Adding* AreaCode *and* AreaName *to the Suppliers and Parts database*

This table is in 2NF since all attributes are determined by the whole key (that is, any value of *SupplierNumber* — the primary key — is always associated with the same, single value of each of the other attributes), but there is a further dependency hidden in the relation, namely *AreaCode* and *AreaName*. Given the *AreaCode* we can always find the *AreaName*. *AreaCode* determines *AreaName* (e.g. *AreaCode* 10 is always associated with England). Hence the insert, update and delete anomalies still apply. Inserting a new area would result in null values for the attributes concerned with suppliers. Changing the area name allocated to a particular code involves multiple changes to be made. Deleting an area may result in losing information about suppliers. Once again it is only necessary to remove these to a separate table to remove the redundancy; hence the relations in Figure 9.4.

Supplier Number	Name	Address	AreaCode		AreaCode	AreaName
S1	Jones	London	10		10	England
S2	Jones	Paris	12		12	France
S3	Smith	London	10		10	England

Figure 9.4   *Splitting* AreaCode *and* AreaName *from Figure 9.3 into a separate table*

Tables in which these further dependencies have been removed (that is, where a non-key attribute is dependent on another non-key attribute) are in third normal form (3NF). In practice the designer does not have to go through this process step by step as there is a simple rule for spotting redundancy in relations. The process of designing relations simply involves allocating attributes to appropriate tables, and splitting tables to eradicate redundancy. In the preceding examples, notice how the foreign keys (*SupplierNumber* and *ProductNumber* in the supplies relation and *AreaCode* in the supplier relation) form the links between relations.

9.2   Enterprise ru¹~

...g ∪ı tne data in
. , ---.> and parts database, the
...ı␣ colloquial expressions are needed.

- Every part has a *PartNumber*.

- Every *PartNumber* is associated with a description.

- There may be more than one part with the same description.

- Each *PartNumber* is allocated to just one part.

- Each supplier has a unique *SupplierNumber*.

- Each supplier has a name, but several suppliers may have the same name.

- Each supplier has an address (which is just the name of a city) and hence there may be several suppliers with the same address since they have their business in the same city.

- Suppliers supply parts in various different quantities.

The rules which apply to the meaning of the data in an enterprise are called 'enterprise rules'. In different enterprises there will be different rules which need to be represented in the information model of that enterprise. Information comes from the relationships between data elements and the tables which we design need to express these relationships.

The relationships which prove to be useful are surprisingly simple. They are the relationships which focus on whether the value of a data element can be associated with only one value of another data element or whether it can be associated with more than one value.

For example, consider the string of characters 030596. Let us accept that this conveys information about a date: the 3rd of May 1996. (Notice that an American would interpret this as the 5th of March 1996 — this interpretive information, the data description, is typically stored in the data dictionary, not in the database.) The data elements are *Day, Month* and *Year*. Values of *Day* come from the domain 01–31, *Month* has a domain 01–12 and *Year* has the domain 00–99.

When looking at these mappings we are asking ourselves 'can the value of day be associated with one or more than one value of month?'. The answer, of course, is 'more than one' since valid dates are 030596, 030796, 030896. The value '03' of the data element *Day* can be associated with more than one value of *Month* ('01'–'12'). (Do not worry that we are talking about different dates. We know that, but that is exactly the semantics — the meaning of the data — which must be represented in the database.) In this case the value of *Month* can be associated with more than one value of *Day* ('01'–'31') as well. Saying that it *can be* associated does not mean that all associations are valid. For example, the value 02 for *Month* cannot be associated with the values 30 or 31 of *Day* (expressing the semantics that February cannot have 30 or 31 days). Such validation of data is not contained in the design of the structure of the relations in a relational model, but has to be stored elsewhere in the system (as a validation check in a program, or as a check constraint in the relational model).

The above examples can be seen as mappings between domains as shown in Figure 9.5. It is useful to think of data relationships as mappings between domain elements.

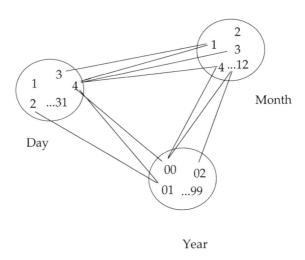

Figure 9.5   *Mappings between domains day, month and year*

Enterprise rules govern the association between data elements. They will be different in different enterprises. In theory we need to examine

the relationships between e~~'
make judgem~~

~~se in
~~sures that each bin
~~~t can only be in one bin. Hence if
~~, we can find the *PartNumber* and if we know the
~~ we can find the *BinNumber*. We say that the relationship
BinNumber:PartNumber is 1:1 (read as 'bin number, part number is one-to-one'). Similarly the relationship *PartNumber:BinNumber* is 1:1.

In enterprise (b), they operate a system which allows them to store several parts in one bin. This is because one of the *BinNumber*s has the value 'outside yard' where all sorts of large and heavy objects are kept. Hence in enterprise (b) the domain of *BinNumber* is {{a01..z99}. 'outside yard'}. To represent the rules in this enterprise, we say *BinNumber:PartNumber* is 1:M (one-to-many), i.e. each bin can contain many (i.e. more than one) parts, but each part can only be in one bin. This relationship could equally well be expressed as *PartNumber:BinNumber* is M:1 (many-to-one).

In enterprise (c), they insist that each bin can contain only one part (i.e. each *BinNumber* is only ever associated with one *PartNumber*) but a part can be found in more than one location because during sale times they have very large stocks and they cannot store all one type of product in a single location. Hence each *PartNumber* can be associated with many *BinNumber*s. *PartNumber:BinNumber* is 1:M, or *BinNumber:PartNumber* is M:1.

Enterprise (d) stores its products all over the place, and some bins can contain lots of different parts. The relationship between *BinNumber* and *PartNumber* is thus M:M (many-to-many). A bin may contain more than one part and a part may be in more than one bin.

Notice that the distinction between type and instance is relevant here. P15 is a value of the data element type *PartNumber*. In the warehouse, we will have many P15s in stock, but we assume that the individual P15s are not further distinguished from one another. Since, in reality, one P15 is indistinguishable from another P15, the database will not distinguish between them either. That is, in the database there will be only one table row for P15.

Of course, not all products are like this and some products are individually identified. For example, there may be plenty of 1600cc engines in the warehouse of a motor manufacturer each having *PartNumber* P13472638 (say). In addition they will each have a unique engine reference number. Whether the enterprise wishes to store details about each individual engine, or whether it only requires details to be kept about a category is, of course, a matter for the enterprise.

Sometimes an identifier represents a single instance of an object (for example, the engine reference number), other times the identifier will represent a category of things (e.g. P13472638 is a 1600cc engine). This distinction can cause problems if it goes unrecognised.

Clearly if the identifier identifies a category of things, the relationships with other data elements will be different from the occasions when an identifier refers to a single physical object. A specific engine could not be located in more than one location! Finally, notice that when we talk of 'many' in terms of the data relationships, we simply mean 'not exactly one'. This could be one, or zero or more than one. Further details of these semantics are captured by the user-oriented data model.

9.3   The dependency diagram

One way to represent the enterprise rules is through a diagrammatic technique knownas a dependency diagram. As a graphical model it is useful for exploring as well as documenting the data relationships. It models the relationships between data elements, or rather the relationship between the values which those data elements can take. The examples in the previous section are shown in Figure 9.6.

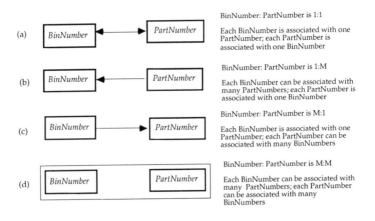

Figure 9.6 showing:

(a) BinNumber ⟷ PartNumber

BinNumber: PartNumber is 1:1

Each BinNumber is associated with one PartNumber; each PartNumber is associated with one BinNumber

(b) BinNumber ← PartNumber

BinNumber: PartNumber is 1:M

Each BinNumber can be associated with many PartNumbers; each PartNumber is associated with one BinNumber

(c) BinNumber → PartNumber

BinNumber: PartNumber is M:1

Each BinNumber is associated with one PartNumber; each PartNumber can be associated with many BinNumbers

(d) BinNumber   PartNumber

BinNumber: PartNumber is M:M

Each BinNumber can be associated with many PartNumbers; each PartNumber can be associated with many BinNumbers

Figure 9.6   *Dependency diagram showing relationships between* BinNumber *and* PartNumber

Notice that the arrowhead ='
where no

... (1985)
...gorous method of
... the notation which is used here is effective
... data relationships and produces a diagram which offers a
clear documentation and easy translation into fully normalised relations.
We shall see later that it is sometimes convenient to use a double
arrowhead for representing that one data element value maybe
associated with many values of another (as opposed to leaving it with
no arrowhead), but for most purposes this clutters the diagram
unnecessarily. It is easier to show which elements are associated with
only one value of another.

9.4   Functional dependencies

The enterprise rule which states that

'each value of data element A is always associated with one, single value
of data element B'

is of particular interest . We say that A determines B (or more precisely
A functionally determines B). We can also say A is a determinant of B,
B is determined by A or B is functionally dependent on A. It is written
A —>B. A and/or B may be composite (i.e. composed of more than one
data element).

Functional dependencies (often abbreviated to FDs) are central to
designing relations which are free from the undesirable properties
(update, insert and deletion anomalies) which were identified in section
9.1. The theory of functional dependencies is well formulated and
understood. In this text, we make this theory available to designers by
presenting it primarily as a diagrammatic technique. However, this does
not mean that the underlying theory will remain hidden and on several
occasions we find that a deeper understanding of the theory is
important.

To say B is functionally dependent on A, or that A determines B means
that if we are given a value of A we can always find, unambiguously,
the value of B. As you can see from the diagrams, it is possible for A to
determine B and B to determine A (as in Figure 9.6(a)) or for there not to

exist a functional dependency (as in Figure 9.6(d)). Here there is a relationship between *BinNumber* and *PartNumber* but neither determines the other; there is a non-functional relationship.

As we build more complex models of the relationships between data elements, we discover that we can make other statements about dependencies. Consider the example in Figure 9.7 which shows the dependencies between five data elements concerned with a customer's order. This diagram represents the following enterprise rules.

1. Each *OrderNumber* is associated with only one *CustomerNumber*, but a *CustomerNumber* may be associated with many *OrderNumbers*.

2. Each *CustomerNumber* is associated with only one *Address*, but the same *Address* may be associated with more than one *CustomerNumber*.

3. Each *OrderNumber* may be associated with many *PartNumbers*, and each *PartNumber* can be associated with many *OrderNumbers*.

4. Each *OrderNumber* and *PartNumber* taken together (written {*OrderNumber,PartNumber*}) is associated with only one *QuantityOrdered*, but a *QuantityOrdered* may be associated with more than one {*OrderNumber,PartNumber*}.

We can easily deduce that there are other enterprise rules which can be derived from the above. (For example each *OrderNumber* can be associated with only one *Address*.) The choice of the rules to model can be critical to good database design.

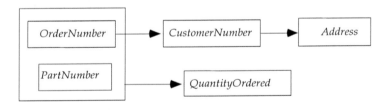

Figure 9.7   *Dependencies on a customer's order*

From these enterprise rules, we can say *OrderNumber* is a determinant of *CustomerNumber*, *CustomerNumber* is a determinant of *Address*, and {*OrderNumber,PartNumber*} is a determinant of *QuantityOrdered*. In a strictly mathematical sense, it is true to say {*OrderNumber,PartNumber*} determines *CustomerNumber*, {*OrderNumber,PartNumber*} determines *QuantityOrdered* and {*OrderNumber,PartNumber*} determines *Address*. However, this distracts from the purpose of examining functional

dependencies which is to capture the ~ ·
an enterprise. The defini⁺⁻
concerned wi⁺ʰ ˄

...ɷutes.

...ɷer,*PartNumber*} to determine
., ɔu the second feature of determinants is:

Determinants can be composite attributes.

Furthermore, since *OrderNumber* determines *CustomerNumber* and
CustomerNumber determines *Address*, it means that given a value of
OrderNumber, we can find the value of *CustomerNumber* and hence find
the value of *Address*. We say that *OrderNumber* determines *Address*
transitively through *CustomerNumber*. The third property of
determinants is:

Determinants are transitive.

This final property is particularly important, because it is the existence
of transitive dependencies within a table which gives rise to much of the
redundancy in a data model. Transitive dependencies must be avoided
within a relation.

There are a number of other rules and axioms which can be stated about
FDs which have less practical significance than those defined above. For
example, there are trivial FDs such as

$$A \longrightarrow A \text{ or } A \longrightarrow A,B$$

In the more concrete terms of the example above

$$CustomerNumber \longrightarrow CustomerNumber \text{ or}$$

$$CustomerNumber \longrightarrow \{CustomerNumber, Address\}$$

Date (1995a) covers the theory. The most important thing from our
perspective is that we are not interested in trivial FDs. We want to
remove transitive dependencies from relations and when considering
functional dependencies, we need to ensure that they are full functional
dependencies (i.e. the determinant does not include any superfluous
attributes).

Consider the following examples (Figure 9.8.) taken from Howe (1989).
By inspection of the dependency diagram, we can establish what the
determinants are and which items are dependent on them.

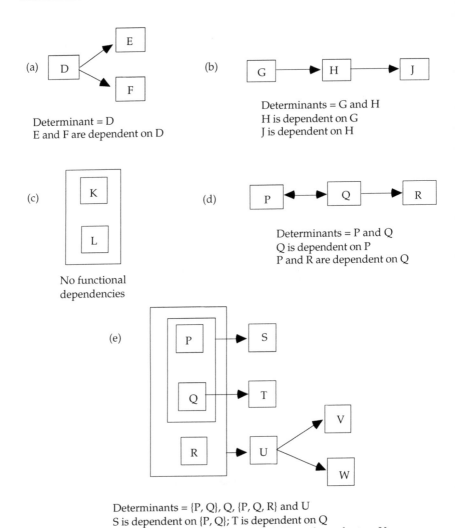

Figure 9.8   *Spotting determinants from dependency diagrams*

9.5   Discussion

Our discussion of normalisation has been quite non-rigorous. A number of assumptions have been made, but left unstated, in order to introduce the ideas of functional dependence as naturally as possible. The

literature on dependency the~~
persist over the b~~
of d~~

. ~~ute (1995a,
~~ can have no meaning outside
~~nnot exist outside of a relation. The problem
~~ to where that relation came from. Did the designer
arbitrarily assign attributes to relations and then start examining the
functional dependencies? Do all attributes begin life in a single,
universal relation? Do all attributes begin in binary relations? These
questions have been considered at length by many of the eminent
database theorists (see Further Reading). The approach adopted by Date
is to *decompose* relations, thereby tacitly assuming the existence of a
universal relation (consisting of all the attributes in the enterprise). The
approach of Bernstein (1976) and others is to *synthesise* (that is build up)
relations from a set of functional dependencies.

Although much of this debate is rather too theoretical for this text, there
are some important considerations. For example, in decomposing
relations we have assumed that relations can be decomposed without
losing any meaning from the data. That is, relations can be *non-loss*
decomposed (i.e. in decomposing the relations, no information is lost in
the process. This is not the case for all the possible decompositions of
relations. There is also the question of preferred decompositions. Are
some decompostions better in some sense than others? The answer to
this question is certainly 'yes'. Some decompositions are better than
others because they retain the semantics of the data.

This leads to the notion of **independence** which is closely allied to the
problems of transitive dependencies. The following is based on Date
(1995a).

If in a relation with attributes (A, B, C) and A —> B and B —> C, then
A —> C (because functional dependencies are transitive). If it is
decomposed into the two relations (A, B) and (A, C), however, the
dependency B —> C is not automatically enforced by the structure of
the relations. It is better, therefore, to decompose it into the relations
(A, B) and (B, C) when the dependency A —> C is automatically
enforced. The former decomposition results in a loss of meaning
whereas the latter does not, because the latter decomposes the original
relation into two *independent* projections. Independence in this sense

means that each of the relations resulting from the decomposition can be updated without regard for the other.

As a concrete example of this substitute *OrderNumber* for A, *CustomerNumber* for B and *Address* for C from the orders example above. The tables (*OrderNumber, CustomerNumber*) and (*CustomerNumber, Address*) are clearly more semantically sensible than (*OrderNumber, CustomerNumber*) and (*OrderNumber, Address*). Besides being more intuitive, the former design means that if the customer changes address then only one relation has to be updated whereas with the latter design every order which the customer had placed would have to be updated.

All these issues bring us back to the purpose of the data models. The purpose of the relational model is to represent as much of the meaning of the data in the enterprise as possible in a non-procedural form suitable for subsequent implementation as a database. The purpose of the dependency diagram is to assist the designer in understanding the desired relationships between the data elements which model the enterprise.

Functional dependence is about the *meaning* — the semantics — of data within the context of the enterprise. It is for this reason that we stressed the importance of enterprise rules. It is the rules which express the meaning of the data and which must be represented in a relational model.

The final point to note is that functional dependencies express *constraints*. To say that *OrderNumber* determines *CustomerNumber* expresses the constraint that in the world of the enterprise in question, an order (represented by the data element *OrderNumber*) is always associated with one customer (represented by the data element *CustomerNumber*).

It is important for the database designer to remember that the relations which are designed represent the constraints which are a feature of the enterprise rules in an organisation. Some of these constraints can be represented in terms of dependencies between data elements. Other constraints are represented by the relational model itself (through the integrity rules). Some of these are implemented in the database language SQL. Other constraints are represented in terms of our model through the data dictionary and may be enforced in some implementations. Other constraints cannot be represented so easily and may only be implemented through defining restricted views of the database or by writing SQL queries as we saw in chapter 8.

9.6   Key points

In ..

                                                                   . . ..uundancy from a set of
                                              ....ng update anomalies.

.. ..iuer to decide how to allocate attributes to relations, the
database designer needs to consider the functional
dependencies which exist in the database.

- One data element is fully functionally dependent on another
  data element if each value of the first data element is always
  associated with just one value of the second data element and
  no subset of the first data element is always associated with just
  one value of the second data element.

- The only way to find out about functional dependencies is to
  examine the relationships which exist between data elements in
  a particular enterprise — these are the enterprise rules.

- Dependency diagrams are a useful graphical technique for
  exploring and representing the enterprise rules.

Further reading

Kent, W. (1981) Consequences of assuming a Universal Relation *ACM Transactions on Database Systems* 6, no. 4 Dec.

Ullman, J. D. (1983) On Kent's 'Consequences of Assuming a Universal Relation' *ACM Transactions on Database Systems* 8 no. 4 Dec.

Kent, W. (1983) The Universal Relation revisited *ACM Transactions on Database Systems* 8 no. 4 Dec.

Maier, D. , Ullman, J.D. and Varadi, M. Y. (1984) On the foundations of the Universal Relation Model *ACM Transactions on Database Systems* 9 no. 2 June

> These papers give a fascinating account of the discussion
> over the existence of a Universal Relation and the desirability
> of finding one, or more! The correspondance between Kent
> and the protagonists is highly readable and serves to remind

us all that we are dealing with semantics more than a rigorous theory.

Bernstein, P. A. (1976) Synthesising third Normal Form Relations from Functional Dependencies *ACM Transactions on Database Systems* 1 no. 4 Dec.

Date, C. J. (1995) *An Introduction to Database Systems* 6th Edition Addison-Wesley, Reading, MA

Date devotes several chapters to the theory of functional dependencies and gives excellent pointers to the original papers.

Howe, D. R. (1989) *Data Analysis for Database Design* Edward Arnold, London

Chapter 6 discusses the topics covered in this chapter.

, --v.ous chapter
, - v.tween data elements. From the
...ι specify the determinants which exist. In this chapter
we describe how to transform the dependency diagram model of
data into a set of fully normalised tables.

After studying this chapter you should be able to:

- spot identifiers from dependency diagrams

- design fully normalised relations given a set of dependencies
  represented as a dependency diagram

- define and use the Boyce/Codd rule (BCNF)

- define multi-valued dependencies.

10.1   Spotting identifiers

In our discussion of the relational data model so far we have established
two important features of the model. First every table has some
combination of attributes which will unambiguously identify each row.
This follows directly from the fact that relations do not have duplicate
rows (therefore every row can be distinguished from the others). The
attribute(s) which fulfil this role is the primary key of the relation. This
identifier cannot be null, must not contain superfluous attributes and
can never take duplicate values. Second we found that if we put all
attributes in a single relation there were some undesirable effects. A
table containing the redundant duplication of data leads to various
anomalies when we try to change the content of the relation by adding
tuples, updating the table or deleting tuples.

In order to design relations which avoid these problems we need to
ensure that all redundancy is eliminated from the tables; we want our
relations to be fully normalised. We can do this directly from the
dependency diagrams.

From a dependency diagram we can deduce what the identifier would
be if we were to put all the data elements into a table. For example in

Figure 10.1, the minimum number of attributes needed to identify the table

Order (*OrderNumber, PartNumber, QuantityOrdered, CustomerNumber, Address*)

is {*OrderNumber,PartNumber*}. This will not be null, will not take duplicate values and does not contain superfluous attributes.

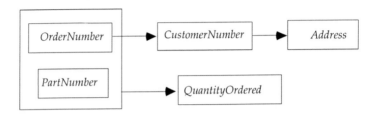

Figure 10.1   *Dependencies on a customer's order*

Consider the examples in Figure 10.2 and satisfy yourself that the identifiers are as indicated if all the attributes are put into a single table. (We will use the notation of underlining table identifiers from now on.)

However, not all these tables are fully normalised. In Figure 10.2(b) H determines J, so any given value of H will always be associated with the same value of J. This is also true of Figure 10.1(d) where R is dependent only on Q. In Figure 10.2(e) there are lots of dependencies embedded in the table.

Referring back to the dependency diagram for the customer's order (Figure 10.1), and the sample occurrences in Figure 10.3, we can see a similar effect. Since *OrderNumber* determines *CustomerNumber,* if we know the value of *OrderNumber* we can always find the value of *CustomerNumber* (e.g. *OrderNumber* 128 will always be associated with *CustomerNumber* C1). So every time the *OrderNumber* appears in a table it will always be associated with the same *CustomerNumber*. The same is true of *CustomerNumber* and *Address* since *CustomerNumber* determines *Address.*

This table contains redundant data, i.e. data which is duplicated unnecessarily. If we delete *CustomerNumber* and *Address* from row 2, the *Address* from row 4, or the *CustomerNumber* and *Address* from rows 5 or 6, we can discover what the values should be by inspecting row 1. This is because an *OrderNumber* is always associated with the same *CustomerNumber* (*OrderNumber* determines *CustomerNumber*) and the *CustomerNumber* is always associated with the same *Address* (*CustomerNumber* determines *Address*). A good test for spotting

Table ($\underline{D}$, E, F)   Table ($\underline{G}$, H, J)

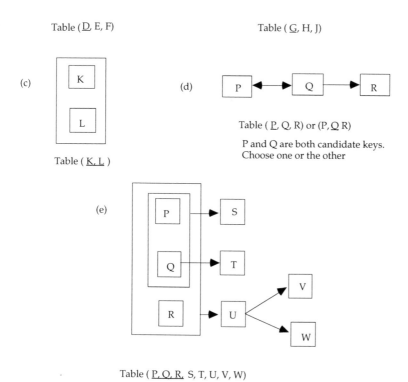

(c)   K

           L

Table ($\underline{K, L}$)

(d)   P ⟷ Q ⟶ R

Table ($\underline{P}$, Q, R) or (P, $\underline{Q}$ R)

P and Q are both candidate keys.
Choose one or the other

(e)   P ⟶ S

       Q ⟶ T

                      V

       R ⟶ U

                      W

Table ($\underline{P, Q, R}$, S, T, U, V, W)

Figure 10.2   *Spotting identifiers from dependency diagrams*

Order	(Order Number,	PartNumber,	Quantity Ordered,	Customer Number,	Address)
	128	P1	500	C1	London
	128	P2	500	C1	London
	137	P7	250	C2	Leeds
	138	P2	520	C1	London
	138	P7	250	C1	London
	138	P4	400	C1	London

Figure 10.3   *Sample occurrences for order example (Figure 7.8)*

10.2   Boyce/Codd Normal Form (BCNF)

In order to eliminate this redundancy, we need to split the single table into several related tables such that in each table **every determinant is a candidate identifier (or candidate key)**. This is known as the Boyce/Codd rule and any table satisfying this condition is said to be in Boyce/Codd Normal Form (BCNF). The order table (Figures 10.1 and 10.3) should thus be split into three tables in order to be in BCNF, as follows. In each of these relations every determinant is a candidate key.

Order (*OrderNumber, CustomerNumber*)

Customer (*CustomerNumber, Address*)

OrderLine (*OrderNumber,PartNumber, QuantityOrdered*)

The table occurrences are shown in Figure 10.4. Order represents the dependency of *CustomerNumber* on *OrderNumber*, Customer represents the dependency of *Address* on *CustomerNumber* and OrderLine represents the dependency of *QuantityOrdered* on {*OrderNumber,PartNumber*}.

Order	(*OrderNumber,*	*CustomerNumber*)
	128	C1
	137	C2
	138	C1

Custom---

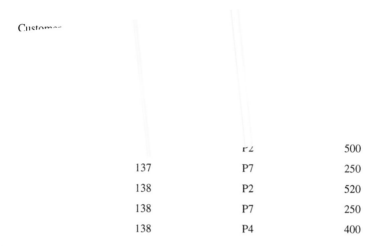

	r2	500
137	P7	250
138	P2	520
138	P7	250
138	P4	400

Figure 10.4   *BCNF relations for order example*

The Boyce/Codd rule is a stronger version of third normal form (3NF) described in section 9.1. It is stronger because it deals with *candidate* identifiers and overlapping identifiers and not just primary keys.

Look at the examples from Figures 9.8 and 10.2. In order to produce a set of BCNF tables, we create tables so that in each table every determinant becomes a candidate identifier. This is shown in Figure 10.5. Notice that in (c), since there are no functional dependencies, we cannot apply the Boyce/Codd rule. Instead we form a table containing, and identified by, the two attributes. Also notice in (d) that there are two candidate identifiers. We return to these problems in the next section.

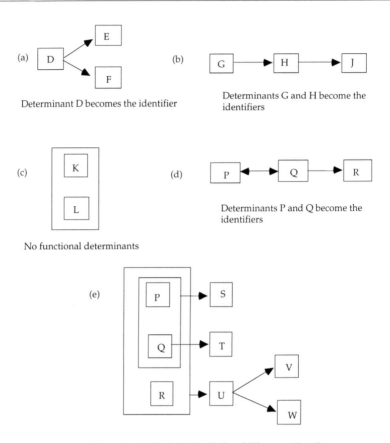

Figure 10.5   Deriving tables in which every determinant is a candidate identifier (i.e. in BCNF)

Following the Boyce/Codd rule that in every table every determinant must be a candidate identifier of that table ensures that all transitive dependencies are automatically eliminated. However, such relations may still contain redundancy. This redundancy arises from the existence of multi-valued dependencies rather than functional dependencies.

10.3 Multi-valued d~~enc~~

~~and~~
~~of~~ almost all redundancy
~~…al~~ Form.

~~…ve~~ also recognised that other relationships exist between data elements. In particular, we have encountered non-functional relationships existing between two data elements and have suggested a rule that these should be put together into their own table with both data elements becoming the identifier. Can we extend and develop these types of relationship?

A non-functional relationship is a particular kind of relationship in which instead of one element determining a single value of another element, it is associated with a set of values. Hence an *OrderNumber is* associated with a **set** of *PartNumbers* (in this case with all possible *PartNumbers*), an employee is associated with a **set** of salaries over time, a subject is taken by a **set** of students. Where these relationships are important, we can represent them in the dependency diagram by a double-headed arrow:

$$A \longrightarrow\!\!> B.$$

It should be clear that a functional dependency is simply a special case of the multi-valued relationship; when B is a single value.

Also notice, that dependencies operate in two directions. Thus A—>>B is ambiguous. Does it imply A—>>B and B—>>A (i.e. there is a M:M relationship between A and B) or does it imply A—>>B and B—>A (i.e. there is a 1:M relationship between A and B). If it is the latter, then we would not show the multi-valued relationship because that is implicit in saying B—>A. If it is the former then we would tend to model the relationship by enclosing both the data elements in a single box (as in Figure 10.5(c)).

In practice we rarely use double-headed arrows in the dependency diagram, because they tend to clutter the model and make it less readable. But for exploring relationships, it can be useful to show multi-valued relationships. Multi-valued relationships exist between many pairs of data elements (indeed all pairs of data elements where there is no functional dependency). However, most of these hold no interest for the enterprise unless they are related through their functional dependency. Most multi-valued relationships are independent. For example, consider the diagram in Figure 10.6.

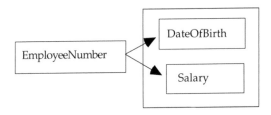

Figure 10.6   *Dependency diagram for employees*

This gives the table Employee (*EmployeeNumber*, *Salary*, *DateOfBirth*). The relationship existing between *Salary* and *DateOfBirth* is represented through their relationships with *EmployeeNumber*. In fact it would be redundant to include the table (*Salary*,*DateOfBirth*) even though both tables are in BCNF. This is because the table (*Salary*,*DateOfBirth*) does not convey any information which cannot be obtained from Employee. Salary and date of birth can be considered as independent facts about an employee. In Date's (1995a) terms, both *Salary* and *DateOfBirth* can be updated without regard for the other (given the dependencies in the diagram). Kent (1983a) describes independence slightly differently, arguing that any particular pairing of *Salary* and *DateOfBirth* does not in itself convey any information. Notice though, that this does not imply that there will never be cause to analyse the relationships between *Salary* and *DateOfBirth*. If this is required, the information can be obtained from the Employee table.

The outcome of this analysis is that when constructing dependency diagrams, the designer must be careful not to model dependencies where independent facts are concerned. For example, an employee may have a number of skills (e.g. translating, cooking, teaching) and a number of languages (e.g. French, German, Spanish). In modelling the relationships between the data elements *EmployeeNumber*, *SkillType*, and *Language* we need to consider if they are dependent, that is, an employee only perform certain skills in certain languages, or are they independent in the sense that an employee has certain skills and certain languages, but it doesn't matter which skill is paired with which language?

The former case has to be modelled as in Figure 10.7(a) and the latter as in Figure 10.7(b).

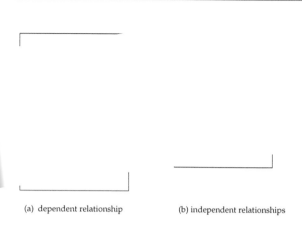

(a) dependent relationship   (b) independent relationships

Figure 10.7   *Employee, skills and languages*

Another way of viewing this is that Figure 10.7(a) represents that an employee only has some skills in some languages and Figure 10.7(b) represents that if he or she has a skill, he or she is deemed to possess that skill in all the languages which he or she has. Figure 10.7(a) represents dependent facts. If either *SkillType* or *Language* have to be updated (perhaps a mistake was made when the data was entered onto the database or the employee acquires a new language or skill) then the other data element has also to be updated. In Figure 10.7(b), however, either can be changed without affecting the other. Thus some multi-valued relationships are independent and some are dependent. It is these multi-valued dependencies which cause problems.

We are now in a position to define a **multi-valued dependency** (MVD).

> *In a relation R with attributes A, B and C, A multi-determines B if the set of B-values associated with any A-value, C-value pair, is independent of the value of C.*

Notice that MVDs occur in relations with three or more attributes and so A—>>B implies that A—>>C as well. Also remember that a functional dependency is a special case of an MVD where the 'set' of values is a single value.

Hence, were we to put the data elements *OrderNumber*, *PartNumber* and *CustomerNumber* into a single table given the usual dependencies

OrderNumber —>>PartNumber

OrderNumber —> CustomerNumber

there would be a multi-valued dependence with the resulting redundancy. Where two or more multi-valued dependencies exist between data elements, they must only be put into a single table if they are dependent on each other. In the above example, *CustomerNumber* is clearly *independent* of *PartNumber*.

Tables in which these MVDs have been removed are said to be in fourth normal form (4NF). Any table in 4NF is also in BCNF. Moreover, any table can be *non-loss decomposed* into its 4NF projections. Much of the theory behind 4NF is due to Fagin (1979) and interested readers should refer to his paper.

Although the concept of MVDs is quite complicated to come to terms with, the use of dependency diagrams can help considerably in establishing whether multi-valued relationships are independent or not. Consider Figure 10.7 again. If the enterprise rule shown in Figure 10.7(a) holds (i.e. an employee has certain skills in certain languages) then it would be quite wrong to represent it as (*EmployeeNumber, SkillType*) and (*EmployeeNumber, Language*) because these tables do not show that only certain pairings of *Language* and *SkillType* are allowed (*SkillType* and *Language* are dependent). Such problems crop up quite frequently when modelling data. It all depends on the enterprise rules which are being modelling. Consider the following examples.

Example 1

In a database storing details about authors, book titles and subject categories. If the book has several authors and several subject categories if each author associated with all the subject categories then represent as two tables (*AuthorName, BookTitle*) and (*BookTitle, SubjectCategory*). If each author is only associated with some categories then represent as a single table (*AuthorName, BookTitle, SubjectCategory*).

Example 2

In a database storing details about products, the operations which they go through and the machines which perform those operations. If the enterprise rule is that a product going through an operation is associated with all the machines which perform that operation then represent it as two tables (*ProductNumber,OperationNumber*) and (*OperationNumber, MachineNumber*). If the rule is that the product is only associated with the machine which actually performed the operation, then represents as one table (*OperationNumber, MachineNumber, ProductNumber*).

Example 3

The final example in this section is taken from Kent (1983a). It again illustrates the different representations of data required if the tables are

to accurately reflect the ent
further pr...

...agents, companies
... interest are *AgentName*,
...actName*. An agent sells many products, an agent
...works for many companies and each company makes many products.
A product can be sold by many agents, a company employs many
agents and a product can be made by many companies.

If the enterprise rules are such that if an agent works for a company and
the company makes a product then the agent is deemed to sell that
product, then the two tables

(<u>AgentName, CompanyName</u>) and (<u>CompanyName, ProductName</u>)

would represent the information and are in 5NF. However, if the agent
only sells certain products for certain companies we would expect the
table (<u>AgentName, CompanyName, ProductName</u>) to result. But this table
contains redundancy, because there are two multi-valued facts about
agents in the same table (i.e. the relationships *AgentName*
—>>*CompanyName* and *AgentName*- —>>*ProductName*). Indeed in this
case there are also two multi-valued facts about companies and
products as well (since *CompanyName* —>>*ProductName*). If we split this
into two tables

(<u>AgentName, CompanyName</u>) and (<u>AgentName, ProductName</u>)

this representation is only valid if the enterprise rule states that if an
agent works for a company and sells a product, then the company
makes that product. Similarly, the other possible decomposition, i.e.

(<u>AgentName, ProductName</u>) and (<u>ProductName, CompanyName</u>)

implies that if an agent sells a product and the product is made by a
company, then the agent works for the company. In short, although
there is redundancy in the table (<u>AgentName, CompanyName,
ProductName</u>), it is not possible to split it into two tables without losing
information. The solution is to split it into three tables

(<u>AgentName, ProductName</u>), (<u>ProductName, CompanyName</u>) and
(<u>AgentName, ProductName</u>)

these are then in 5NF.

This class of problems is the most general type of dependency which we have encountered. It is called Join Dependency (JD) and relations which are consistent with the constraints are said to be in Project–Join normal form (PJ/NF), or in fifth normal form (5NF). PJ/NF is the final normal form for relations (with respect to the operators project and join) and MVDs are a special case of JDs. Whereas MVDs can be dealt with by splitting the relation into two of its projections without losing any information, JDs require three or more projections in order to remove the redundancy without losing information. This can best be seen with the aid of an example, and for this we turn to Bill Kent's (1983a) paper on the five normal forms.

AGENT	COMPANY	PRODUCT
Smith	Ford	car
Smith	Ford	truck
Smith	GM	car
Smith	GM	truck
Jones	Ford	car
Jones	Ford	truck
Brown	Ford	car
Brown	GM	car
Brown	Toyota	car
Brown	Toyota	bus

AGENT	COMPANY	COMPANY	PRODUCT	AGENT	PRODUCT
Smith	Ford	Ford	car	Smith	car
Smith	GM	Ford	truck	Smith	truck
Jones	Ford	GM	car	Jones	car
Brown	Ford	GM	truck	Jones	truck
Brown	GM	Toyota	bus	Brown	car
Brown	Toyota			Brown	bus

All these three tables are in fifth normal form

Figure 10.8   *Agents, Companies and Products problem*

[Figure 10.8] 'illustrates a case in which the rule about agents, companies, and products [i.e. if an agent sells a certain product and represents the company making that product, then he sells that product for that company] is satisfied, and which clearly requires all three record types in the normalised form. Any two of the record types taken alone will imply something untrue.

The problem of 5NF arises because the multi-valued facts are not independent. The same problems would occur in earlier examples. If only certain skills could be performed in certain languages (for example German Cooking does not exist), if only certain subjects could be related to certain authors, if only certain machines could operate on certain products. It is the symmetric nature of the constraints which creates the additional problems of 5NF.

However, in all the discussions of MVDs, if the enterprise rules are modelled correctly, then the tables which result will be in 5NF. The agents, companies and products database would be modelled as in Figure 10.9 which gives the three tables (*AgentName, CompanyName*), (*CompanyName, ProductName*) and (*AgentName, CompanyName*) which are in 5NF.

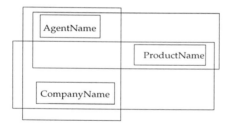

Figure 10.9   *Dependency diagram for agents, companies and products database*

Drawing the model carefully and then constructing tables such that every determinant becomes a candidate identifier and every multi-valued dependency is put in its own table, will ensure the resulting tables are in 5NF.

10.4   Key points

This chapter has been concerned with designing fully normalised tables; tables which represent the information content of the enterprise as a relational data model which minimises the redundant duplication of data.

- Avoiding redundancy is important because of anomalies which can arise if data is redundantly duplicated.

- The Boyce/Codd rule states that very determinant in a table must be a candidate identifier for that table.

- Spotting identifiers is easily done by inspecting the dependency diagram and spotting determinants is also easy from a dependency diagram.

- Multi-valued relationships also exist and where there are two dependent relationships they should be put into their own table, with all related data elements becoming the identifier.

- The problem is not one of designing relations, it is one of drawing accurate dependency diagrams.

Further reading

Simsion, G. (1994) *Data Modelling Essentials: Analysis, Design and Innovation.* International Thompson Publishing, Boston, MA

> Simsion provides an excellent discussion of both basic and advanced normalisation.

Date, C. J. (1995) *An Introduction to Database Systems* 6th Edition Addison-Wesley, Reading MA

> Once again, Date gives a good introduction to functional, multi-valued and join dependencies and pursues the definitions with more rigour than we have done here.

Kent, W. (1983a) The five normal forms *Communications of the ACM* vol 26 no. 2 Feb.

> A clear and concise guide to the different 'Normal Forms'

Smith, H. C. (1985) Database design: composing fully normalised tables from a rigorous dependency diagram *Communications of the ACM* vol 28 no. 8 Aug.

> An interesting article using a more rigorous form of the Martin notation

... produce a
.... the semantics of the data and which
.... the problems of redundancy. However, it is important to recognise that developing the diagrams helps the analyst/designer to understand the data more clearly. The diagrams represent the data. The designer needs to explore dependencies. In this chapter we look at a number of examples of data modelling using dependency diagrams.

After studying this chapter you should be able to:

* understand the process of bottom-up modelling

* consider the enterprise rules from different perspectives

* develop a fully normalised database for a small application.

11.1   A methodology for relational modelling

In chapter 5 we discussed a number of approaches to developing models. One of these was called 'bottom-up' modelling. This approach is characterised by the designer working with detailed aspects of a problem and combining these into larger units. In the case of developing a data model, bottom-up modelling involves looking at a group of related data elements and, by drawing dependency diagrams and considering the dependencies which exist between them, grouping the elements into full normalised relations. This approach is complementary with the top-down modelling approach provided by the entity-relationship model (chapter 12).

The designer must first identify and name the data elements which are relevant to the problem. Any data elements which are calculated from other data elements should be identified and recorded. All data elements should be recorded in a data dictionary. At this point it is also important to identify any implicit data elements. These issues were discussed in chapter 2, where we found that *GrossWage*, for example, was calculated from *Payment* and where *Grade* was implicit in the description of the data requirements. We return to this example in section 11.3.

Once the relevant data elements have been identified, it is necessary to look carefully at the enterprise rules as these represent the meaning of data in a particular enterprise which we want to represent. Previous chapters have provided a number of examples of different enterprise rules in different enterprises. For example, the different relationships between *BinNumber* and *PartNumber* in section 9.3 or the different possible relationships discussed in section 10.3. From these enterprise rules the obvious dependencies can be identified and sketched by using dependency diagrams. Some of the dependencies will not be so obvious and here the designer should explore various possibilities. How does the meaning of the data vary if different dependencies are considered? The designer should write out some sample occurrences of the data to check whether the dependencies are sensible and consider what impact there will be if certain data elements are put together into a table. Writing out sample occurrences is a good way to check for redundancy in relations and redundancy indicates that some functional or multi-valued dependencies have been missed. The designer can use the concept of independence to help in these deliberations; do not keep two or more facts about some data element together which are dependent on each other.

The process of exploring the enterprise rules, representing them as a dependency diagram, writing out occurrences, checking for redundancy and trying other alternatives will continue until a suitable representation is established. The designer will iterate and check several times before the enterprise rules are properly understood and represented as a dependency diagram. Once the diagram is complete, it is a simple operation to produce a set of normalised relations directly from the diagram according to the rules established in chapter 10 — the Boyce/Codd rule which states that very determinant in a table must be a candidate identifier and for multi-valued relationships where there are two dependent relationships they should be put into their own table, with all related data elements becoming the identifier.

Applying this methodology will ensure that the designer produces a fully normalised set of tables. The purpose of doing this is *not* so that this set of tables is immediately implemented as a relational database. The purpose of doing this is to understand the data in an enterprise. The method of implementation involves many other considerations. (Although it would always be *possible* to implement this model as a relational database, this may be undesirable because of other demands on the data.) The relational modelling approach described here is a central part of first level design (as is explained in chapter 14).

........(a) represents the relationships between S(= student), J(= subject) and T(= teacher). The enterprise rules stated are that:

1. each student is taught by one teacher for each subject

2. a teacher only teaches one subject, but a subject may be taught by many teachers.

Hence T is dependent on {S, J} and J is dependent on T. Figure 11.1(a) shows the dependency diagram. Following the methodology described in section 11.1, we should now construct the tables from the dependency diagram and write out some occurrences to check that there is no redundancy. In this case we find that the resulting tables, (S, J, T) and (T, J) are not fully normalised. (S, J, T) contains redundancy as shown in Figure 11.1(b). The teacher's name is redundantly duplicated for each student taking the subject (we are assuming that students teachers and subject are identified by their names in this example).

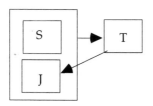

(a) Dependency diagram for students, subjects and teachers

Subject (J)	Student (S)	Teacher (T)
Maths	Brown	Prof. A
Maths	Rico	Prof. A
Computing	Brown	Prof. B

(b) Occurrences of student, subject, teacher relation

Figure 11.1   *Student, teacher and subject database*

The problem here is that the enterprise rules have been badly thought out. A more interesting set of rules is as follows:

1. A teacher only teaches one subject, but a subject may be taught by many teachers.

2. A student can be taught by many teachers, a teacher can teach many students.

After all, if a teacher only teaches one subject, if you know the student's teacher you can find the subjects he or she is taking. The dependency diagram for these enterprise rules is shown in Figure 11.2.

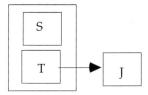

Figure 11.2   *Alternative dependency diagram for student, teacher and subject database*

From the rules, the dependencies are J is determined by T (as before), and there is a non-functional relationship between S and T. The dependency diagram in Figure 11.2 results and the tables (T, J) and (T, S) represent the information and are fully normalised. However, these tables do not automatically enforce the dependency of T on {S, J} — i.e. that a student is taught by only one teacher for each subject. The example data from Figure 11.1(b) would appear as follows given the design resulting from Figure 11.2.

Student (S)	Teacher (T)		Teacher (T)	Subject (J)
Brown	Prof. A		Prof. A	Maths
Rico	Prof. A		Prof. B	Computing
Brown	Prof. B			

This design means that we could insert a new teacher for Maths, say 'Prof. C' easily enough but we could also insert a tuple {Brown, Prof. C.} in the (Student, Teacher) table which would violate the rule which said that a student is taught by one teacher for each subject. Thus the relational model is unable to enforce all constraints automatically. Some constraints have to recorded outside the structure of the relations. In an SQL database a table constraint enforcing the rule could be specified.

These ....

...sider the time sheet and narrative for CND (engineering) which we encountered in chapter 2 (Figure 2.3). To establish the tables required to represent the data, firstly write down all the data elements in a data dictionary. Where any data element can be calculated from others, show the calculation along side (see Figure 11.3).

Data element Name	Value Set	Description
Name	any characters	Employee's name
DepartmentNo	numeric (integer)	Department number
WeekNo	numeric (integer)	Payroll week number
EmployeeNo	numeric (integer)	Works payroll number
DayName	any characters	Abbreviated day name
Date	DD/MM/YY	English date including year
JobNo	numeric	Number as issued by job controller
JobDescription	any characters	General purpose job title
HoursWorked	numeric (decimal)	Hours worked on a task (allow for half hours only)
TaskName	any characters	Name of task
Payment	numeric (decimal)	Amount paid for an hourly rate
TotalHours	numeric (decimal)	Total hours worked this week
GrossWage	numeric (decimal)	Total payment for this week

Figure 11.3   *Data element list for CND (engineering) application*

Now consider whether there are any other data elements which are implicit in the description or calculations.

From inspection, we have Grade (this is given in the narrative) and *HourlyRate* which must be stored somewhere, in order to arrive at the *Payment*.

The designer can now begin to look at the dependencies. However, one point is worth noting first. In computer systems there is often a choice as to how to represent some piece of information. We can represent it in a declarative manner through representing the relationships between data elements. Alternatively the same piece of information can be represented in a procedural fashion, i.e. by a formula or piece of program code. Consider the example above, where

Payment = NumberOfHours × HourlyRate.

It is clear that a dependency exists as shown in Figure 11.4(a) and the resulting table and occurrences in Figure 11.4(b).

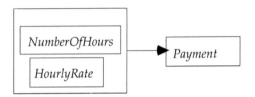

(a) Dependency of Payment *on* NumberOfHours *and* HourlyRate

NumberOfHours	HourlyRate	Payment
0.25	10.00	2.50
0.50	10.00	5.00
0.75	10.00	7.50
....	....	....
10.00	10.00	100.00
0.25	10.10	2.525
0.50	10.10	5.05
.... and so on	.... and so on	.... and so on

(b) Table and occurrences resulting from dependency in (a)

Figure 11.4   *Payment problem*

However, this appears to be a fairly silly way of representing something that can so easily be represented as the procedure:

Payment = NumberOfHours × HourlyRate.

There is no guarantee that we can cover all possibilities by representing the information as a table, and besides, the table will rapidly become

Ignoring calculated data elements, the designer can now begin to model the relationships between the other data elements which are not calculated from others. The 'obvious' ones are shown in Figure 11.5.

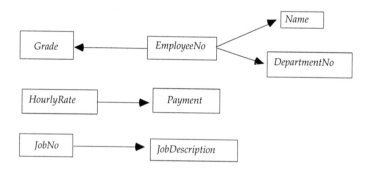

Figure 11.5   *CND (engineering) 'obvious' dependencies*

Although, in real life, some of these may require detailed investigations, it is clear that an *EmployeeNo* is associated with one *Grade*, *Name* and *DepartmentNo*, an *HoulyRate* is associated with a *Payment* and a *JobNo* is associated with a *JobDescription*. These data elements can be crossed off the data dictionary. This leaves the following data elements to be considered.

Data element Name

WeekNo

DayName

Date

HoursWorked

TaskName

Clearly a *WeekNo* is associated with several *Date*s and several *DayNames*, the same day name can be associated with several week numbers and dates, but a date will only be associated with one day name and one week number. This gives the dependency diagram in Figure 11.6.

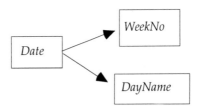

Figure 11.6   *Dependencies on Date*

Dealing with *TaskName* is more difficult. It must be related to *JobNo* but the relationship is many to many. Each *JobNo* associated with many *TaskNames* and a *TaskName* can be associated with many *JobNos* (Figure 11.7).

Figure 11.7   *Many to many relationship between* JobNo *and* TaskName

This is satisfactory to some extent, but on re-reading the description we discover that tasks are completed in sequence, and this information is not shown. The table resulting from the above dependency diagram is (*JobNo, TaskName*) and since tables must not be row-order dependent, we cannot represent the sequencing information. We have to invent a data element, *SequenceNumber*, in order to represent this information (*cf.* chapter 2).

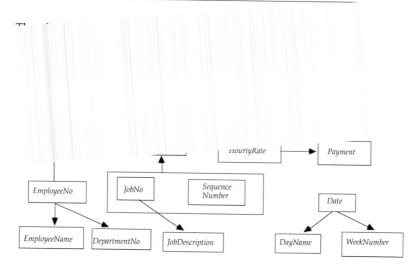

Figure 11.8   *CND (engineering). Second try.*

This leaves the question of what determines the hourly rate and the number of hours? From the narrative, 'hourly rate ... varies with the grade of employee and the task'. Hence

$$\{Grade, TaskName\} \longrightarrow HourlyRate.$$

11.5   Completing and checking

From inspection of the time sheet, we can see that the number of hours is filled in for each job and task done. However, since the same *JobNo* and *TaskName* can be done on different days, these two items are not sufficient to determine *HoursWorked*. (Look at lines 5 and 12 of Figure 2.4 where 'Computer table, Finishing' appears associated with 2 hours and 3 hours respectively.) It appears then that *JobNo*, *TaskName* and *Date* are required to determine *HoursWorked*. The possibility that the same *TaskName* is performed more than once on the same *JobNo* on the same *Date* (and hence may be associated with more than one value of *HoursWorked*) can be handled either by inventing another sequence number, or by totalling the hours on a given day. We will choose the latter. But notice that this means that we have changed the meaning of the data element. *HoursWorked* no longer means the hours worked on a task it means the total hours worked on a task on a particular day.

The final dependency diagram is shown in Figure 11.9.

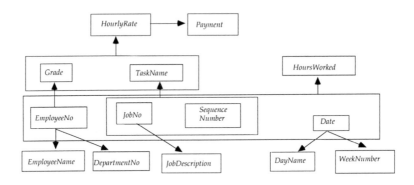

Figure 11.9   *Final dependency diagram for CND (engineering)*

To construct the fully normalised table types, it is now simply a question of inspecting the diagram and ensuring that every determinant becomes the identifier (or candidate identifier) of a table and that the only attributes in the table are those directly determined by the identifier. This produces:

E   (*EmployeeNo*, Name, Grade, DepartmentNo)

J   (*JobNo*, Description)

S   (*JobNo, SequenceNumber*, TaskName)

D   (*Date*, WeekNo, DayName)

W   (*EmployeeNo, JobNo, SequenceNumber, Date*, HoursWorked)

P   (*Grade, TaskName*, HourlyRate)

H   (*HourlyRate*, Payment)

from which the pay can be calculated for any given week and tasks done and hours worked can be analysed. The data values available to us from the time sheet are shown below, and the advantages of the structure should be apparent. Changing pay scales is easy, storing additional details of jobs (customer details, etc.) and work done doses not present many problems. In short the relations offer a highly flexible structure. However this is not to say that this is exactly how the system would be implemented. This is a conceptual model, and whilst it may become the final design, such decisions are deferred until later.

E	(*EmployeeNo*,	Name,	Grade,	DepartmentNo)
	159	I. Willis	07	06

S

(*JobNo,*	*SequenceNumber,*	*TaskName*)
0123	1	smoothing
0123	2	welding
0123	3	bending and joining
0067	6	loading
0067	2	welding
0066	4	painting
0066	3	scraping
0066	5	finishing
0066	2	welding

D

(*Date,*	*WeekNo,*	*DayName*)
230396	14	Monday
240396	14	Tuesday
250396	14	Wednesday
260396	14	Thursday
270396	14	Friday

W	(*Employee No,*	*JobNo,*	*Sequence Number,*	*Date,*	*Hours Worked*)
	159	0123	1	230396	6
	159	0123	2	230396	2
	159	0066	3	240396	3
	159	0066	4	240396	1
	.....etc.	.....etc.	.....etc.	.....etc.	.....etc.

P	(*Grade,*	*TaskName,*	*HourlyRate*)
	07	smoothing	A
	07	welding	K
	07	scraping	A
	07	finishing	A
	07	bending & joining	C
	07	painting	A
	07	loading	B

H	(*HourlyRate,*	*Payment*)
	A	7.00
	B	6.50
	K	10.00
	C	10.00

11.6   Key points

In this chapter, we have established a bottom-up method of data modelling.

*   Begin by identifying the data elements which are of interest through observation, discussions and other analyses we can establish the enterprise rules which express the relationships between data elements.

*   Represent these rules using dependency diagrams.

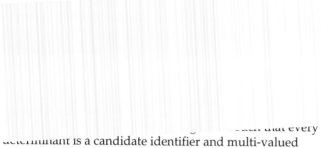

~~~~~~ ~~~~ every
~~~~~~~~~~ is a candidate identifier and multi-valued
dependencies have their own table, ensuring that there are no
dependent MVDs in the same table.

Further reading

Howe, D. R. (1989) *Data Analysis for Database Design* Edward Arnold,
London

> Chapters 6 and 7 give the best tutorial on dependency
> diagrams (Howe calls them determinancy diagrams) which I
> have seen and is thoroughly recommended.

Simsion, G. (1994) *Data Modelling Essentials: analysis, design and
innovation.* International Thompson Publishing, Boston, MA

> Although he does not use dependency diagrams in the same
> way as I have used here, Simsion discusses many of the
> important issues in chapter 7 of his book.

... previous chapters is a good user-centred model for explaining and documenting the relationships amongst data elements. However, in most information systems, there will be hundreds or thousands of data elements and hence tens or hundreds of thousands of possible relationships. Even the model for a single document, (e.g. the work sheet in chapter 11) becomes quite complex and so to examine all the functional and non-functional dependencies existing in a 'real' system becomes a mammoth task. The problem is comparable to the example given in chapter 5 of trying to travel the length of Britain using a set of 1:50000 scale maps. The model is inappropriate for the purpose as it is too detailed, too fine grained. Even if we could draw an accurate dependency diagram for the whole of a system, the model offers no perspective of the area. We are bogged down in detail or, in the words of the old adage, 'we cannot see the woods for the trees'.

The entity-relationship (usually abbreviated to E-R) model offers a solution to the problems of scale and practicability, by modelling the relationships between groups of data elements rather than individual data elements.

After studying this chapter you should be able to:

- understand what an entity-relationship model is

- understand how an E-R model relates to the ideas expressed through functional dependencies

- understand the components and constructs of an E-R model

- understand that E-R models are one type of semantic data models

- understand and use the concepts of entity, attribute, relationship

- understand the similarities and differences between entities, attributes and relationships

- develop simple E-R models.

12.1   The E-R model

The E-R model stems from the work of P. P-S. Chen in 1976. Since then it has developed into a branch of computer science and there are regular conferences on the usefulness and uses of the model. It was originally proposed as an alternative to the relational model, but in recent years the compatibility of the two have been recognised. The entity-relationship model offers a solution to the problems of scale and practicability, by modelling the relationships between groups of data elements rather than individual data elements. We call these groups 'entities' which means 'things of interest to our enterprise'. As we shall see, there is nothing fundamentally different between the E-R model and the dependency diagram except for the scale of the model. However, the E-R model has some attractive features not possessed by the dependency diagram which result from the property that it deals with larger units. The E-R model is a highly flexible and powerful tool for exploring information needs. It offers a graphical language for discussing and thinking about what the information system has to deal with.

Before we go any further it is important to notice the difference between relationships and relations. Relationships are associations between things, whereas relations are the tabular data structures which provide a good way of capturing particular relationships.

As with the relational model, the E-R model is grounded in set theory and hence demonstrates a certain mathematical rigour. The term 'entity set' is sometimes used in preference to 'entity type' to emphasise this. As usual in data modelling, we must distinguish between the 'type' (the general category) and the 'occurrences' (the specific instances) of an entity. The concept of a domain is also present in the E-R model, but is often referred to as a 'value set'. In this text, however, we do not use the E-R model with too much precision (indeed most people I know use it slightly differently). We use it as an effective way of capturing the meaning of data in an organisation and as a rich language for discussing concepts.

A completed E-R model consists of a diagram (the E-R diagram), a corresponding set of fully normalised (i.e. in 5NF) relations and additional information such as descriptions of the entities and relationships, assumptions which have been made and constraints which could not otherwise be represented within the model. A complete E-R model in this sense can then be used as a formal specification of the database and given to the database administrator for subsequent implementation on a computer. Before the E-R model becomes such a formal model, however, it will go through various levels of refinement as details of the information requirements are understood. During this

.... However, it is usual to include some definition of an entity in terms of its constituent data elements and related tables. The E-R diagram alone is usually too ambiguous to be used as the basis of a database design, so entity descriptions are needed to accompany the diagram.

The E-R model is a top-down approach to data modelling. It begins with general concepts and fills in the details until a suitable level of accuracy is achieved and data elements are grouped together in a meaningful way. This can be compared with the bottom-up approach of dependency diagrams and relational modelling which begins with the definition of data elements and collects them together into groups by examining the data dependencies. However, it must be remembered that these are essentially complimentary approaches. It is the final grouping of the data elements (i.e. the set of relations) which is important, not the method of getting there. If you are like me, however, you will not wish to deal with the details until you have an overall picture of the problem. E-R modelling facilitates the production of such a picture.

E-R modelling provides a number of advantages over relational modelling, particularly at the earlier stages of database design. The model can represent some additional features of the meaning of the data which can help to overcome the problems of null values. The model does not get cluttered with detail and provides an immediate pictorial representation of the major things of interest to the enterprise. It also provides a useful exploratory model which can help the analyst discover new relationships and new pieces of data. Finally, it is simpler in the early stages of data modelling to deal with groups of elements (entities) as represented by the relation identifiers than it is to deal with the myriad of relationships between data elements.

12.2   From dependencies to entities

Consider a simple dependency diagram showing the relationship between employees and their departments (Figure 12.1).

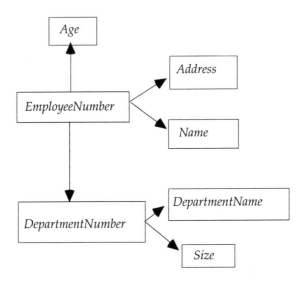

Figure 12.1   *Employee and department data dependency diagram*

As there are no multi-valued relationships, we can apply the Boyce/Codd rule and collect the data elements together into tables ensuring that in each table every determinant is a candidate identifier of that table. The determinants are *EmployeeNumber* (determines *Name*, *Address* and *DepartmentNumber*) and *DepartmentNumber* (determines *DepartmentName* and *Size*). The diagram in Figure 12.1 thus gives the tables;

Employee   (*EmployeeNumber, Name, Address, Age*)

and

Department   (*DepartmentNumber, DepartmentName, Size*)

in which the determinants (*EmployeeNumber* and *DepartmentNumber*) became the table identifiers. The dependency *EmployeeNumber —>DepartmentNumber* is the dependency which forms the relationships between the two things, Employee and Department in a relational model representation. *DepartmentNumber* is a foreign key in Employee.

Since an identifier identifies something, we can deal with the things identified rather than with the individual data elements. The things identified are the groups of data elements collected together in the relations. In this case *EmployeeNumber* identifies the relation Employee and *DepartmentNumber* identifies the relation Department. It makes sense, then, to deal with these relations and the relationships between

, ... Department is M:1. In E-R terms we say the relationship between the entities Employee and Department is many-to-one (M:1). In the notation of the E-R model this is expressed as shown in Figure 12.2. The relationship can also be read from right to left, in which case we say Department:Employee is 1:M (Department to Employee is one-to-many).

Entity descriptions

Employee   (*EmployeeNumber*,....

Department   (*DepartmentNumber*,...

Figure 12.2   *E-R model for M:1 relationship between Employee and Department*

In an E-R model, the entity is shown in the round cornered box with the entity description shown underneath. The entity description corresponds to the definition of a relation and we use the notation of underlining the relation's identifier. Data elements are shown in italics and entity names are shown in plain text. The unclosed brackets in the entity (relation) definition indicate that there are, or may be, other attributes of the entity but since they are directly determined by the identifier (i.e. the tables are fully normalised) we choose to ignore them for the present in order to maintain the simplicity of the model. Relationships between entities are shown by joining the entity boxes with a line. The 'crow's foot' indicates a 'to-many' relationship and the single line indicates a 'to-one' relationship. This notation is able to show 1:1, 1:M, M:1 and M:M relationships.

As the relationship is shown explicitly on the diagram by means of the line joining the entities, it allows us to name and describe what we mean by the relationship. This can help to clarify the meaning of the relationship and is particularly important when there is more than one relationship between entities. An example of this is shown in Figure 12.3.

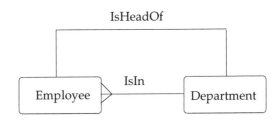

Entity descriptions

Employee   (*EmployeeNumber*,...

Department   (*DepartmentNumber*,...

Relationship descriptions

IsIn   An employee is in a department

IsHeadOf   An employee may be head of a department

Figure 12.3   *Naming relationships on an E-R diagram*

An important advantage of the E-R model over a dependency diagram is that it can capture some additional information; some further semantics of the enterprise rules. One of the most important of these is: does an entity have to participate in a relationship or is participation optional? For example, does an employee have to belong to a department, or is this relationship optional? Does a department have to have an employee in order to exist, or is the enterprise happy to store details of departments which do not have any employees?

In the dependency diagram, saying *EmployeeNumber —>
DepartmentNumber* does not say whether or not *every EmployeeNumber* is associated with just one *DepartmentNumber*. In the E-R model we are able to make such statements. We use the notation of including a filled dot beside the entity if it has to participate in a relationship, and an open dot (think of it as an 'o' for optional) beside the entity if it does not have to participate in that relationship. This is known as the membership class or participation condition of an entity with respect to a particular

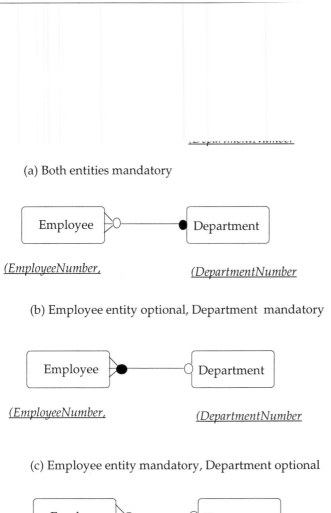

(a) Both entities mandatory

(EmployeeNumber,   *(DepartmentNumber*

(b) Employee entity optional, Department mandatory

(EmployeeNumber,   *(DepartmentNumber*

(c) Employee entity mandatory, Department optional

(EmployeeNumber,   *(DepartmentNumber*

(d) Both entities optional

Figure 12.4   *Mandatory and optional relationships*

12.3   Semantic modelling

There are many different versions of the E-R model and it has become central to most methodologies of information systems development. Several authors describe a form of semantic modelling which demonstrates the characteristics which we attribute to the E-R model. The principle of semantic modelling is to view the world as a collection of objects (entities) which have properties (attributes) and associations (relationships). In previous chapters we have encountered the work of Sundgren (1975) and Langefors (Langefors and Sundgren, 1975) who describe the world in this way. Other authors such as ter Bekke (1992) use similar terminology. Although our approach is based on the work of Chen (1976), it is freely adapted to include the principals of other semantic models. For a discussion of the similarities of the different semantic models see Further reading.

One area which receives considerable attention is the notation used in the diagram. Some authors argue that an entity should always be shown as a 'soft box', i.e. a box with rounded corners (a convention which is used here). This is to distinguish it from the physical objects in the system such as files. Others prefer an ellipse to a box. Others like to make the relationship lines more explicit by representing relationships as diamonds or circles. Others show attributes as ovals attached to entity boxes. The most popular notation is probably the 'crows foot' for representing a 'many' relationship (as is used here). In several texts the E-R model is referred to as a 'crows foot' diagram. Similarly other practitioners prefer to represent an optional relationship by a dotted line and call it a non-obligatory relationship. Other terms such as obligatory relationships, partial and total dependency, bubble diagrams, data structure charts, etc. abound and serve to confuse the literature, whilst all referring to essentially the same model. When reading other authors, then, care must be taken to ensure that the same concept is being discussed, even though a different word may be used.

As mentioned above, in this text, the notation of the model is not the most important aspect since the E-R diagram is not expected to act on its own as a formal representation of the information requirements. It is the relational model which defines the computer-oriented, formal view. The E-R model is used as a means of arriving at such a representation. In addition the E-R model is more understandable by the users of the system and can be used as a basis of discussion between users and system designers. Many important pieces of information about the enterprise cannot be represented diagrammatically and it is quite appropriate to include comments along with an E-R diagram.

For example, sometimes an entity may participate in only one of two relationships (exclusive relationships) whereas at other times it must

Figure 12.5 shows an example where the additional constraint on the data is shown on the E-R diagram, namely that an employee is either the head of a department or just an ordinary employee but is not permitted to be both. A department on the other hand must have a head and at least one ordinary employee. There is no need for an arc indicating that Department must participate in both relationship because participation in both the is in and is head of relationships is already mandatory.

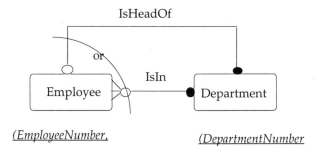

Figure 12.5   *Example of an exclusive relationship*

Another aspect of entity-relationship and other semantic models is the idea of entity sub-types. This area is particularly important when the E-R model is being used as part of a object-oriented approach to information modelling (see chapter 16). Sub-types can be shown by including an entity box inside another (see Figure 12.6). However, the designer needs to be careful here as one of the difficulties with dealing with sub-types is knowing exactly what the semantics being represented are. For example, can an instance of an entity be in more than one sub-type? Are the sub-types mutually exclusive? Must an instance belong to a sub-type? Must the sub-types cover all possible instances? Unfortunately there are no simple answers to these questions, so once again a flexible approach is preferred and the definition of a sub-type as used here is simply that a sub-type has the same attributes as its super-type and participates in the same relationships as its super-type. The converse is not true in that a sub-type may have some additional attributes or some additional relationships from its super-type.

An example of the concept and the notation is shown in Figure 12.6. In this enterprise there are two types of depot ('major' and 'minor'). One type has the facilities to service vehicles and the other type does not. Hence the different relationship and attribute of the 'major' type from the 'minor' type. The Major sub-entity (or entity sub-type) participates in the Maintains relationship and has an additional attribute *ContactName*. All Depots participate in the Operates relationship and have attributes *DepotNo, Address* and *Phone*.

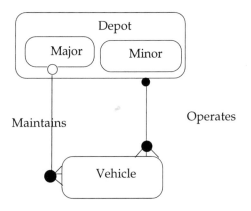

Entity descriptions

Depot	(*DepotNo, Address, PhoneNo*)
Major	(*DepotNo, ContactName*)
Vehicle	(*RegistrationNo, Make, Model*)

Relationship descriptions

| Operates | A depot operates vehicles |
| Maintains | A major depot routinely maintain vehicles |

Figure 12.6   *Illustrating entity sub-types*

In order to deal with situations involving multiple relationships between entities, several authors have introduced the concept of a 'Role'. This is the part or function which an entity is playing in a particular

relationsh... ...section

...help alleviate the problem, it introduces ...plexity.

There are many varieties of semantic models which use slightly different notations and employ slightly different rules in order to represent what are essentially the same concepts. Some methods insist that relationships can only be represented by the lines on the diagram and should not have attributes representing relationships (as they do in the relational model). Other versions, sometimes called pure entity models, insist that the primary key/foreign key mechanism as used in the relational model must appear in the entity descriptions. Some methods allow entities and relationships to have attributes. Some methods insist that only entities can have attributes (entity-attribute-relationship models — EAR models) whereas others permit relationships to have attributes (entity-relationship-attribute models — ERA models). Other methods, usually called binary data models, insist that an entity can only have one attribute in addition to its identifying attribute. Some methods allow for relationships to exist between several entity types whilst others only permit relationships between two entity types.

This text adopts a deliberately flexible approach. As is explained in the next few sections there are very few definite strong criteria which can be used to distinguish entities from attributes from relationships. The purpose of the model is to capture the meaning of the data in an enterprise and to provide a representation which can map onto a set of relations, or onto other representations such as an object-oriented implementation and which provides an accurate and useful pictorial representation of the information needs of the enterprise.

12.4 Entities

An entity (type) is simply a 'thing'. Anything real or conceptual which is of interest to the enterprise. It could be an object (car, machine, product, room, etc.), a person (customer, supplier, employee, etc.), an event (manufacturing operation, course enrolment, placement of order, holiday booking, etc.) or a concept (a schedule, plan, order, etc.).

The important criterion for depicting something as an entity is 'are we (the enterprise) interested in this thing?' i.e. do we want to store data about it. There is no restriction on what entities are nor how many there are. For example in Figure 12.4 there are two relationships between the entities Employee and Department. This could have been modelled using entities DepartmentHead, Employee and Department. We might have shown DepartmentHead as a sub-type of Employee (as long as all department heads are full employees). E-R modelling is subjective. It seeks to focus attention on important aspects of the enterprise.

Although E-R modelling is subjective, there are certain guiding principles which can be used to help the designer to spot entities. Firstly, an entity is often something which is described as being 'distinctly identified'. This feature stems from Chen's original paper, but is not further elaborated there. The significance of insisting that entities must be distinctly identified is that the designer can specify a data element which is the entity's identifier, just as a relation must have a primary key in the relational model.

Secondly, an entity is *not* a data element, but a collection of data elements given a useful name. Occasionally an entity does consist of a single data element (corresponding to a unary relation), but the entity is the concept and not the data element.

Thirdly, it is unlikely to be a document. Usually we are interested in the information conveyed by the document not the document itself. Consider 'order'. This is often an entity in a sales processing system, but 'order form' is not. Once again notice that in entity-relationship modelling, we are interested in the thing, the concept of an order, not in the piece of paper. However care must be taken here. If the order form has to be authorised by someone then perhaps we are interested in the form itself in addition to the concept of an order. The important aspect of understanding entities is to consider what the enterprise wants to store data about, so that we can identify the data needed to provide information. We are not concerned with the method currently used to convey information (such as an order form).

Fourthly, it is often tempting to create entities for which we have words! This can be dangerous as we try and fit our concepts into our language. The E-R diagram provides an alternative language for talking about abstract ideas of information so do not worry if there isn't a suitable word for the concept. The E-R model encourages designers to discover concepts which may be obscured by common language.

Finally, an entity has attributes. It will always have an identifying attribute and usually has other attributes as well. If you choose something as an entity, but cannot find a suitable identifier then it is wise to reconsider your choice. However, sometimes you will need to

... attribute is a data element associated with an entity. In mathematical terms an attribute can be defined as a mapping from an entity or relationship (set) to a domain (value set). It may describe the entity, identify the entity, categorise the entity or express a relationship between entities. The employee entity in section 12.2 had the attributes *EmployeeNumber, Name, Address, Age* and *DepartmentNumber*. Some attributes being descriptive (*Name, Address*), some categorising (*Age* might categorise the employee into an Age group), another identifying (*EmployeeNumber*) and *DepartmentNumber* representing the relationship between employees and departments.

The choice of attributes is again quite arbitrary, it depends on the enterprise and what interests us. However an attribute is a data element and not an abstract concept. Kent (1981) gives the example of 'hair colour'. Is this an attribute of person or is colour an attribute of the entity hair which has a relationship with the entity person? Presumably in most systems it would be the former, but in a hairdressing system it could be the latter as 'hair' (type, colour, thickness, etc.) is something of interest to that enterprise and hence will become an entity.

One person's attribute is another person's entity.

To be on the safe side, we can consider anything to be an entity. If it turns out that an entity has no attributes apart from its identifier (every entity must have an identifier), has a 1:M relationship with another entity, and the participation condition of the entity in that relationship is mandatory, then it can probably become an attribute of the other entity.

For example, if I choose Customer to be an entity with an identifier of *CustomerNumber* (quite likely) and surmise that Name (identifier *CustomerName*) and Address (identifier *CustomerAddress*) might also be entities then the E-R model would appear as in Figure 12.7.

What information is there to store about addresses or names apart from their values? Information about the values which a data element can take is stored in the domain of that data element. It is difficult to envisage what attributes Address can have. If *CustomerAddress* determines some other data elements such as *Area* then of course it will be an entity. (If one data element determines another, it will have to be the identifier of a table in order for the tables to be in BCNF. If a table exists it will be an entity.)

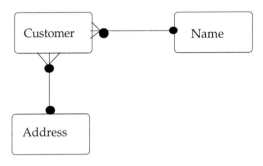

Entity descriptions

Customer   (*CustomerNumber,...*

Name   (*CustomerName,...*

Address   (*CustomerAddress,...*

Figure 12.7   *Possible entities in Customer application*

```
┌─────────────────┐
│                 │
│    Customer     │
│                 │
└─────────────────┘
```

Entity descriptions

Customer   (<u>*CustomerNumber,*</u> *CustomerName, CustomerAddress*)

Figure 12.8   *Customer data as attributes*

If there are no attributes for Name and Address (apart from their identifiers) then I can represent the information as in Figure 12.8. The entity is Customer. It has attributes *CustomerNumber, Customer Name* and *CustomerAddress.*

The logic of this should be apparent if we consider the relations associated with each entity. The M:1 relationships (Customer:Address and Customer:Name) are represented by posting the identifiers as foreign keys. Hence, since the membership classes of all entities are mandatory, the same data values will be stored in the unary relations for Address and Name as is stored in the Customer entity. Where the

.... particular significance. There may be more than one relationship between the same entities. We can name relationships if there is any ambiguity, but often there is not and naming is unnecessary. Relationships operate in both directions, e.g. an employee 'is in' a department, a department 'has got' many employees.

Relationships are fundamental to the provision of information. As we have seen the attributes of an entity have 1:M relationships with that entity. Functional dependencies are particular forms of relationships.

Here, we are dealing with relationships between entities. Relationships have:

- degree — i.e. the number of entities participating in the relationship. A binary relationship has degree = 2, ternary has degree = 3. In general, n entities participate in an n-ary relationship.

- complexity (or *cardinality*) — this maybe a 1:1 relationship, M:1, 1:M or M:M. A many-to-many relationship is often referred to as a complex relationship.

- participation conditions (or membership class) —is it mandatory or optional for the entity to participate in a relationship.

Relationships are not fundamentally different from entities or attributes as we demonstrate below (section 12.7). If we are interested in the relationship itself then it is often better to represent it by an entity. A relationship can and often does have attributes and in these circumstances, it should be represented as an entity. All M:M relationships and relationships between three or more entities can be redefined as entities. This is known as 'decomposing' a complex relationship.

For example, Figure 12.9 shows a M:M relationship between suppliers and parts. A supplier can supply many parts and any part may be supplied by many suppliers. We want to store information about Suppliers and Parts even if they do not participate in the relationship (it is optional on both sides). The relationship is thus 'supplies'.

y M:M relationship can be decomposed into two relationships of 1:M
d M:1 with a newly created entity intervening. In other words, a M:M
relationship can always be replaced by an entity which has a M:1,
mandatory relationship with each of the original entities. The supplies
relationship in Figure 12.9 becomes the supplies entity in Figure 12.10.

Notice that the identifier of the Supplies entity is the concatenation of
the identifiers of the other two entities (indeed so is the identifier of the
Supplies relationship in Figure 12.9), and that it is always mandatory for
the new entity to participate in the relationship. This must be so, since
the new entity contains the identifiers of the other entities.

Entity descriptions

Supplier   (*SupplierNumber*, Name, Address)

Part   (*PartNumber*, Description)

Figure 12.9   *Many-to-many relationship*

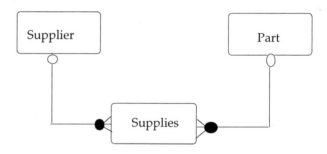

Entity descriptions

Supplier   (*SupplierNumber*, Name, Address)

Part   (*PartNumber*, Description)

Supplies   (*SupplierNumber, PartNumber*,...

Figure 12.10   *Supplies relationship as an entity*

This can be generalised to three or more entities as shown in Figure
12.11. Once again, notice that the newly created entity has a M:1,

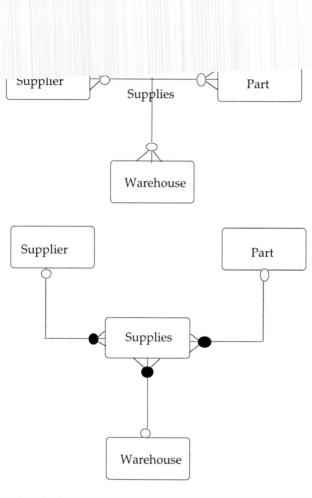

Entity descriptions

Supplier   (<u>SupplierNumber</u>, Name, Address)

Part   (<u>PartNumber</u>, Description)

Supplies   (<u>SupplierNumber, PartNumber</u>), WarehouseNumber, ...

Warehouse   (<u>WarehouseNumber</u>, ...)

Figure 12.11   *Decomposing a complex relationship between three entities*

The entity resulting from the decomposition of a M:M (or M:M:M, etc.) may not be the entity which is interesting to that enterprise. For example, if a supplier supplies parts to a particular warehouse, the meaning of the Supplies entity is somewhat ambiguous. Does it mean the parts which *were* supplied from a warehouse by a supplier on a particular day, or the parts which *can be* supplied? Are there other interpretations which are valid? What is the enterprise interested in and what did the designer intend by the entity?

Relationships can exist between four entities, e.g. if a supplier uses a particular haulage company when supplying to different warehouses. Relationships between five or more entities are unusual, but not impossible.

This ability to decompose complex and n-ary relationships into their simple, binary equivalents (i.e. 1:M relationships involving only two entities) is very useful as it helps us to discover entities which may otherwise have been overlooked. However, there is nothing wrong in leaving complex relationships represented as such. The relationship still has its corresponding table and the identifier of that table is still the concatenation of the identifiers of the participating entities. The advantage of decomposing relationships — and one which should not be underestimated — is that it highlights the relationship and forces the designer to consider its meaning, and relationships with other entities, in detail.

12.7   Entity, attribute or relationship?

The choice of entities depends on what is interesting to the enterprise. For example, consider the relationships between employees and the cars which they may drive in different enterprises. In Figure 12.12 (enterprise 1) there are three entities; Employee, Car and Driver. In enterprise 2 (Figure 12.13) there are two entities, Employee and Car, as there are in enterprise 3 (Figure 12.14). In enterprise 4 (Figure 12.15) the drivers are a sub-type of Employee. They all model similar relationships, but model them in different ways because the different enterprises are interested in different aspects of the available information. There is no 'correct' solution. The choice of entities, relationships and attributes depends on what the enterprise is interested in. The designation of something as an entity shows that we are interested in it, and will be storing data about it.

Figure 12.12 has entities Employee, Driver and Car. An Employee does not have to be a Driver, but a Driver must be an employee. A driver must be associated with a car, but a car can be associated with 0, 1 or M drivers. The existence of a Driver entity suggests that we want to store

Entity descriptions

Employee   (*EmployeeNumber*,...

Driver   (*EmployeeNumber*, *CarNumber*)

Car   (*CarNumber*,...

Figure 12.12   *Enterprise 1 Employees drive cars represented as an entity*

Entity descriptions

Employee   (*EmployeeNumber*,...

Car   (*CarNumber*,...

Drives   (*EmployeeNumber, CarNumber*)

Figure 12.13   *Enterprise 2. Employees drive cars represented as a relationship*

In this enterprise (Figure 12.13) we do not require any information about drivers other than the car which they can drive. Not all employees are car drivers. There is no Driver entity, but the Drives relationship will have its own relation (see section 12.8).

Entity descriptions

Employee   (*EmployeeNumber,...*

Car   (*CarNumber,...EmployeeNumber*

Figure 12.14   *Enterprise 3. Employees drive cars represented as an attribute*

In this enterprise (Figure 12.14) employees do not have to have a car, but all cars must be assigned to employees. The data about drivers is thus represented as an attribute in the Car relation. Figure 12.15 shows an enterprise representing information about cars and drivers using subtypes. There are Driver and Non-Driver sub-types of the Employee entity. Only Driver sub-types participate in the Drives relationship. The Driver employees have the additional attributes shown.

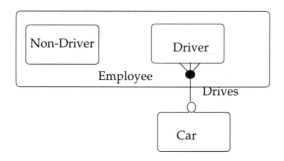

Entity descriptions

Employee   (*EmployeeNumber,...*

Driver   (*EmployeeNumber,...DrivingLicenceNumber,...CarNumber*

Car   (*CarNumber,...*

Figure 12.15   *Drivers as a sub-type of Employee*

In his book *Data and Reality* Kent (1978) devotes several chapters to discussing the difference between an entity, attribute and relationship. It is a stimulating and often amusing account and comes to the conclusion

... ...p...,..... .. ..p...... .... participation conditions in relations. We have seen that relationships are represented in relations by the inclusion of the identifier of one entity as an attribute of the other, that is, by posting the identifier when it becomes a foreign key. We also know that foreign keys are allowed to take null values in the relational model, but that we should avoid null values if possible. However, in the E-R model if the participation condition of an entity is optional then null values will occur for the foreign key of the corresponding relation for the instances which do not participate in the relationship. In order to avoid this some simple rules need to be applied.

1:M relationships

If the participation condition of the entity on the 'many' side is mandatory, post the identifier of the entity on the one side as an attribute of the entity on the many side (see examples in Figures 12.4(a) and 12.4(c)).

If the participation condition of the entity on the 'many' side is optional, create a separate table for the relationship. The identifier of the relationship table is the identifier of the entity on the many side (see examples in Figures 12.4(b), 12.4(d) and 12.13).

If the participation condition of both entities is mandatory and the entity on the one side has no attributes apart from its identifier, then this entity can be removed (see Figures 12.7 and 12.8).

1:1 relationships

If one entity is optional post the identifier of the optional entity as an attribute of the mandatory entity (see example in Figure 12.14).

If both entities are mandatory, the attributes can often be merged.

If both entities are optional create a separate relation for the relationship. Either identifier can become the relationship identifier (see Figure 12.16).

M:M relationships

Always create a relationship table. The identifier is the concatenation of the two (or more) entity identifiers (Figures 12.10 and 12.11).

Entity descriptions

Employee   (*EmployeeNumber*,...

Car   (*CarNumber*,...

Drives   (*EmployeeNumber*, CarNumber,....

    OR   (*CarNumber*, EmployeeNumber,...

Figure 12.16   *Employees drive cars both sides optional*

12.9   Entities and relations

Entities are things of interest to the enterprise. An attribute is a data element associated with an entity. An entity has a M:1 association with its attributes. Relationships exist between entities. Relationships have degree (the number of entities participating), membership class (is it mandatory or optional for the entities to participate) and complexity (relationships are 1:1, 1:M, M:1 or M:M).

Entities and relationships are represented by relations (tables). An entity (or relationship) occurrence is a tuple (table row). An entity (or relationship) type is a relation header (table type). Entities (or relationships) can therefore be referenced by their identifiers, which are the identifiers (primary keys) of the corresponding relations. Entities and relationships, together with their corresponding relations provide a subjective model of the information content of the database. They model the enterprise rules.

There is thus a very close correspondence between the E-R model and the relational model. Indeed in the methodology provided in this text, *together* they form the information model. The E-R model being the main user-oriented part of the information model and the relational representation being the computer-oriented part. This relationship can be shown clearly with the following examples.

Functional dependencies become the attributes of an entity (Figure 12.17) with the determinant becoming the identifier. Secondly, multi-valued relationships (M:M relationships between data elements) require

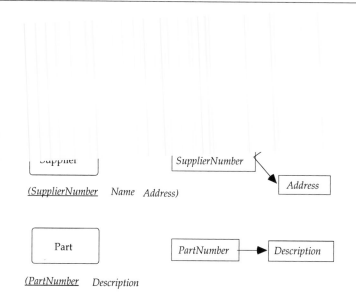

Figure 12.17   *Functional dependencies and entities*

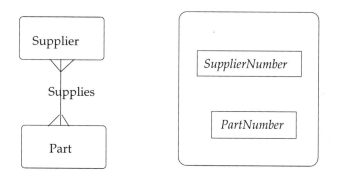

Entity descriptions

Supplier   *(SupplierNumber,...*
Part   *(PartNumber,...*
Supplies   *(SupplierNumber, PartNumber,....*

Figure 12.18   *M:M relationships in the dependency diagram and E-R model*

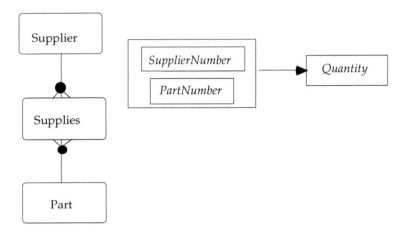

Entity descriptions

Supplier   (*SupplierNumber*...
Part   (*PartNumber*,...
Supplies   (*SupplierNumber, PartNumber, Quantity*)

Figure 12.19   *M:M relationships determining another data element*

12.10 Key points

In this chapter we have explored some basic features about the entity-relationship model and how it relates to the relational model.

- The E-R model consists of a diagram showing the entities in boxes joined by relationships shown as lines along with entity descriptions.

- The E-R model is more abstract than the relational model which makes it more suitable for the early stages of data modelling.

- The E-R model is a semantic data model which is able to represent more semantics of the enterprise than the relational model.

- Entities are things which we want to store data about. They correspond to relations and have an identifier and possibly other attributes.

...ng taken.

Further reading

Veryard, R. (1992) *Information Modelling: practical guidance* Prentice Hall, Englewood Cliffs, NJ

> Chapter 2 of Veryard's book gives an informal, but easily accessible discussion of E-R modelling.

Simsion, G. (1994) *Data Modelling Essentials: analysis, design and innovation.* International Thompson Publishing, Boston, MA

> A good discussion from a practitioner's perspective.

Modell, M. (1992) *Data Analysis, Data Modelling and Classification* McGraw-Hill, New York

> This book provides a thorough discussion of data models in general.

Kent, W. (1978) *Data and Reality* North-Holland, Amsterdam

> See his discussion of entities, attributes and relationships.

Bubenko, J. A. (ed.) (1983)*Information Modelling* Chartwell-Bratt, Lund, Sweden

> Although the papers in this book were first presented in 1979, there are several interesting and useful accounts of different aspects of semantic modelling in general and of entity relationship modelling in particular. The papers are mostly very theoretical and hard going, but important for readers interested in research in the area.

....c C-R model provides a good
graphical representation of the information, but it is the relations
which capture the information in a rigorous form. It is important
to recognise the connection between entities, relationships,
relations and information. The E-R model can also be seen as a
'map' of the database or information structure and can be used to
test whether the structure can be navigated in an appropriate
manner. In this chapter we look at a number of examples of how
the E-R model can be used.

After studying this chapter you should be able to:

- understand the similarities and differences between the E-R
  model and the relational model

- identify and remove connection traps from an E-R model

- understand the relationship between E-R constructs and
  multi-valued dependencies

- be able to design relations which accurately represent the
  participation conditions of relationships.

13.1   Traversing the terrain

One of the desirable features of the E-R model is that it provides a map
of the information system. Relationships can be thought of as paths
which join the entities together. The designer can check the model to
verify that certain paths exist. In particular, the E-R model can be
checked against the process model (see section 5.4) to ensure that all
processes can be completed.

However, even before checking the E-R model against the process
model it must be checked against the enterprise rules. As discussed
previously, the data model is a model of the enterprise rules made of
data. It is a representation of these rules expressed by the static
relationships between data elements. Whilst the dependency diagram
and relational model capture the relationships between data elements,

the E-R model captures the relationships between groups of data elements.

Consider the following example.

Figure 13.1 shows the E-R model that represents the data requirements of a school's 'outward bound' centre.

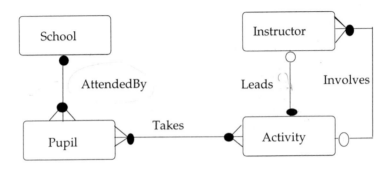

Entity descriptions

School	(*SchoolName*, Address)
Pupil	(*PupilName*, Age, SchoolName)
Activity	(*ActivityCode*, ActivityDescription, InstructorId)
Instructor	(*InstructorId*, InstructorName, StaffStatus, ActivityCode)
Takes	(*PupilName, ActivityCode*)

Figure 13.1   *E-R model for Outward Bound*

From Figure 13.1 we can see that various logical paths exist in the model. For example if I wish to know the name of the instructors leading the activities which a particular pupil took, I can find the activities which the pupil took from the Takes relationship and for each activity I can find the *InstructorId* of the instructor which I can use to find the name of the instructor from the Instructor table. If I want to know which schools have been involved with a particular activity description, I can find the *ActivityCode* from the Activity table, find all the pupils associated with that activity from the Takes table and find the school details for each pupil by using the *SchoolName* in the Pupil table to access the School table.

You should be able to see how this can be accomplished by using a number of relational operators (i.e. SQL data manipulation statements — see chapter 8). For example to find the schools which have been involved with a particular activity description, horse riding say, I

1. Select

...now complicated that would become if the SQL statements were embedded in one another.) Using the E-R model in this way means that various user queries can be checked to ensure that the model can deal with them. The designer must verify that all the required paths through the model are indeed possible.

13.2   Connection traps

Although pairs of entities may have been related accurately during the modelling stages, it is often the case that paths connecting three or more entities have not been considered. It is these paths which may result in a misrepresentation of the required information. This problem is sometimes referred to as 'semantic disintegrity', but a more common term is 'connection trap'. The problem is referred to only fleetingly by Date (1995a), but is discussed in some length in Howe (1989). Connection traps only occur when the information requirements of the enterprise require three or more entities to be traversed in order to retrieve information. There are two sorts of connection trap identified by Howe (1989), the fan trap and the chasm trap.

Fan traps

Any relationship between three entities of the form M:1, 1:M is potentially ambiguous. Whether or not the ambiguity arises or is important depends on the enterprise rules. Consider the example in Figure 13.2. The enterprise rules are as follows.

Each department is in one division and each division has many departments. Each employee is in one division and each division has many employees.

The E-R model in Figure 13.2(a) represents the specified enterprise rules correctly. However, it does not represent the relationship between Employee and Department, and if this is important information to the enterprise, then the model must be changed to show this. To see why it does not show which employee is related to which department, consider the table occurrences in Figure 13.2(b). From these occurrences it can be seen that employees E1, E2 and E3 are all in Division K2 as are departments D1, D2 and D3. However, there is no connection between an employee and a department. The three employees could all be in department D2 or in department D3 or E1 could be in D3 with E2 and E3 in department D1, and so on. Any number of interpretations can be made from the data stored in the relations.

Entity descriptions

Department   (*DepartmentNumber,.....DivisionNumber*)

Division   (*DivisionNumber,.....*

Employee   (*EmployeeNumber,.....DivisionNumber*)

(a) E- R model of fan trap

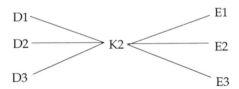

(b) Occurrence diagram for fan trap

D1,.............K2   E1,.............K2   K1,...............

D2,.............K2   E2,.............K2   K2,...............

D3,.............K2   E3,.............K2   K3,...............

Department relation   Employee relation   Division relation

(c) Sample occurrences for fan trap

Figure 13.2   *Fan trap between Employee and Department*

Fan traps do not always result in lost information. In the example in Figure 13.3, the model shows that a room may have many telephones in it and may have many employees assigned to it. In this case there might

be no requirement to connect individual emplo
telephones. If an employee is assig
automatically associated
rule in many
ho

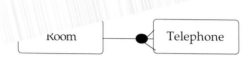

Entity descriptions

Employee   (*EmployeeNumber*,................*RoomNumber*)

Room   (*RoomNumber*,...............)

Telephone   (*TelephoneNumber*,..............*RoomNumber*)

Figure 13.3   *No fan trap because an Employee associated with a room is associated with all telephones in that room*

In other cases information is not lost because there is never a need to traverse a particular path either because such information is not required or because there is an alternative path between the entities which can be used.

Chasm traps

Chasm traps can occur when there exists an optional relationship between entities. In such cases a path between entities may not exist for certain entity occurrences (because not all entity occurrences have to participate in the relationship) and hence information is lost. The example in Figure 13.4 shows an example and table occurrences of a chasm trap. Here the problem is to determine which warehouse *BinNumber* B14 is in. The only occasions when this information is represented is if a bin has a part assigned to it. Since B14 is not related to a part, there is no connection between that particular bin and a warehouse.

As with fan traps, not all chasm traps result in lost information, but all entities with a non-obligatory membership class must be examined to check that they do not create chasm traps.

Removing connection traps

The problems of connection traps can be easily overcome, by introducing the relationship which is missing. The connection trap only arises because a relationship has been overlooked. Once the required relationship has been included in the model, the other relationships can be examined to see if they are necessary or if one of them can be removed. In Figure 13.5 the example from Figure 13.2 has had the relationship Employee : Department added, and as a result the Employee : Division relationship can be removed. The relationship between Employee and Division can be discovered, unambiguously by traversing through the Department entity. In Figure 13.6 the relationship between Warehouse and Bin has been introduced and hence the Warehouse : Part relationship can be removed. However, it is not always the case that relationships can be removed when another is introduced as we see later.

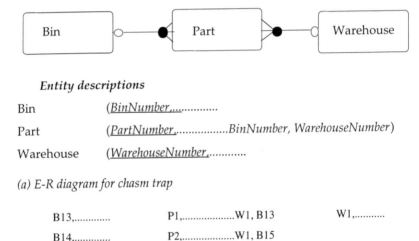

Entity descriptions

Bin   (*BinNumber,................*

Part   (*PartNumber,.................BinNumber, WarehouseNumber*)

Warehouse   (*WarehouseNumber,............*

(a) E-R diagram for chasm trap

B13,.............	P1,...................W1, B13	W1,...........
B14,.............	P2,...................W1, B15	
B15,.............		
Bin relation	Part relation	Warehouse relation

(b) Sample occurrences for chasm trap

Figure 13.4   *Chasm trap between Warehouse and Bin*

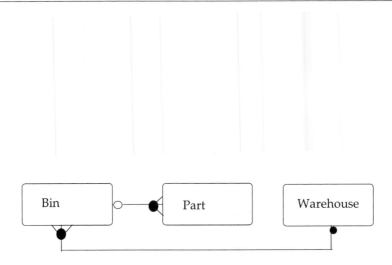

Figure 13.6   *Removing the connection trap from Figure 13.4*

Connection traps can be checked for towards the end of the data modelling process. The analyst need only examine optional relationships and relationships of the form M:1, 1:M and ask: 'Does the system need to traverse this entity in order to represent information.' Notice that connection traps only occur between entities with another intervening. In the examples given the connection traps are between Department and Employee and Warehouse and Bin and not between adjacent entities. Also notice that the fan trap occurs with two relationships, M:1 followed by 1:M and not between relationships 1:M followed by 1:M, 1:M followed by M:1 or M:1 followed by M:1. Connection traps can be overcome by introducing a relationship between the disconnected entities, but all other relevant relationships must then be re-examined to see if they are required.

13.3   The need for information

Consider the following case. It illustrates how the E-R diagram can be used to highlight difficulties and form the basis of debate about the importance of certain information requirements. Imagine the discussions taking place between the system designer and the system users.

The diagram in Figure 13.7 is an attempt at an E-R model of the retail stock control system for a 'High Street' chain store. The company wishes to maintain records of each article in each shop. An article is identifiable by an *ArticleNumber* consisting of the *ProductNumber* and a

SequenceNumber and the data to be stored includes *DateReceived* in the shop, the *DateSold* and *Price*. There are several depots which deliver to shops according to the products required. Each product is handled by one depot only.

If we decompose the M:M relationships we discover that there are several connection traps (Figure 13.8). There is a fan trap around Shop so that depots cannot be related to products. There is a fan trap around Product so articles cannot be connected with shops. Apart from the fan traps, there is a potential chasm trap around Product.

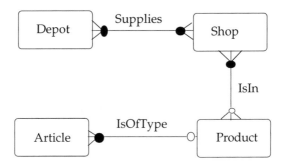

Figure 13.7   *Attempt at E-R diagram for High Street chain store*

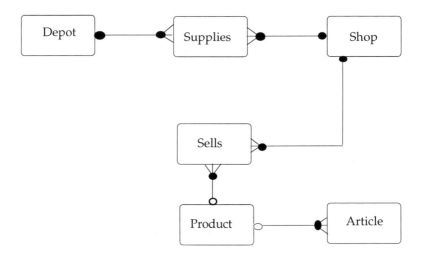

Figure 13.8   *Expanded version of Figure 13.7 showing M:M relationships as entities*

From the narrative th

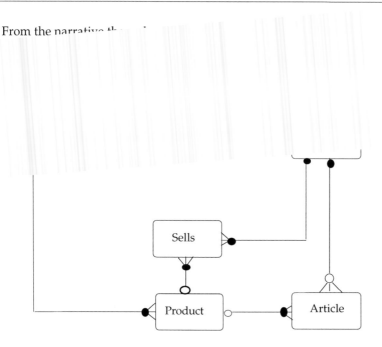

Entity description

Depot	(*DepotNumber*,...
Supplies	(*DepotNumber, ShopNumber*,...
Shop	(*ShopNumber*,...
Article	(*ProductNumber, SequenceNumber*, DateReceived, DateSold, Price)
Product	(*ProductNumber*,...

Figure 13.9   *Expanded version of Figure 13.8*

The original Sells relationship appears to be redundant now that Article is connected with shop. However, since the Product:Article relationship is optional for Product, we can only discover the products which a shop sells if it has some articles. If it is a new product, it can not be related to a shop. Furthermore, Article is optional with respect to Shop (the article might be in the depot) and so another chasm trap results.

The fan trap between Supplies and Sells is significant because it means we do not know which products are supplied by which depots to which shops. Presumably depots do not supply all products to all shops (they are dependent facts about the shop (*cf.* section 10.3)). The argument here is rather involved. Since Product:Depot is M:1 if we know the products which a shop sells (from the Sells entity) we can find the depot which supplies each product and hence deduce the information provided by the Supplies entity. It appears as if we can remove Supplies, but the optional membership class of Product with Sells may be significant. We can only discover which depots *can* supply which shops if the shop has a product in stock which was supplied by that depot. Since we cannot guarantee that this will always be the case, the Supplies entity must be retained. Once again the problem is caused by the chasm trap between Depot and Sells. A new product will not have a row in the Sells table and therefore will not be connected with Shop. If the depot does not already supply a shop with products, there is no way of connecting Depot and Shop unless we maintain the Supplies entity. Of course if this information is not of interest to the enterprise, then the Supplies entity can be discarded. The connection traps around Shop and Depot are no longer significant because of the alternative route through Product which is the relationship 'supplying at present' rather than 'can supply'.

Once again we can see that the final model and the significance of the relationships depends on the enterprise rules and the information which is required. The E-R model forces us to discuss exactly those questions.

13.4   Information and multi-valued relationships

In the entity-relationship model, any M:M relationship followed by another M:M relationship will produce a fan trap when the relationships are replaced by an entity. Consider the example in Figure 13.10.

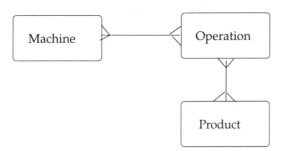

Figure 13.10   *Two M:M relationships*

The E-R model of Figure 13.10 represents the enterprise rules that a machine can perform many operations and an operation can be performed on many machines. An operation relates to many products and a product can undergo many operations.

From the di...

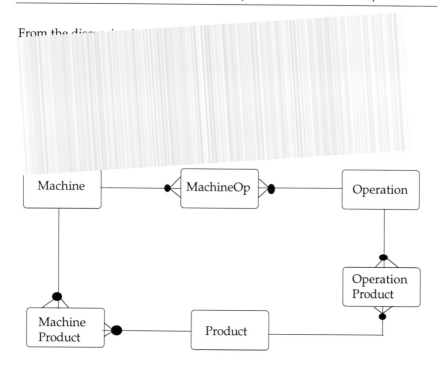

Entity descriptions

Machine	(*MachineNumber*,...
MachineOp	(*MachineNumber, OperationNumber*,...
Operation	(*OperationNumber*,...
OperationProduct	(*OperationNumber, ProductNumber*,...
Product	(*ProductNumber*,...
MachineProduct	(*MachineNumber, ProductNumber*,.....

Figure 13.11   *Expanded version of Figure 13.10 plus additional relationship between Product and Machine represented as an entity*

Far from alleviating the fan trap around operation resulting from expanding the relationships in Figure 13.11, the introduction of the relationship between Product and Machine has created two more fan traps! The model now has fan traps around Machine, Operation and Product. How can this problem be overcome?

One method of overcoming this problem is to consider the M:M:M relationship between the three entities Machine, Product and Operation.

(Equivalently we can consider the M:M relationship between MachineOp and Product, the one between OperationProduct and Machine or between MachineProduct and Operation). This results in the creation of a new entity MachineOperationProduct which has a mandatory M:1 relationship with the three original entities (by decomposing the complex relationships — see section 12.6). Whenever two consecutive M:M relationships are encountered in an E-R model, it is wise to examine the alternative of representing them as a single, ternary relationship. This is shown in Figure 13.12. Notice that the original M:M relationships are now redundant.

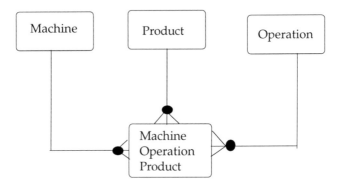

Figure 13.12   *Expanded ternary relationship between machine, product and operation*

The question now arises as to whether or not this representation captures the enterprise rules, and whether the associated table

(*MachineNumber, OperationNumber, ProductNumber,...*)

contains redundant data.

The MachineOperationProduct entity is appropriate if the Operation, Machine and Product entities are not independent of each other, i.e. if we want information on which machine *performed* which operation on which product. However, if there is any independence between the entities then the MachineOperationProduct entity will contain redundancy. For example if we require information on which machines *can* perform which operations, which machines *can* operate on which products or which products *can* undergo which operations, the entities MachineOp, MachineProduct and OperationProduct avoid the redundancy. Indeed if all three of these are needed then the model of

Figure 13.11 is

...ups are required between them, and at
others three relationships are required. In some cases it is possible that
four relationships are required between the three entities. Three binary
relationships expressing what might happen and one ternary
relationship representing what has happened. It all hinges on whether
the relationships are dependent or not.

To illustrate this, we return to the agents, companies and products
example of section 10.3 (see Figure 13.13). Agents work for companies,
companies make products and agents sell products. However, agents
do not necessarily sell all products and companies do not necessarily
make all products, but if an agent sells a certain product and represents
the company making that product then he sells that product for that
company. In addition we now add the requirement that we need to
know which products an agent did sell for which company.

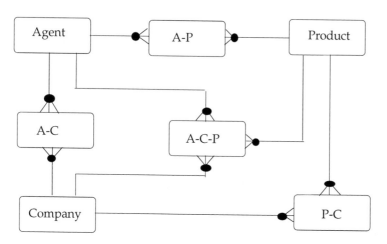

Figure 13.13   *Agents/Companies/Products/Problem*

The entities in Figure 13.13 represent the following information:

- Agent   contains details of all agents

- A-P   contains information on which products an agent
             sells

- Product   contains details of all products

- P-C   contains information on which products are made by
             which companies

- Company   contains details of all companies

- A-C   contains information on which companies each agent
             works for

- A-C-P   contains information on which product a particular
             agent sold and the company he or she was
             representing when he or she sold it.

All the above tables are in fifth normal form and all are required to
capture the information required.

Multi-valued dependencies are dictated by the rules of the enterprise
and the only way to find out about them is to ask the users of
information system. In the E-R model MVDs show up as M:M
relationships between three (or occasionally four or five) entities which
result in fan traps. The fan traps result in lost information if the entities
are *dependent* on one another (hence the need for the A-C-P entity
above). Where the entities are *independent* no information is lost through
the fan trap.

An alternative way of viewing this was examined in Figure 13.3 in
relation to the employees, rooms and telephones. We argued that the
fan trap around room was not significant because an employee was
associated with *all* the telephones in a room. No information is lost if
one entity is related through another entity to all occurrences of a third
entity.

Thus in the Employees, Skills, Languages example (section 10.3), the
Employee-Skill combination (representing the skills which an employee
has) is related to all occurrences of the Employee-Language combination
(representing the languages which an employee has), i.e. they are
independent facts about employees. The dependency diagrams and E-R
diagrams for this are shown in Figure 13.14.

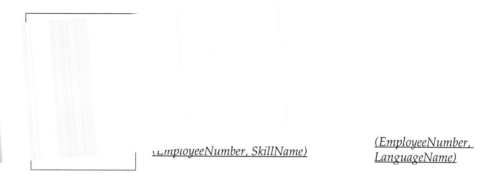

(EmployeeNumber, SkillName)

*(EmployeeNumber,
LanguageName)*

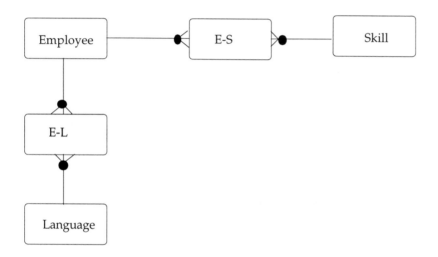

Entity descriptions

Employee	*(EmployeeNumber,...*
E-S	*(EmployeeNumber, SkillName,...*
Skill	*(SkillName,...*
E-L	*(EmployeeNumber, LanguageName,..*
Language	*(LanguageName,...*

Figure 13.14   *Alternative representations for Employee has skills and languages (independently)*

13.5   Key points

In this chapter we have looked at how the E-R model can be used to explore relationships and to expose problems with the model.

- The E-R model provides a 'map' of the information system.

- The designer can check that the model represents all required information by traversing from one entity to another.

- Fan traps can result in lost information and appear on the model as a M:1 relationship followed by a 1:M relationship.

- Chasm traps can result in lost information and appear on the diagram where there is an optional participation of an entity in a relationship.

- Different enterprises will require different information and it is important to check exactly what the model does represent.

- Multi-valued dependencies show up on the E-R model as fan traps.

Further reading

Howe, D. R. (1989) *Data Analysis for Database Design* 2nd Edition Edward Arnold, London

> Chapter 11 presents an excellent treatment of connection traps.

...............several chapters to
.... the details of the data model. The data model consists of
the a user-oriented model (the E-R model) and a computer-
oriented model (a set of fully normalised relations). The purpose of
this chapter is to present a methodology for producing a model of
an application and once again to show the relationship between
the E-R and relational data models.

After studying this chapter you should be able to:

- describe the contents of an information model

- describe the stages of information modelling

- produce a complete E-R model for a simple application.

14.1 The information model

The (conceptual) information model consists of three parts as shown in
Figure 14.1. The reason for including the word 'conceptual' in
parentheses in the previous sentence is to remind you that there are
many other aspects to developing a complete information model
implemented on a database. The conceptual information model has to
be tailored to the particular processing needs of the enterprise and has
to be implemented bearing in mind the constraints imposed by any
hardware and software which is to be used (see Figure 14.2 and
discussion later in this section).

The techniques described so far — relational modelling, normalisation,
using dependency diagrams and using the E-R model — have been
concerned with the development of a conceptual information model.
However, the information model requires us to develop two conceptual
models: a conceptual data model and a conceptual process model. These
models are then checked for consistency, and any necessary
modifications are made, when we produce the data processing model.
This, then, is the first level information model (the data model, the
process model and the data processing model), otherwise called first
level design (1LD, see Figure 14.2).

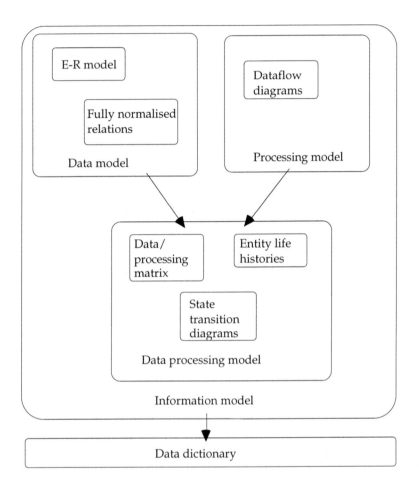

Figure 14.1   *Components of the information model*

In this chapter we concentrate on developing a comprehensive data model, deferring discussion of the process model and data processing model until chapter 15.

Figure 14.2 illustrates the processes involved in information modelling. The information model (1LD), along with some information about the volumes and frequency of transactions is the input to second level design. Second level design is concerned with adapting the first level design to the specific requirements of the processing required. It may be that the first level design consists of so many tables that it would not achieve an acceptable level of performance if it were implemented in that form   Th

...olved in third level design, but if it is a
hierarchical DBMS, or if the system is to be implemented without using
a DBMS, then major changes may be required to the original model.

The approach of moving from first to second to third level design may
seem rather long-winded, but it is important for a number of reasons.
The first level design provides a transaction independent view of the
information content of the system. The data model is enterprise
dependent because the data model will only reflect the things of interest
to that enterprise. In particular, the existence of connection traps will
vary between enterprises depending on the enterprise rules governing
the semantics of the data. The second level design is enterprise and
transaction dependent, but is still independent of hardware and
software. Hence the second level design can be used to evaluate
alternative implementations and to assist in the selection of hardware
and software. It is only when the restrictions of a particular
implementation method are known that it is necessary or desirable to
produce the internal model in the form of process and data physical
definitions.

It is important to remember that this process does not equate with the
design of the entire information system. In particular we will not cover
data collection in any depth nor will we mention the design of peoples
jobs, the method of interacting with the computer or the strategic
decisions involved in selecting an information area. We offer no
guidelines on project planning, establishing the feasibility of the
information system or of its implementation. Similarly we say nothing
about the design of forms, codes, screens and reports nor of the
techniques for analysis of the requirements of users. This discussion is
limited to showing how the techniques so far described can be brought
together into a useful methodology for producing an information model.
There are many detailed methodologies available which will not be
discussed here (e.g. Yourdon, 1989; Lewis, 1994). Some follow a similar
procedure, others differ in their emphasis. The issue is not which is
best, it is which is applicable, easy to use and accurate. The approach
described here meets these criteria.

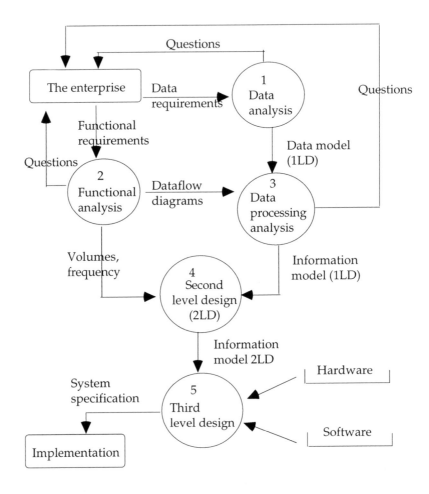

Figure 14.2   *Stages in information modelling*

14.2   Using the E-R model to help in data analysis

Identifying data elements and their value sets is the first part of data analysis. It is also important to understand how those data elements can be aggregated into entities and how those entities are associated with one another. In this section we return to the case of CND Engineering (Figure 14.3) and provide an annotated example of how the construction of an E-R model forces the analyst to analyse what entities and relationships are required in order to represent the data requirements.

						rate	(£)
Mon	23/3	0123	Supermarket trolley	6	Smoothing	A	42.00
				2	Welding	K	20.00
Tues	24/3	0066	Computer table	3	Scraping	A	21.00
				1	Painting	A	7.00
				2	Finishing	A	14.00
		0067	Hospital trolley	1	Loading	B	6.50
				2	Welding	K	10.00
Wed	25/3	0123	Supermarket trolley	8.5	Bending & joining	C	85.00
Thurs	26/3	0067	Hospital trolley	6	Painting	A	42.00
				2	Loading	B	14.00
Fri	27/3	0066	Computer table	5	Welding	K	50.00
				3	Finishing	A	21.00
			Total hours	41.5		Gross wage	332.50

CND (engineering) is a small firm based in Derby. It manufactures a variety of products in its factory, processing bought in steel bars, tube, wire, etc. and finishing the processes off by painting the completed articles. Each job is for one customer and is given a unique job number. Every week, all employees complete a job sheet which records the work which they have done during that week. Employees work for a single department and their gross wage is calculated using the figures on the job sheet multiplied by an hourly rate which varies with the grade of the employee and the task. For each job there are a set number of tasks which must be completed in sequence. However, an employee does not necessarily work on all tasks associated with a job.

Figure 14.3   *CND (engineering) Job Sheet*

One of the advantages of looking at CND (engineering) is that you are already familiar with it from chapters 2 and 11. Indeed we would hope that using the top-down technique of E-R modelling will result in the same set of relations as the bottom-up method of relational modelling. This gives you a chance to compare the methods and to see the strengths and weaknesses of each.

The first thing to do when developing an E-R model of an application is to read through the application description, study the documents and then jot down your 'first guess' entities and to sketch the important relationships. A handy guide to the choice of entities is to look for nouns in the description. Verbs often indicate likely relationships. Whilst doing this, look for candidate entity identifiers and possible relationships. You cannot go wrong at this stage!

For example, from the description of CND (engineering), I choose the following entities and relationships.

Entities	*Relationships*
Product	Manufacture
Job (identifier *JobNo*)	WorkIn
Customer	SequenceOfTasks
Week	WorksOn
Employee (has an attribute *Grade*)	
Department	
Task	
Steel	

The designer can now attempt a first sketch E-R diagram (mine is shown in Figure 14.4). Whilst doing this the designer should include any relationship names. Other relationships will also be discovered which seem likely to be important. Designers should use the fact that they are drawing a model to help in thinking about the enterprise and what is important. At this stage it is important to keep in mind that each entity will require an identifier and to reflect on what that identifier might be.

14.3   Developing the model

Once the first sketch has been produced, it is important to examine the diagram and for each entity, ask 'what data do we want to store about this entity?'. If there is any doubt about the answer, the entity should be left in the model, but if the designer is convinced that the application is

not concerned with this the

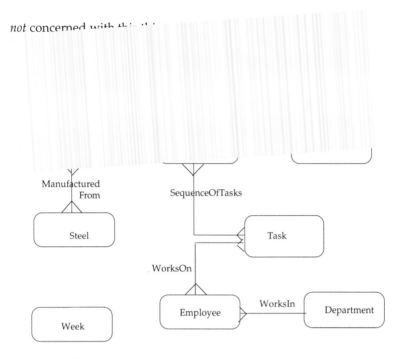

Entity descriptions (outline)

Job   (*JobNo*,...

Employee   (*EmployeeNo, Grade*,...

Figure 14.4   *First sketch ER diagram for CND (engineering)*

Once a first sketch E-R diagram has been produced it is also important to examine each relationship and ask whether there is some data to store about that relationship. Remember that any M:M relationship can be replaced by an entity which then has a M:1 relationship with each of the entities originally in the M:M relationship. All M:M relationships should be decomposed during the early stages of data analysis. The advantage in decomposing a M:N relationship in this way is that it forces the data modeller to question exactly what this thing is and to consider if it has any attributes of its own or relationships with other entities. Also recall that the identifier of the newly created entity will be the concatenation of the identifiers of the two entities originally associated through the M:M relationship.

We can now re-draw the E-R diagram of Figure 14.4, removing the entities which are no longer required and decomposing the M:M relationships. At this point we also provide outline entity descriptions

and pause to consider to what extent any of the newly discovered
entities is likely to be important. For example, in this case the WorksOn
relationship does seem important in this enterprise — the Task which an
Employee works on is central to recording data such as the number of
hours spent working on a particular task. The SequenceOfTasks seems
important in order to store data about which tasks need to be
undertaken in which order for a particular job. The next version of the
E-R diagram is shown in Figure 14.5.

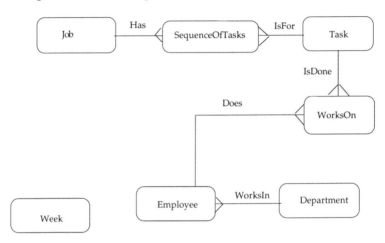

Entity descriptions (outline)

Job	(*JobNo*,...
Task	(*TaskName*,...
SequenceOfTasks	(*JobNo, TaskName*,...
Employee	(*EmployeeNo, Grade*,...
WorksOn	(*EmployeeNo, TaskName*

Figure 14.5   *Developing the E-R diagram 'discovering' WorksOn and
SequenceOfTasks entities*

Once an outline model has been produced, it is a good idea to look back
at the list of data elements which have been identified from the
document analysis and description analysis. The list of data elements, as
given in Figure 2.6 is:

Name

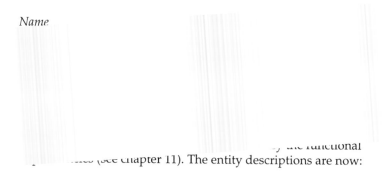

..., ... (see chapter 11). The entity descriptions are now:

Job	(*JobNo, JobDescription,...*
Task	(*TaskName,...*
SequenceOfTasks	(*JobNo, TaskName,...*
Employee	(*EmployeeNo, Grade, Name.,..*
WorksOn	(*EmployeeNo, TaskName*

This leaves

HoursWorked	*DayName*	*Date*

unaccounted for. In addition we have yet to discover a relationship with Week.

We now use the E-R diagram to help us think further about the data. First, let's consider dates and weeks. There is clearly a relationship between *DayName*, *Date* and *Week*. Each date is in only one week, but a week has many dates in it. A day name is associated with many dates (there are lots of Tuesdays, for example), but each date can only ever have one day name. We might model these relationships as illustrated in Figure 14.6.

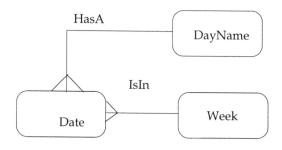

Figure 14.6 *Considering entities concerned with dates*

The designer now needs to question these entities; what data is there to store about them — now or in the future? We soon discover that there is no data to store about DayName. It is not clear whether there is data to store about Week, but there may be attributes such as whether it is a holiday week and so on. Since there is no data to store about DayName, we can better represent it as an attribute of Date giving the entity descriptions;

Date   (*Date*, DayName,...

Week   (*WeekNo*,...

and a 1:M relationship between Week and Date.

The E-R diagram can be used to help us think about other relationships (Figure 14.5). In this case, we can recognise that WorksOn can store data about the tasks which particular employees have done, or are scheduled to do. It does not tell us anything about *when* they were done, however, since there is no relationship with Date. The SequenceOfTasks entity can store data about which tasks have to be done for a Job, but as it stands, it doesn't say anything about the *sequence* in which those tasks were done (or could be done)! Once again it can be useful to utilise the methods of bottom-up modelling to explore the details of entities, by exploring the dependencies or writing out occurrences of the entities. From the work sheet we can see that some occurrences of SequenceOfTasks are:

0123   Smoothing

0123   Welding

0123   Bending & Joining

0066   Scraping

0066   Painting

0066   Finishing

0066   Welding

The SequenceOfTasks entity does not say anything about the sequence in which tasks are, or can be, performed on a job because we cannot assume that the entity occurrences will be stored in the order in which they were presented above. If the ordering of the entity occurrences is changed, the information about sequence would be changed!

Recall the discussion about this problem from chapter 11 when we were developing a relational model of this application. If we want to store data about the sequence in which tasks are done on a particular job, we need to uncover a hidden data element. This we might call *SequenceNo*. It is a sequential number which, when concatenated with a *JobNo*, will only ever be associated with a single Task (such as 'welding' or 'boltino') Th...

...... m ngure 14.7.

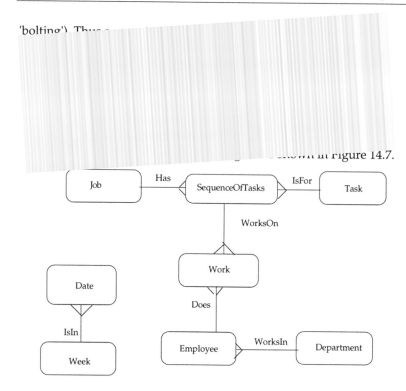

Entity descriptions (outline)

Job	(*JobNo*, *JobDescription*.,..
Task	(*TaskName*,...
SequenceOfTasks	(*JobNo, SequenceNo*,...
Employee	(*EmployeeNo*, Grade, Name.,..
Work	(*EmployeeNo, JobNo, SequenceNo*
Date	(*Date*, DayName,...
Week	(*WeekNo*,...

Figure 14.7 *Dealing with the Work entity*

Although the model is becoming a better representation of the application it is still not complete. Firstly, we have to consider whether the Work entity in Figure 14.7 really does represent the relationships which we want. In fact it still does not, because as it stands we have no way of knowing *when* the employee did the work. We need now to consider the relationship between Work and Date. Once again this is

M:M (the work may be spread over several days and many pieces of work will be done on any one day). Decomposing this relationship provides a new Work entity which now has the identifier {*EmployeeNo, JobNo, SequenceNo, Date*}.

Now we apply the 'litmus test' for entities; is there any data to store about this? The answer to this is 'yes, the number of hours worked'. Hence although it has taken a long time to uncover the Work entity, it certainly appears important. The process of data modelling as a part of data analysis has revealed something fundamental to the whole application.

The final part of this problem is dealing with rates and payments. From the application description, we know that a task has a number of rates associated with it which vary with the grade of the employee. There is thus a M:M relationship between Task and a possible entity, Grade. We can represent this as an entity GradeForTask, say (identifier {*TaskName, Grade*} and apply two tests for entities — (a) is there any data which we want to store about this thing or (b) does it have a relationship with anything else. The answer to this question is provided in the application description where it says '...an hourly rate which varies with the grade of the employee and the task'. Thus, *HourlyRate* is either an attribute of GradeForTask, or an entity which has a relationship with GradeForTask.

Some care is required here. The data element *HourlyRate* is a code (A, K, C, etc. are shown on the sample work sheet) which is associated with a monetary amount, represented by the data element *Payment*. Go back to the list of data elements to confirm this. Hence there is an entity which represents the hourly rates and associated payment amounts. Call this entity Rate. It then has a 1:M relationship with GradeForTask. *HourlyRate* is thus the identifier of Rate and not an attribute GradeForTask. (Notice that if there were not this distinction between codes and amounts, the payment amount would be an attribute of GradeForTask and a Rate entity would not be necessary.) This portion of the model is shown in Figure 14.8.

14.4   Checking the model

We are now in a position to put Figures 14.7 and 14.8 together. The model can then be checked to ensure that it effectively represents the data requirements. Whilst checking the model, the analyst can specify the participation conditions of all the entities in the relationships. This process gives the model shown in Figure 14.9, which is a completed conceptual data model of the data requirements at CND (engineering).

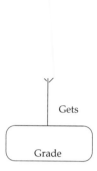

Entity descriptions (outline)

Grade	(*Grade*,...)
Task	(*TaskName*,....)
GradeForTask	(*Grade, TaskName*)
Rate	(*HourlyRate*, Payment)

Figure 14.8   *Dealing with rates of pay*

Notice, however, that when specifying the participation conditions, you are specifying some important constraints on the data. For example, SequenceOfTasks is optional with respect to the WorksOn relationship. This means that data can be stored about the sequence of tasks on a job *before* any work is undertaken. If this relationship had been mandatory the data would have constrained so that information about the sequencing of tasks would only be available once the job had been scheduled and allocated to an employee. This would seem to be too fierce a constraint. Participation conditions are a vital part of conceptual modelling, but the analyst needs to be aware of the impact which such conditions have.

The model must also be checked to determine whether there are any other constraints or assumptions which the designer has made which cannot be expressed through the E-R model. Just as the relational model cannot represent all the relationships between data elements and relations (see, e.g., section 11.2), so the E-R model cannot represent all constraints. It represents more than the relational model and can be annotated with comments to cover inclusive and exclusive relationships and so on, however, there often remain important aspects of the data model which need to be provided in narrative form. Three important assumptions have been listed in Figure 14.9 — these will need to be verified with the users at CND (engineering). Assumptions serve to define the scope of the system, to establish what the data model can and cannot represent.

Constraints on the other hand are sometimes needed to represent features which cannot be shown on the model, or which cannot be shown easily on the model. Although there do not seem to be any of these in CND (engineering), in other applications there could be constraints such as 'only employees in department 06 can do welding' or 'every job must include at least one employee with a grade of "supervisor" '. These constraints cannot be represented easily in E-R terms and are better represented in narrative form, listed after the entity and relationship descriptions in the model.

Another aspect of checking the model is to ensure that the various paths through the model are appropriate to the application and can deliver the information required. When checking the paths through the model it is important to look out for connection traps (chapter 13). For example does the E-R model in Figure 14.9 enable CND (engineering) to calculate the employees gross wage for a given week? Can we find out which jobs include the bending and joining task? For the first of these, we would start from Employee using *EmployeeNo*, and find the employee's grade from the Employee table. From the Work entity we can find out the number of hours which the employee has worked on each of the {*JobNo*, *SequenceNo*}s within a range of dates and from this we access the SequenceOfTasks entity to find which Task this is. Taking the *TaskName* and *Grade* we can find the appropriate hourly rate from the GradeForTask entity which allows us to retrieve the payment from Rate. This provides enough information to perform the calculation. To discover which jobs include bending and joining, it is simply necessary to retrieve the job numbers from the SequenceOfTasks entity which match the given value of *TaskName*.

Whilst looking at the various paths through the model, the designer should look out for connection traps. In Figure 14.9 there appears to be a fan trap around Task and another around Grade. However, neither of these result in any lost information because if an employee is associated with a Grade then he or she is associated with *all* the occurrences of GradeForTask associated with that *Grade* and similarly if a Job is associated with a *TaskName* then it is associated with *all* the GradeForTask occurrences which relate to that *TaskName*. The *HourlyRate* is dependent on the *TaskName* and *Grade* and is independent of both the *JobNo* and the *EmployeeNo*.

We now consider the possible chasm traps in the WorksOn, DoneOn, Does, IsFor, HasA, Gets and IsOf relationships. (Recall that chasm traps can only occur b̶e̶t̶···

... ...ask since HasA is mandatory with
respect to GradeForTask. However, 'welding' may not be associated
with a value of SequenceOfTasks since IsFor is optional with respect to
Task. This does not appear to result in any lost information because I
cannot see any need to traverse these relationships in this order.
GradeForTask provides information about the hourly rates for tasks and
it does not matter whether any particular task is related to a job. A
similar argument means that there is no information lost through the
IsOf relationship.

The optional participation of Task in HasA means that a given task may
not be associated with an hourly rate. If a new task is required on a job,
'hammering', say, then someone might submit a worksheet which
includes the task of 'hammering', but the database would not be able to
retrieve the hourly rate for this task. Although this does result in lost
information, it is exactly the sort of information which the managers of
CND (engineering) would like to know about. It is a management
decision whether to make HasA mandatory with respect to Task
(meaning that whenever a new task is added to the database the hourly
rates associated with that task must also be added) or whether to have
an exception condition programmed into the system which alerts
managers if someone submits a work sheet for a task which has no
hourly rates. The fact that we have considered this chasm trap has
revealed an important aspect of the data requirements which the
managers need to consider. An analogous argument holds for the Gets
relationship — what should happen when a new grade is added?

The optional participation of Date in DoneOn means that for a given
WeekNo, there might be no occurrences of Work. But if there is no work
done on a date then that is precisely the information which is required,
so no information is lost. Similarly, the optional participation of
Employee in Does and SequenceOfTasks and WorksOn do not result in
lost information as there is never a need to traverse these relationships
unless the occurrences exist.

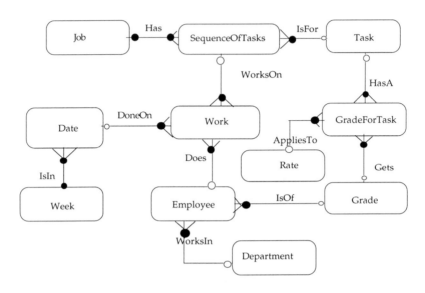

Entity descriptions

Job	(*JobNo*, JobDescription)
SequenceOfTasks	(*JobNo, SequenceNo*, TaskName)
Task	(*TaskName*)
GradeForTask	(*TaskName, Grade*, HourlyRate)
Rate	(*HourlyRate*, Payment)
Grade	(*Grade*)
Employee	(*EmployeeNo*, Grade, Name)
Department	(*DepartmentNo*)
Work	(*EmployeeNo, JobNo, SequenceNo, Date*, HoursWorked)
Date	(*Date*, DayName, WeekNo)
Week	(*WeekNo*)

Figure 14.9   *Completed EAR conceptual data model for CND (engineering) application*

Relationship d

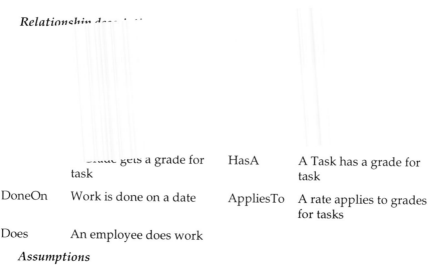

	gets a grade for task	HasA	A Task has a grade for task
DoneOn	Work is done on a date	AppliesTo	A rate applies to grades for tasks
Does	An employee does work		

Assumptions

The same task may be performed more than once on a job.

The application does not deal with scheduling work (since Work is mandatory in DoneOn).

The application only deals with Jobs on which the tasks have been scheduled

Figure 14.9   *concluded*

14.5   Completing the model

The process of checking the E-R model has revealed a number of things which need to be checked with the systems users. What the data analysis has done is to expose these aspects of the system which may otherwise have gone unnoticed. Apart from the issue of the optional participation of Task in HasA and Grade in Gets, the model in Figure 14.9 is complete. We have checked that the model can provide the required information and indeed the database design which results from the E-R model is the same as that which resulted from the relational approach used in chapter 11. There will almost certainly be no need for relations corresponding to the Week, Grade and Task entities since they consist of a single data element which already exists as a posted identifier in other relations. Although department is in a similar position, it is more likely that other data will need to be kept about departments and so Department may be implemented as a relation. These are considerations which related primarily to the implementation of the model and consequently are outside the scope of the conceptual model. The designer will need to take the conceptual model and modify it in the light of the processing requirements at CND (engineering) as the design moves to the second level design (section 14.1).

Data analysis is something which is not easy, but which comes with practice. It is important to use the construction of a conceptual data model as an aid to analysis. Producing the model exposes holes in the designer's understanding of the application. In real life, the designer would be able to go directly to the system users and ask them to clarify points. When developing models away from a real situation it is often necessary to make assumptions. The model works just as well here, in identifying the assumptions which have to be made.

This example has also demonstrated that data analysis is an iterative process. The analyst does not simply identify all the data elements and then proceed to produce a model. Constructing the model will force the analysts to check the definition of data elements or to uncover implicit data in the system. In the CND example, we uncovered the data element *SequenceNo*, for example.

14.6   Key points

In this chapter we have concentrated on the data modelling aspect of information modelling.

- The information model consists of data models, process models and data processing models.

- The process of information modelling includes second and third level designs in addition to the first level design (the conceptual model) described here.

- Data elements, their descriptions and value sets are discovered from documents and the application description along with the major entities and entity identifiers.

- The designer then examines relationships between entities, decomposing all M:M relationships and considering the meaning of the entity which is created as a result.

- The designer needs to focus on the meaning of entities, as specified by the entity's identifier and on the central concerns of data analysis; 'does the application require data about this thing' and 'does this thing have relationships with anything else'.

- The designer iterates around these activities, using bottom-up techniques where appropriate to clarify the meaning of entities

...providing entity and relationship descriptions and any constraints and assumptions.

Further reading

Lewis, P. (1994) *Information Systems Development* Pitman, London

This book describes an approach to data modelling placing it in the context of a soft systems approach to information systems development.

Veryard, R. (1992) *Information Modelling: practical guidance* Prentice-Hall International, London

A practical approach to information modelling.

...pics which we have looked at so far in this book have all been to do with just a part of information modelling. In chapter 14, the components of the information model were identified as the data models, process models and data processing models. Whilst we are still concerned primarily with the conceptual information model (first level design), in this chapter we bring all these aspects together to illustrate the process and products of information modelling. The example illustrates the process from identifying the information needs (*cf.* chapter 1), the data elements and values (*cf.* chapter 2), the data dictionary entries (*cf.* chapter 4), process and data processing models (*cf.* chapter 5), relational modelling and normalisation (*cf.* chapters 9–11), some relational operations (*cf.* chapter 8) and the E-R modelling (*cf.* chapters 12–14). The example concerns the information needs of Jackie Jones and her music shop.

After studying this chapter you should be able to:

* develop an information model for a medium sized application

* understand the interrelationships between the components of information modelling

* be able to use the various models and modelling techniques in a way which is suitable for the problem at hand.

15.1   Overview

Jackie Jones wants to set up a database which will help her manage her small music shop. The database should be capable of dealing with the sales, purchasing and stock control of her products. It is expected that, once Jackie gets used to using the system, she will wish to make various *ad hoc* inquiries such as sales trends of different types of recordings, slow moving stock and so on. In particular the system should be able to:

* record data on regular sales

- record data on special orders placed by customers

- enable some elementary sales analysis to be undertaken and for data to be recorded on the purchase orders placed by Jones with suppliers

- record data on deliveries and returns.

General description

In 1995 Jackie Jones invested her savings in a small record shop, and formally opened 'Disco Jones' on New Year's Day 1996. Business soon became very brisk with an average of 1000 people visiting the shop each day culminating in 200 actual sales. However, at peak times, Jackie makes as many as 500 sales in a day. She keeps a range of about 4000 cassette tapes and compact discs (CDs) in stock, many of which are a single copy, although for the most popular she may keep as many as 300 copies. Customers spend a lot of time browsing around the shelves or asking Jackie for particular recordings.

The current manual system, which the database is to replace, works as follows. When a sale is made, customers are given a receipt (Figure 15.1) with details of the recordings they have bought. Jackie retains a carbon copy of this receipt and enters details from it on a ledger (Figure 15.2). The receipt is also used to update the stock record cards (Figure 15.3). The volume of sales is quite considerable and has led to Jackie spending an increasing amount of time updating the stock record cards and ledger at the end of the day. Receipts are then filed in a loose leaf folder.

A large notice encourages customers who cannot find the recordings they require to place special orders through 'Disco Jones'. A form is available for this purpose (Figure 15.4) and customers are required to pay a £5 deposit. This is necessary because Jackie found that many customers did not honour their orders and left her with unwanted stock. When the ordered item is received a postcard is sent informing customers that their order is ready for collection (Figure 15.5). Jackie feels that this service earns her a large amount of goodwill, but she freely admits that it is a 'headache' to run as she has to deal with 30–40 special orders each week. The £5 deposits have to be kept separate with details of the order and postcards have to be completed, addressed and paid for! Some customers are still defaulting but Jackie is afraid to re-sell their orders just in case they should claim them sometime in the future. Jackie admits that the service is out of hand and badly needs 'tidying up'. In particular, she would like to vary the amount of deposits, but at present this appears too complicated to consider. Similar problems are experienced with the discs which she has from time to time on 'special offer'.

An important aspect of Jackie's

...week. Consequently she
...keep at least one week's stock of recordings, based on
the maximum number sold in a week during the past six months. The
most popular recordings are kept in much larger quantities. Deliveries
are received once or twice a week from each supplier accompanied by a
delivery note (Figure 15.7). All goods received are checked for damage
and poor quality goods are returned with a covering note (Figure 15.8).
This happens about once a week. Sometimes inferior goods get past
Jackie's visual inspection and are sold to customers. Rectifying these
errors causes an irritating amount of administrative work.

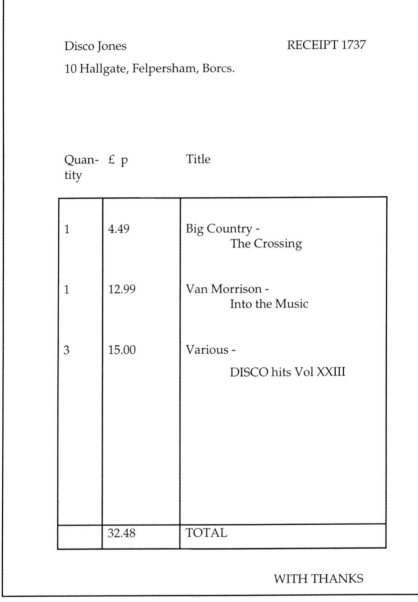

Figure 15.1   *Receipt*

Date	Qty	Description				
					41	00
	10	Fallen Idol - Silly Wizard	87202		40	30
	10	Silly Costumes - Bucks Fizz	87202		39	20
	1	Born in the USA - Bruce Springsteen	1733	3 50		
	1	Heroes - David Bowie	1734	1 99		
	1	Sky 3 - Sky	1735	1 99		
	1	Pop Go the Classics - NDO	1736	0 59		
	15	Meaningless Lyrics - A McCartney/Jackson compilation	87219		57	00
	1	The Crossing - Big Country	1737	4 49		
	1	Into the Music - Van Morrison	1737	2 49		
	3	Disco Hits Vol XX111 - Various	1737	4 50		

Figure 15.2   *Ledger*

Record: With the Beatles Release date: 11/64		Artist: The Beatles RRP. £3.99					
W/beg 5/2	B/fward balance 12	W/beg 12/2	B/fward balance 21	W/beg 19/2	B/fward balance 7	W/beg 26/2	B/fward balance 9
I	11	I I	19	I I	5	I I I	6
I I	9	I I I	16	I	4	I I	4
I I I	6	I I	14	I I I I	0	I I I I	0
I I	4	I I I I	10	Out of stock	Out of stock	+25	25
I	3	I I I	7	+10	10	I I I I I	21
+20	23			I	9	I I I	18
I I	21						

Figure 15.3   *Stock record card*

Disco Jones   SPECIAL ORDER

CUSTOMER . . . . Jack Sneed

ADDRESS   17 Birbeck Avenue
                       Worcester

TITLE   ARTIST   LABEL   DATE
End of the World   Disaster Area Oblique   21/8/96

£5 DEPOSITED RECEIVED

Figure 15.4   *Special order form*

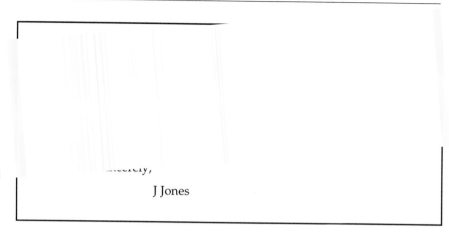

                   J Jones

Figure 15.5   *Post card*

Date 5/8/96

order number

E321

Purchase Order

To: From:

Texas Records Ltd   Disco Jones

Unit 17, Riverside   10, Hallgate,
Industrial Estate   Felpersham

Market Banton   Borcs.

BO9 4LE

Disc Number	Artist and Title	Quantity
K31728	The Crossing - Big Country	10
P91316	Fallen Idol - Silly Wizard	10
K21131	Silly Costumes - Bucks Fizz	10
P61214	Meaningless Lyrics - McCartney and Jackson	15

Notes

Figure 15.6   *Purchase Order*

Disc no.	Artist/title	Quantity
P61214	Meaningless Lyrics - McCartney and Jackson	15

Figure 15.7   *Delivery Note*

date 12/8/96	Returns Note

To:

Texas Records Ltd Unit 17, Riverside Industrial Estate Market Banton BO9 4LE	Disco Jones 10, Hallgate, Felpersham Borcs.

Disc Number	Quantity	Reason
P61214	10	crumpled covers

Figure 15.8   *Returns Note*

15.2   Analysis

The first part of the process of developing an information model is concerned with sketching the areas under scrutiny and beginning to compile a data dictionary. This activity will help to clear the mind and establish the scope of the model. From the scenario if appears that Jackie Jones is interested primarily in:

1. Recording details of sales made. Let's call this system MAKESALE.

2. She is also interested in keeping details of sales and deliveries so that she knows how much she has in stock of a particular CD or tape. Let's call this system STOCK.

3. She wants to

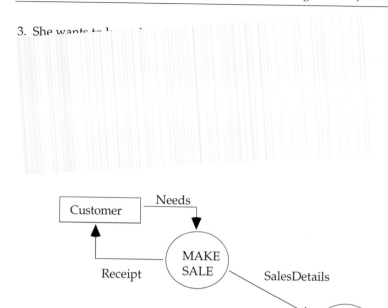

Figure 15.9   *'First shot' analysis of main systems (processes) at Disco Jones*

In Figure 15.9 we are concentrating solely on the data that is involved in the system. We are not concerned with physical problems. The model of the systems, or functions, involved is a dataflow diagram (DFD) as described in chapter 5. However, the first shot analysis is unsatisfactory for a number of reasons. Firstly there are two distinct sorts of sales — those that involve the customer coming into the shop and selecting his or her choice and those that involve special orders being made. Secondly it is difficult to see what the System STOCK actually does. What is its purpose? Thirdly, the PURCHASE system involves the placing of orders with suppliers and the handling of deliveries. This system consists of two separate (but related) functions each with its own purpose and hence would be better shown as such.

Taking these criticisms into consideration we can re-do the analysis as shown in Figure 15.10.

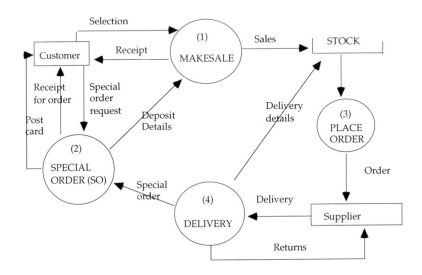

Figure 15.10   *Process analysis — second try.*

The second try analysis seems more satisfactory. STOCK is now represented as a store of data rather than a function. The creation of SO and DELIVERY appears to be vindicated by the number of inputs and outputs which each has. This is not to say that the representation is 'correct', nor that it only takes two tries before a suitable model is created. Figure 15.10 appears to offer a good starting point for further analysis and appears to reflect some significant features of Disco Jones. We can define the systems as follows.

1. MAKESALE concerns the recording of moneys received, discs sold and the production of receipts. It may include methods for selecting discs and analyses of sales.

2. SO concerns the recording of special orders and deposits, the production of receipts and the notification of customers when the delivery is received. In addition SO must hand details of deposits to the MAKESALE system when the customer pays the full amount.

3. PLACE ORDER concerns the selection of suppliers, the analysis of stock in order to determine the quantity to be ordered and the recording of orders placed. It may also include the printing of orders.

4. DELIVERY concerns the receipt of deliveries, checking deliveries and recording details against orders placed. In addition it should be able to identify discs on special orders and notify the SO system when they are

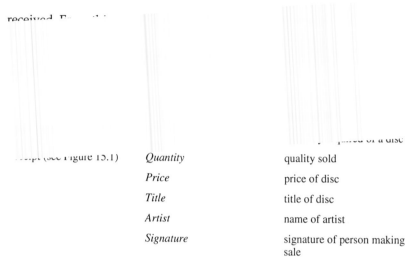

received F.

...p. (see Figure 15.1)   *Quantity*   quality sold

                         Price   price of disc

                         Title   title of disc

                         Artist   name of artist

                         Signature   signature of person making
                                             sale

Notice that the other elements on receipt are either fixed (such as the name and address at the top and 'with thanks' at the bottom) or calculated (such as the price £15.00 on line 3 and the total at the bottom). We do not include these data elements in the data dictionary at present. Also notice that the heading 'title' on the receipt is in fact two data elements i.e. *Artist* and *Title* (refer to chapter 2 for analysis of documents).

Data flow	Data element name	Description
Sales	*Artist*	as above
	Title	as above
	Quantity	as above
Receipt for order (Figure 15.4)	*CustomerName*	customer name
	CustomerAddress	customer address
	Title	as above
	Artist	as above
	LabelName	Name of disc label (record company)
	SODatePlaced	date SO was placed
	DepositReceived	deposit received 'yes' or 'no'
	Signature	as above
Special order request	*Title*	as above
	Artist	as above

Data flow	Data element name	Description
Post card (see Figure 15.5)	*CustomerName*	as above
	DiscType	'single', 'album', etc.
	Artist	as above
	Title	as above
Order	*SupplierName*	supplier name (i.e. ▼
	SupplierAddress	suppliers address
	Artist	as above
	Title	as above
	? LabelName	as above
	DiscNumber	disc identification n
	QuantityOrdered	quantity ordered
	PODatePlaced	date order placed

Presumably there could be several discs ordered on one order. The queries (?) indicate that we don't know whether such data elements exist, but it seems likely that they would. In a 'live' analysis, of course, the analyst would resolve such queries by discussing them with the appropriate people. In our case, we must make do with making sensible assumptions.

Data flow	Data element name	Description
Delivery (Figure 15.7)	*Artist*	as above
	Title	as above
	DiscNumber	as above
	? LabelName	as above
	QuantityReceived	quantity received
Returns (Figure 15.8)	*Artist*	as above
	Title	as above
	DiscNumber	as above
	LabelName	as above
	QuantityReturned	quantity returned
	Reason	reason for returning
Special order	*Artist*	as above
	Title	as above
	LabelName	as above

		Quantity Received minus Quantity Returned)
Stock (Figure 15.3)	*Title*	as above
	Artist	as above
	ReleaseDate	date of release of disc
	RRP	recommended selling price
	WeekBeginningDate	week beginning date
	WeekSales	number of sales
	QuantityAccepted	as above

We have examined all the documents and explored all the dataflows and data stores. We can now compile a provisional data dictionary of the data elements involved in the system. This is shown below.

Data element name	Value set	Description
Artist	any characters	Name of group, singer, etc.
Category	A	category of disc, e.g. F = folk, R = Rock, etc.
CustomerAddress	any characters	customers address
CustomerName	any characters	customers name
DelNoteNumber	?	delivery note number
DepositAmount	Money	Amount of deposit received for each disc (in pounds)
DepositReceived	Alphabetic	Y = deposit received N = deposit not received
DiscNumber	?	Disc identification number
DiscType	Alphabetic	A = Album, S = Single, etc.
LabelAddress	any characters	address of record company
LabelName	any characters	Label, i.e. record company
OrderNumber	?	purchase order number

Data element name	Value set	Description
PODatePlaced	Date	Date order was placed with supplier
Quantity	Numeric	quantity sold on one sale
QuantityAccepted	Numeric	quantity accepted into stock
QuantityOrdered	Numeric	quantity ordered on one order
QuantityReceived	Numeric	quantity of one disc received on a delivery
QuantityRequired	Numeric	Quantity of a disc required by a customer
QuantityReturned	Numeric	quantity returned to supplier
Reason	any characters	reason for returning discs
Receipt Number	?	receipt number
ReleaseDate	MM/YY	date disc was released month and year only
ReturnDate	Date	date of return
RRP	Money	recommended selling price
SellingPrice	Money	actual price charged on a sale
Signature	any characters	authorisation. Just hold person's initials
SODatePlaced	Date	date special order was placed: DD/MM/YY
SpecialOfferPrice	Money	Special offer price
Supplier	any characters	Supplier name
SupplierAddress	any characters	Supplier address
Title	any characters	Title of disc
WeekBeginningDate	Date	week beginning date
WeekSales	Numeric	total sales for a week

Although all deposits are only £5 at present, this could change in the future, so a data element *DepositAmount* seems sensible. However it is doubtful whether the *DepositReceived* data element is required. A number of value sets (marked ?) will have to be more carefully specified Such decisions can be left until later.

The above analysis raises many questions which would have to be reviewed by discussing the matter with the system owner (Jackie Jones in this case). In particular, the system has made no provision for any

15.3   The data model

The analysis has also provided us with the basis for developing a data model. It is clear that we are interested in:

- Sales

- Special orders

- Customers

- Suppliers

- Discs

- Deliveries

- Labels (= record companies)

and hence these will become the entities in our entity-relationship model. The first shot E-R diagram is shown in Figure 15.11.

Disc is clearly central to this system. A disc can be identified by *DiscNumber* and is related to a single label. A disc can come from many suppliers and a supplier can supply many discs. A delivery is related to only one supplier but may include many discs. A disc will appear on many deliveries. A sale may be for many discs, as could a special order. A disc will appear on many sales and many special orders. Both sales and special orders relate to a single customer.

The next step in the process is to replace all M:M relationships by an entity and to examine what the entity is and whether or not we are interested in it. In addition we must select identifiers for those entities which do not have them. The results of this process are shown in Figure 15.12.

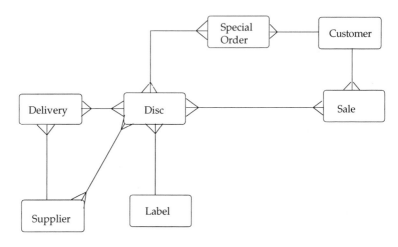

Entity Descriptions

Customer	*(CustomerNumber,...*
Delivery	*(DelNoteNumber,...*
Disc	*(DiscNumber,...*
Label	*(LabelName,...*
Sale	*(ReceiptNumber,...*
SpecialOrder	*(?????,...*
Supplier	*(SupplierName,...*

Figure 15.11   *1st try E-R diagram*

Figure 15.12 must now be examined to see how accurately it reflects the enterprise rules, to establish if any entities or relationships are redundant and to pinpoint important relationships which are missed out or ambiguous.

The SODisc entity relates a special order to a *DiscNumber*. It is, therefore, equivalent to a line on a special order. The example special order which we have (Figure 15.4) has only one line, but the wording of the postcard suggests that more than one disc could be ordered. Although there does not appear to be any additional data which needs to be kept about a line on a special order it would seem safer to retain the entity for the time being. A similar argument can be made for DiscSale which relates a disc to a receipt, DeliveryDisc which associates discs with deliveries and SupplierDisc which records which discs can be obtained from which suppliers. DiscSale has an obvious attribute — *Quantity* — being the quantity sold of a particular disc on a particular sale. DeliveryDisc has attributes *QuantityReceived* and *QuantityReturned*

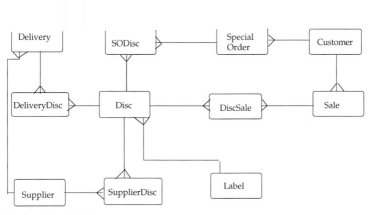

Entity descriptions

Customer	*(CustomerNumber,...*
Delivery	*(DelNoteNumber,...*
DeliveryDisc	*(DelNoteNumber, DiscNumber*
Disc	*(DiscNumber,...*
DiscSale	*(DiscNumber, ReceiptNumber*
Label	*(LabelName,...*
Sale	*(ReceiptNumber,...*
SODisc	*(SONumber, DiscNumber*
SpecialOrder	*(SONumber*
Supplier	*(SupplierName,...*
SupplierDisc	*(SupplierName, DiscNumber,*

Figure 15.12   *Expanded 1st try E-R diagram*

If we continue the analysis process using the E-R diagram (Figure 15.12) as the basis for questions, we can make some further observations at this point. Firstly, the relationship between Sale and Customer appears to be redundant. We do not want to know who bought which discs, just which discs were sold. In another enterprise this may be important data to keep, but in a cash sale system such as at Disco Jones, the data is not required. Secondly, we have no record of orders placed with suppliers. This oversight can be rectified by introducing an entity Order which has a M:M relationship with Disc, and a M:1 relationship with Supplier. Once again the M:M relationship can be replaced by an entity which will have M:1 relationships with the other two entities. As with SODisc, DeliveryDisc and DiscSale, it will have an attribute of quantity — in this case *QuantityOrdered*. The relevant part of the model is shown in Figure 15.13.

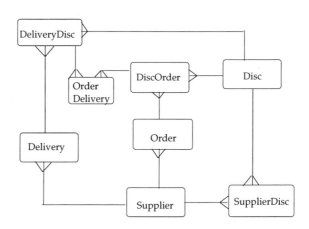

Entity descriptions

Delivery	*(DelNoteNumber,...*
DeliveryDisc	*(DelNoteNumber, DiscNumber*
Disc	*(DiscNumber,...*
DiscOrder	*(DiscNumber, OrderNumber, QuantityOrdered,...*
Order	*(OrderNumber,...*
OrderDelivery	*(DiscNumber, OrderNumber,...*
Supplier	*(SupplierName,...*
SupplierDisc	*(SupplierName, DiscNumber....*

Figure 15.13   *Introducing the Order and DiscOrder entities*

This appears satisfactory, but on closer inspection it can be seen that there is no connection between orders placed and deliveries received. There are 1:M relationships fanning out from both Disc and Supplier and hence this appears to be a fan trap (see chapter 13). It is likely that a direct connection between deliveries and orders is required, otherwise it is impossible to tell which delivery relates to which order. Some sample data is shown in Figure 15.14.

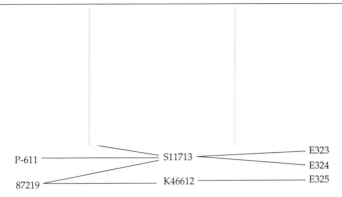

DiscNumber S11713 was ordered on *OrderNumbers* E323 and E324. Other orders were placed (E322 for P61214 and E325 for K46612). Deliveries were made for *DiscNumber* S11713 on delivery notes 87224, P-611 and 87219 (other deliveries being made for discs P61214 (*DelNoteNumber* 87224) and K46612 (*DelNoteNumber* 87219). Which delivery relates to which order? If this information is important, then there must be a direct relationship to avoid the connection trap.

Figure 15.14   *Connection trap around Disc*

A similar argument to that presented above will show that there is a connection trap around Supplier, though it is unlikely that SupplierDisc will be involved. This entity effectively lists which discs are available from which suppliers and hence does not need to be connected to Order or Delivery and so no information is lost.

The question now arises as to which relationship to introduce. The relationship between Delivery and Order is M:M. A delivery could relate to many orders and an order could be delivered in several deliveries. Introducing an entity for the M:M relationship produces fan traps around Delivery and Order (try this for yourself) and hence does not remove the ambiguities. The relationship between DeliveryDisc and DiscOrder is also M:M, but when this is replaced by an entity no further fan traps are introduced. It is, therefore, the best solution. The OrderDelivery entity is shown in Figure 15.13; it represents information about which discs were delivered against which orders.

Notice that these ambiguities would have remained unexamined if we did not replace M:M relationships by an entity. However, once the relationships have been analysed, there is no harm in replacing an entity with a relationship, particularly if it has no obvious attributes. We have done this with SupplierDisc, calling it CanSupply.

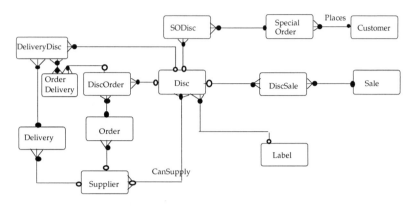

Entity descriptions

CanSupply	*(SupplierName, DiscNumber)*
Customer	*(CustomerNumber,...*
Delivery	*(DelNoteNumber,...*
DeliveryDisc	*(DelNoteNumber, DiscNumber,* QuantityReceived, QuantityReturned, ..*
Disc	*(DiscNumber,...*
DiscOrder	*(DiscNumber, OrderNumber,* QuantityOrdered,...*
DiscSale	*(DiscNumber, ReceiptNumber,....*
Label	*(LabelName,...*
Order	*(OrderNumber,...*
Order Delivery	*(DelNoteNumber, OrderNumber, DiscNumber,*
Sale	*(ReceiptNumber,...*
SODisc	*(SONumber, DiscNumber, QuantityRequired,...*
SpecialOrder	*(SONumber,.......*
Supplier	*(SupplierName,...*

Figure 15.15   *2nd Try E-R diagram*

In addition to the above amendments, we can now specify the participation conditions of all relationships. The second attempt E-R diagram is shown in Figure 15.15.

The model is beginning to take shape. The participation conditions are mostly self-evident, but notice that we only store details of customers who have placed special orders (Customer is mandatory in the Places relationship). Also SODisc, DiscSale, DiscOrder and DeliveryDisc must relate to Disc, but details of a disc may be stored even if it is not involved with the other entities. The only requirement is that a disc must have a label and must have a supplier. These restrictions may

The final point to look at at this stage is the existence of chasm traps —
i.e. relationships which may not exist for certain occurrences and which
may result in lost information. This involves examining the optional
relationships to see if there is ever a pathway using that relationship
which would lose information if the occurrence did not exist.
Frequently there are alternative pathways which circumvent the chasm
trap, so it is not a problem.

The optional relationships around supplier will not cause chasm traps
because orders and deliveries can already be related to discs through the
DeliveryDisc and DiscOrder entities. However problems do exist
relating special orders to deliveries. This is because of the fan trap
around Disc rather than the chasm traps. However it is important to
obtain information on deliveries of special orders because we want to
notify customers when their disc is received. We need to introduce a
M:1 relationship between SODisc and Order so that we can overcome
this problem. We can now produce the 3rd attempt E-R model by
dealing with the above comments and allocating the attributes to their
tables. In allocating attributes we must ensure that the tables are all
fully normalised. The result of this is shown in Figure 15.16.

All attributes have been assigned with the exception of *SpecialOfferPrice*.
This cannot be assigned to Disc because not all discs have a special offer
price and so some occurrences of Disc would have null values. In order
to avoid this, we need to create a new entity, SpecialOffer, consisting of
the data elements (*DiscNumber, SpecialOfferPrice*). In fact we should
create a separate entity for returns which would include the data
elements *DelNoteNumber, DiscNumber, QuantityReturned, ReturnDate* and
Reason, because the return details will be null for some deliveries. We
leave this option out of the model for the time being.

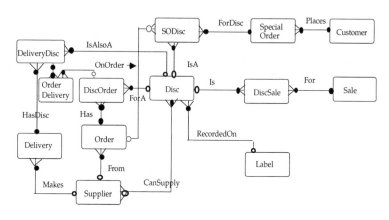

Entity descriptions

Delivery	*(DelNoteNumber,...*
Supplier	*(SupplierName, SupplierAddress)*
Disc	*(DiscNumber, title, artist, DiscType, ReleaseDate, RRP, Category)*
CanSupply	*(SupplierName, DiscNumber)*
DeliveryDisc	*(DelNoteNumber, DiscNumber, QuantityReceived, QuantityReturned, ReturnDate, Reason)*
Order	*(OrderNumber, PODatePlaced)*
DiscOrder	*(DiscNumber, OrderNumber, QuantityOrdered)*
Label	*(LabelName, LabelAddress)*
Sale	*(ReceiptNumber, signature)*
Customer	*(CustomerName,. CustomerAddress)*
SpecialOrder	*(SONumber, SODatePlaced)*
SODisc	*(SONumber, DiscNumber, QuantityRequired, DepositAmount)*
DiscSale	*(DiscNumber, ReceiptNumber, Quantity, SellingPrice)*
OrderDelivery	*(DelNoteNumber, OrderNumber, DiscNumber)*

Figure 15.16   *3rd try E-R model. Most attributes assigned.*

The first level E-R model is nearly complete. The main task remaining is to post identifiers in order to represent the relationships. However, one aspect is still annoying me. The OrderDelivery, DiscOrder and DeliveryDisc entities seem cumbersome and unnecessarily complicated. Hence before completing the process, it is wise to examine the dependencies between the various data elements so that we are satisfied that we have an accurate and suitable model.

{*OrderNumber, DiscNumber*} determines the *QuantityOrdered*

and

{*DelNoteNumber,DiscNumber*} determines the *QuantityReceived.*

This gives the dependency diagram in Figure 15.17.

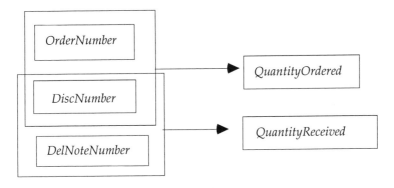

giving tables

DiscOrder   (<u>*OrderNumber, DiscNumber,*</u> *QuantityOrdered*)

DeliveryDisc   (<u>*DelNoteNumber, DiscNumber,*</u> *QuantityReceived*)

Figure 15.17   *Dependencies in order-delivery problem.*

However, there are other dependencies to consider. There is a multi-valued relationship between *OrderNumber* and *DelNoteNumber* and another between {*OrderNumber,DelNoteNumber* } and *DiscNumber*. These are shown in Figure 15.18.

The question facing us is which is the solution best able to capture the semantics of the data? To help us consider this, we need to use some (fictional) sample data.

OrderNumber 123 was placed for *DiscNumbers* 1387 and 1389. When a delivery was not received, a further order (*OrderNumber* 131) was placed for *DiscNumbers* 1387 and 1389. Later still *OrderNumber* 182 was placed

for *DiscNumber* 1421. Two deliveries were then received.
DelNoteNumber D12 was for *DiscNumbers* 1387 and 1389 and
DelNoteNumber D15 covered the remaining quantity of 1389, 20 of 1387
and the order for 1421. The DiscOrder and DeliveryDisc tables are
shown in Figure 15.19.

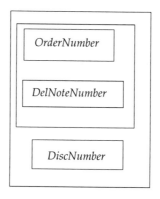

giving tables

OrderDel   (*OrderNumber, DelNoteNumber*)

OrderDelivery (*OrderNumber, DelNoteNumber, DiscNumber*)

Figure 15.18   *Further dependencies in order-delivery problem.*

DiscOrder	(OrderNumber,	DiscNumber,	QuantityOrdered)
	123	1387	30
	123	1389	50
	131	1387	30
	131	1389	50
	182	1421	25
DeliveryDisc	(DelNoteNumber,	DiscNumber,	QuantityReceived)
	D12	1387	40
	D12	1389	40
	D15	1389	60
	D15	1387	20
	D15	1421	25

Figure 15.19   *Sample data for dependencies in Figure 15.17*

182

and

OrderDelivery	(OrderNumber,	DelNoteNumber,	DiscNumber)
	123	D12	1387
	123	D12	1389
	123	D15	1389
	123	D15	1387
	131	D12	1387
	131	D12	1389
	131	D15	1389
	182	D15	1421

Figure 15.20   Sample data for dependencies in Figure 15.18

If we now examine the sample data in the form of the dependencies in Figure 15.18 we have some sample data as shown in Figure 15.20.

On first sight, it appears that the OrderDelivery table contains redundancy; the order to which a delivery relates is duplicated unnecessarily In rows 1 and 5 we have {D12, 1387} appearing and in rows 2 and 6 we have {D12, 1389} and rows 3 and 7 we have {D15, 1389}. However if we use the OrderDel table and join it with DeliveryDisc on *DelNoteNumber*, we get the result shown in Figure 15.21.

The join in Figure 15.21 implies several things which are untrue. In particular that *OrderNumbers* 123 and 131 contained *DiscNumber* 1421 and that *OrderNumber* 182 contained *DiscNumber* 1387 and 1389. Similar problems occur when joining OrderDel with DiscOrder on *OrderNumber* (try this yourself).

The three tables DiscOrder, DeliveryDisc and OrderDel represent the three possible projections of OrderDelivery (if we ignore the quantity columns), but any two projections joined together do not reconstitute the original OrderDelivery table. These projections and joins are shown in Figure 15.22 (refer to chapter 8 for a discussion of project and join).

OrderNumber	DelNoteNumber	DiscNumber	QuantityReceived
123	D12	1387	40
123	D12	1389	40
123	D15	1387	20
123	D15	1389	60
123	D15	1421	25
131	D12	1387	40
131	D12	1389	40
131	D15	1387	20
131	D15	1389	60
131	D15	1421	25
182	D15	1387	20
182	D15	1389	60
182	D15	1421	25

Figure 15. 21　　OrderDel join DeliveryDisc on DelNoteNumber

(OrderNumber,	DelNoteNumber)
123	D12
123	D15
131	D12
131	D15
182	D15

(OrderNumber,	DiscNumber)
123	1387
123	1389
131	1387
131	1389
182	1421

(OrderNumber,	DelNoteNumber,	DiscNumber)
123	D12	1387
123	D12	1389
123	D15	1387
123	D15	1389
131	D12	1387
131	D12	1389
131	D15	1387
131	D15	1389
182	D15	1421

(OrderNumber,	DelNoteNumber)
123	D12
123	D15
131	D12
131	D15
182	D15

(DelNoteNumber,	DiscNumber)
D12	1387
D12	1389
D15	1389
D15	1421
D15	1387

(OrderNumber,	DelNoteNumber,	DiscNumber)
123	D12	1387
123	D12	1389
123	D15	1389
123	D15	1421
131	D12	1387
131	D12	1389
131	D15	1389
131	D15	1421
182	D15	1389
182	D15	1421
182	D15	1387
123	D15	1387
131	D15	1387

(OrderNumber,	DiscNumber)
123	1387
123	1389
131	1387
131	1389
182	1421

(DelNoteNumber,	DiscNumber)
D12	1387
D12	1389
D15	1389
D15	1421
D15	1387

(OrderNumber,	DelNoteNumber,	DiscNumber)
123	D12	1387
123	D12	1389
123	D15	1389
131	D12	1387
131	D12	1389
131	D15	1389
182	D15	1421
123	D15	1387
131	D15	1387

Figure 15.22　　*The three projections and joins of OrderDelivery table.*

The problem...
There is redundancy if we mean that a given disc
a given disc was on a delivery, but there is no redundancy if we mean
that a disc was delivered on a given *DelNoteNumber* and against an
OrderNumber. I suggest that it is the latter which is important and that a
new data element *QuantityDelOrd*, i.e. quantity delivered against an
OrderNumber is required. The final dependency diagram and tables is
shown in Figure 15.23.

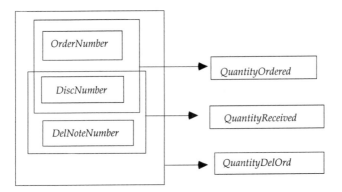

giving tables

DiscOrder	(*OrderNumber, DiscNumber*, *QuantityOrdered*)
DeliveryDisc	(*DelNoteNumber, DiscNumber*, *QuantityReceived*)
OrderDelivery	(*OrderNumber, DelNoteNumber, DiscNumber,* *QuantityDelOrd*)

Figure 15.23　　*Dependencies and tables for orders and deliveries problem*

The result of this analysis is the new attribute for the entity
OrderDelivery. Although this appears to render DeliveryDisc
redundant (because a projection of OrderDelivery will provide the same
information), we will keep DeliveryDisc in order to show any returns
information which there may be. DiscOrder is not redundant because of
the optional relationship with OrderDelivery. The final amendment is to
show the special offer price for some discs by introducing the entity
SpecialOffer. The final, 1st level E-R model is shown in Figure 15.24.

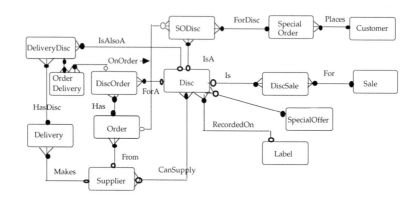

Entity descriptions

CanSupply	*(SupplierName, DiscNumber)*
Customer	*(CustomerName,CustomerAddress)*
Delivery	*(DelNoteNumber, DateReceived, SupplierName)*
DeliveryDisc	*(DelNoteNumber, DiscNumber, QuantityReceived, QuantityReturned, ReturnDate, Reason)*
Disc	*(DiscNumber, Title, Artist, DiscType, ReleaseDate, RRP, Category, LabelName)*
DiscOrder	*(DiscNumber, OrderNumber, QuantityOrdered,)*
DiscSale	*(DiscNumber, ReceiptNumber, Quantity, SellingPrice)*
Label	*(LabelName,,LabelAddress)*
OnOrder	*(SONumber, DiscNumber, OrderNumber)*
Order	*(OrderNumber, PODatePlaced, SupplierName)*
OrderDelivery	*(DelNoteNumber, OrderNumber, DiscNumber, QuantityDelOrd)*
Sale	*(ReceiptNumber, signature, DateSold)*
SODisc	*(SONumber, DiscNumber, QuantityRequired DepositAmount)*
SpecialOffer	*(DiscNumber, SpecialOfferPrice)*
SpecialOrder	*(SONumber, SODatePlaced, CustomerName)*
Supplier	*(SupplierName, SupplierAddress)*

Figure 15.24   *First level E-R model for Disco Jones*

in detail.
Whereas the E-R model was used as the ...
DFDs are essentially a logical design of the new system, specifying the
functions which are required and for the time being ignoring how they
will be accomplished. Initially we will not refer to the E-R model in the
use of names for data stores.

System 1 MAKESALE

In order to complete the MAKESALE process, the customer must come
into Disco Jones and make a selection. Jackie then has to check the stock
levels to verify the choice and then, if all is well, record the sale, issue a
receipt and update the ledger. This is shown in Figures 15.25 to 15.28.

In the case of MAKESALE it is only necessary to have two levels of
DFDs to describe the system. In a larger system it may be necessary to
introduce further levels. Notice how all the dataflows and datastores
are described in terms of their data elements. These have already been
defined in the data dictionary. The construction of the DFDs forces the
analyst to think very carefully about the logic of the system.

It is clear that the output dataflow from check stock requires a data
element to indicate that the required quantity is available. It is this
element, *InStockFlag*, which differentiates the dataflow Selected from
Selection-D. Also notice that the Not available dataflow requires further
details represented by a data element which we have called *Message*.
This too is undefined at present. *Message* could be simply 'the quantity
you require is not available', but it would be much more useful to
indicate what quantity is available, when the required quantity will be
available and/or how to place a special order. The content of *Message*
needs to be ascertained because it will effect the data which must be
available to the Check stock procedure. We will make the assumption
that details of quantities on order and estimated delivery dates must be
available to Check stock procedure. This is shown in Figure 15.28.

In DFD 1.3 (Figure 15.27) notice the existence of a datastore called
Control. Clearly data must be available about the *ReceiptNumber* and
Date to be used on the receipt so that process 1.3.1 can perform its
function. It is common in computerised systems to have a small file of
control information such as this. Finally notice that we are saying
nothing about the actual organisation of the data at this point. We are
simply declaring what data is required, not how it is logically or
physically stored.

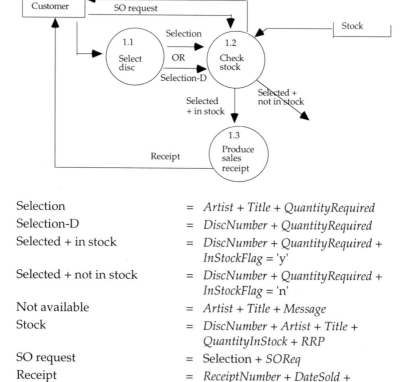

Selection	=	*Artist + Title + QuantityRequired*
Selection-D	=	*DiscNumber + QuantityRequired*
Selected + in stock	=	*DiscNumber + QuantityRequired +* *InStockFlag* = 'y'
Selected + not in stock	=	*DiscNumber + QuantityRequired +* *InStockFlag* = 'n'
Not available	=	*Artist + Title + Message*
Stock	=	*DiscNumber + Artist + Title +* *QuantityInStock + RRP*
SO request	=	Selection + *SOReq*
Receipt	=	*ReceiptNumber + DateSold +* *TotalMoney +* for each *DiscNumber* *[Artist + Title + SellingPrice +* *Quantity]*

Figure 15.25   *Level 1 DFD for MAKESALE*

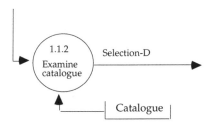

Catalogue   = *DiscNumber + Artist + Title + Price +*
                                              LabelName + ReleaseDate + Category +
                                              Type

Figure 15.26   *DFD 1.1 Select Disc*

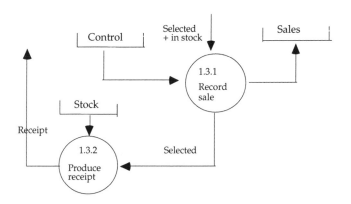

Sales   = *ReceiptNumber + Date +*
                                              [DiscNumber, + Quantity +
                                              SellingPrice]

Control   = *ReceiptNumber + Date*

Selected   = *ReceiptNumber + DateSold +*
                                              SellingPrice + Quantity + DiscNumber

Figure 15.27   *DFD 1.3 Produce receipt*

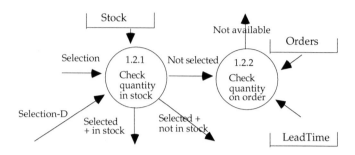

Not selected   = Selection-D + *QuantityInStock*
Orders   = *DiscNumber + SupplierName +*
                                  QuantityOnOrder + PODatePlaced
LeadTime   = ?

Figure 15.28   *DFD 1.2 Check Stock*

System 2 Special Order (SO)

The second major function of the information system is to deal with the placing of special orders. Although in the current system Jackie imposes a single £5 deposit for each order, in the new system she will be able to specify the deposit amount for each disc required. The process involved in Special Order are, therefore, decide deposit and issue a receipt. The actual placement of the order will be dealt with in the Place Order system. Figure 15.29 shows the DFD for Special Order. There is no need for a series of levelled DFDs in this system.

System 3 Place Order

The third system is the Place Order system. In order to accomplish this function, the system must facilitate analysing order requirements, selection of supplier and the making out of an order. This is shown as a DFD in Figures 15.30 and 15.31.

Notice that the Analyse requirements process (process 3.1, Figure 15.31) must take into account special orders, re-orders and new orders. It is unlikely that this part of the system can be precisely specified at this point because the existence of accurate, up-to-date data will probably change the way that Jackie operates. It is just these *ad hoc* analyses of data which gives the database approach to information systems development such appeal. We can only guess at the likely data which will be required and provide Jackie with a flexible system so that she can analyse data when and how she wishes.

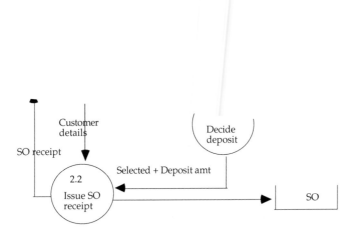

Selected + Deposit amt	=	*Selected + DepositAmount*
SO receipt	=	*SONumber + [Title + Artist +*
		DepositAmount + QuantityRequired]
SO	=	Customer details + *SONumber +*
		Date + [DiscNumber + DepositAmount
		+ QuantityRequired]
Customer details	=	*CustomerName + CustomerAddress*

Figure 15.29   *Special Order*

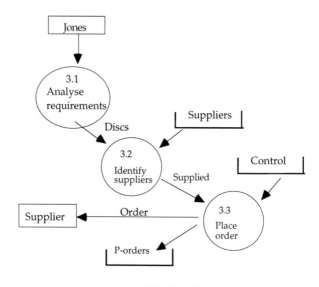

Discs	=	DiscNumber + QuantityOrdered
Supplied	=	[DiscNumber + QuantityOrdered] + SupplierName + SupplierAddress
Order	=	OrderNumber + Date + Supplied
Control	=	OrderNumber + Date
Suppliers	=	SupplierName + SupplierAddress + [DiscNumber] + Discounts
P-orders	=	OrderNumber + SupplierName + [DiscNumber + QuantityOrdered]

Figure 15.30   *Place Order System*

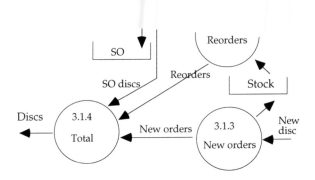

SO trigger	⎫	Exactly what event triggers
Reorder trigger	⎬	processes 3.1.1, 3.1.2 and 3.1.3 is as
New disc	⎭	yet undetermined. It could be 'end
		of day', 'end of week', 'every
		Wednesday afternoon' or a number
		of other events

Discs	= *DiscNumber + Artist + Title +*
	LabelName + QuantityToOrder
SO discs	= *DiscNumber + Artist + Title +*
	LabelName + QuantityToOrder
Reorders	= *DiscNumber + Artist + Title +*
	LabelName + QuantityToOrder
New orders	= *DiscNumber + Artist + Title +*
	LabelName + QuantityToOrder

Figure 15.31   DFD 3.1 Analyse requirements

System 4   Receive Delivery

The final system to be specified in the process model is the Receive
Delivery system. This requires the delivery to be checked and the
quantities accepted to be recorded. In addition, any discs which are on a
special order must be identified and a postcard sent to the customer.
The DFDs are shown in Figures 15.32 to 15.34.

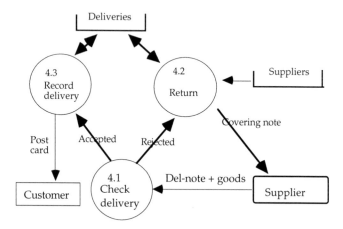

Delivery note	= *DelNoteNumber + Date +* *SupplierName + [DiscNumber +* *QuantityReceived]*
Accepted	= *DelNoteNumber + SupplierName +* *[DiscNumber + QuantityAccepted]*
Rejected	= *DelNoteNumber + SupplierName +* *[DiscNumber + QuantityReturned +* *Reason]*
Covering note	= Rejected + *SupplierAddress*
Deliveries	= Accepted + *[QuantityReturned +* *Reason]*

Figure 15.32   *Receive Delivery*

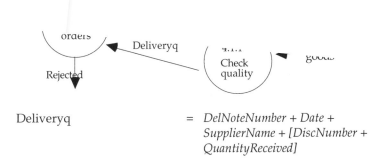

Deliveryq   = *DelNoteNumber + Date +*
                                          SupplierName + [DiscNumber +
                                          QuantityReceived]

Figure 15.33   *DFD 4.1 Check delivery*

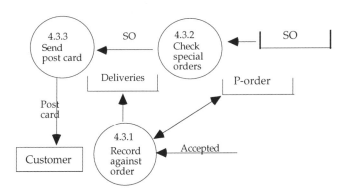

Figure 15.34   *DFD 4.3 Record delivery*

The levelled set of DFDs constitute the process model of the required information system at Disco Jones. As with all the models used, it is a subjective representation and others may disagree with the labels used, the levels chosen, or the content of the dataflows. The important feature is that it is a good representation and consistent in itself. The bubbles show the activities which have to be carried out in response to the events which occur. The dataflows show the data which must be transmitted from one function to another and the datastores show the data which must be available so that a function can be completed. Each function (or process) must have enough data flowing in from the dataflows and data stores to enable it to produce the output dataflow.

We summarise the events and processes in Figure 15.35.

Event	Processes
1. Potential customer arrives	1.1 Select disc
	1.2 Check stock
	1.3 Produce receipt
2. Customer wants to place a special order	
	2.1 Decide deposit
	2.2 Issue SO receipt
3. Jack wants to order from his supplier	
	3.1 Analyse requirements
	3.2 Identify suppliers
	3.3 Place order
4. Jack receives a delivery	4.1 Check delivery
	4.3 Record delivery
	4.2 Return (if necessary)
1.1 Select disc	1.1.1 Browse shelves or
	1.1.2 Examine catalogue
1.2 Check stock	1.2.1 Check quantity in stock
	1.2.2 Check quantity on order
1.3 Produce receipt	1.3.1 Record sale
	1.3.2 Produce receipt
3.1 Analyse requirements	3.1.1 Special order req.
	3.1.2 Reorders
	3.1.3 New orders
	3.1.4 Total
4.1 Check delivery	4.1.1 Check quality
	4.1.2 Check orders
4.3 Record delivery details against order	
	4.3.1 Record against order
	4.3.2 Check special orders
	4.3.3 Send postcard

Figure 15.35   *Summary of events and processes*

The next stage in the design of the information system is to examine which processes are to be computerised and which are not, i.e. to establish the location of the human–computer interface. In a larger system this may be quite a complicated task because of the costs involved in putting some processes on the computer. For example, it may require additional terminals to be installed because of the physical layout of the business, or extra storage space may be needed to hold additional data required for a particular process.

computer system.

It is important to remember that one of the great strengths of the dataflow diagram is that it is a conceptual model rather than a physical model. Many methodologies recommend removing all references to physical objects (such as shelves and postcards in this case) so that new systems do not instantiate out-moded methods of working. However, once again we are faced with the problem that this book cannot do justice to all the details of methods, so our process model will remain a step away from a fully conceptual process model. Similarly at this point in the development of an information system the designer would consider a number of options as to where the human–computer interface should be and which processes will remain manual as opposed to computerised. Accordingly we present the completed process model for Disco Jones in Figure 15.36 with the human–computer boundary shown without further analysis.

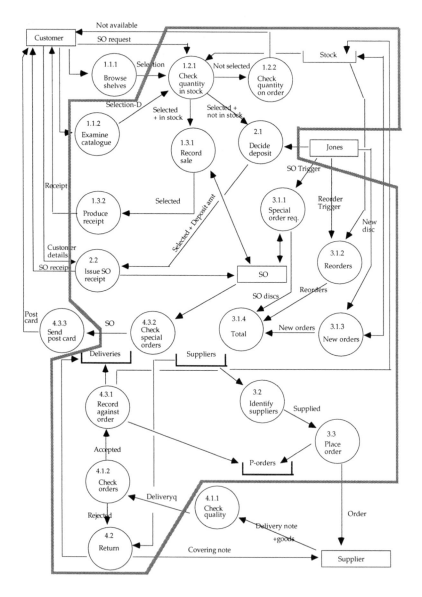

Figure 15.36   *Final, whole process model for Disco Jones showing the human-computer boundary*

matrix cross references data and p⸺
structure diagram which depicts the events which effect the ⸺
entity (occurrence), from the creation of that occurrence to its removal
from the system. The state transition diagram focuses on how a system
changes state. The data/process matrix for Disco Jones is shown in
Figure 15.37. The process of cross referencing the data and process has
uncovered the following problems:

1.2.1 *QuantityInStock* is not recorded anywhere! Hence we cannot
perform function 1.2.1.

1.2.2 Lead time data is not stored, so we cannot complete function 1.2.2.

2.1 How will *DepositAmount* be decided? What data is required?

2.2 Do we need to store *DepositAmount* on Disc entity?

3.1.1 There is a need for a flag to indicate that a special order has been
included on a purchase order. This is done by Table OnOrder.

3.1.2 Need for *QuantityInStock* .

4.3.1 Need for *QuantityInStock.*

QuantityInStock is clearly an important data element which can easily be
accommodated by including it as an attribute of disc since the
dependency *DiscNumber* ⸺> *QuantityInStock* clearly exists.

Lead time may be dependent on *SupplierName* or may be dependent on
{*SupplierName, DiscNumber*}. We shall assume that it is dependent on
SupplierName and therefore becomes an attribute of Supplier.

DepositAmount is more complicated. How does, or will, Jackie calculate
deposits? It may depend on a whole host of factors such as the price of
the disc, the time and trouble needed to obtain it, etc. It is unlikely that
it will be an attribute of disc because special orders are by definition for
the rarer discs which Jackie may not even have on file. This, in fact,
raises another tricky problem. According to the ER model a special
order can only be accepted if it participates in a relationship with the
Disc entity (Figure 15.24). This may cause problems when a disc is to be
ordered which is not on file. Process 2.2 must be extended to allow for
adding occurrences to the disc relation. Returning to deposit, the
solution appears to be to let Jackie enter it each time or to provide a
default option if she requires.

Taking into account the above changes, we can now be reasonably sure that the data model and the process model both offer good representations of the conceptual information system at Disco Jones. The data/process matrix (Figure 15.37) verifies this as all processes, which are to be computerised, can access the data which they require and all the data is used by some process or another. However, we must not lose sight of the fact that there will be other processes required of the system which cannot be anticipated. These are the *ad hoc* inquiries which Jackie may wish to perform.

The analysis so far does suggest that we have made a good choice of entities. We could now examine what events change the entities and how entity occurrences are created and destroyed using the entity-life-history model. ELHs should be produced for all entities. Almost always an entity will need to be effected by events which enable occurrences to be added, amended and deleted. Sometimes we will not wish to delete occurrences, but a facility to amend must be available in case mistakes are made. On other occasions amendments might be forbidden by system auditors. This would be the case in an accounting system when amendments are forbidden for security reasons.

However, the real power of ELHs is when an entity changes state a number of times, which is not the case in this application. The real advantage of drawing ELHs is to check that all entities do indeed have appropriate create, update and delete processes defined. Similarly the state transition perspective can be useful particularly for real time systems. Since Disco Jones is a transaction-based system, state transitions are unlikely to provide great insight. Accordingly we do not develop these models here.

Figure 15.37   *Data/Process matrix for Disco Jones (facing)*

Delivery													
DelNoteNumber													
DateReceived													
SupplierName													--
Disc													
DiscNumber	R	R				A			A				
Title	R	R				A			A				
Artist	R	R				A			A				
DiscType	R					A			A				
ReleaseDate	R					A			A				
RRP	R					A			A				
Category	R					A			A				
LabelName	R					A			A				
DiscOrder													
DiscNumber			R							A	R		
OrderNumber			R							A	R		
QuantityOrdered			R							A	R		
DiscSale													
DiscNumber				A	R			R					
ReceiptNumber				A	R			R					
Quantity				A	R			R					
SellingPrice				A	R								
Label													
LabelName									A				
LabelAddress									A				
OnOrder													
SONumber							A						RD
DiscNumber							A						RD
OrderNumber							A						RD
Order													
OrderNumber										A	R		
PODatePlaced										A	R		
SupplierName										A	R		
OrderDel'vyDisc													
DelNoteNumber											AU	AU	R
OrderNumber											AU	AU	R
DiscNumber											AU	AU	R
QuantityDelOrd												A	
QuantityReturned											AU		
Reason											AU		
ReturnDate											AU		
Sale													
ReceiptNumber				A	R			R					
signature				A	R								
DateSold				A	R			R					
SODisc													
SONumber				D		A							
DiscNumber				D		A	R						
QuantityRequired				D		A	R						
DepositAmount				D		A							
SpecialOffer													
DiscNumber	R												
SpecialOfferPrice	R												
SpecialOrder													
SONumber				D		A							
SODatePlaced				D		A							
CustomerName				D		A							
Supplier													
SupplierName									A	R		R	
SupplierAddress									A	R		R	

15.6   Conclusion

In this example, we have not covered all the details of design. No doubt readers will find inconsistencies and pieces missed out. However, the chapter has, hopefully, demonstrated the method and highlighted many of the problems of system design. If readers are concerned about the amount of documentation provided and the open admission that the design is not complete, then they are not alone. Information system design is complex and it is one of the major problems of current approaches to system design that documentation is so time-consuming and fraught with errors and oversight.

There is no way round this problem apart from constant and thorough checking and re-checking. However, there is a light at the end of the tunnel in the form of automated aids for system design. Computer-based tools called CASE (computer aided software engineering) exist which facilitate the drawing and (far more important) the maintenance of diagrams such as DFDs and E-R diagrams. One of the problems with using diagrammatic tools for documentation is that they are so difficult to amend and so the pressure is on the analyst to bend the world to fit the model rather than to re-draw the model to fit the world.

Fortunately this state of affairs is coming to an end and there are several effective information system design CASE tools with automated aids for consistency checking and maintenance of the data dictionary.

One approach for the company venturing into the area of system design is to adopt one of the proprietary methodologies. There are a vast number of these available on the market today, which have been well described in other publications. However, the problem with adopting a specific methodology is that it may be strong in some areas, but weak in others. The approach taken here is to make available a number of tools which can be used as and when required within a framework of what is needed in an information system, i.e. within the framework of producing an information model.

15.7   Key points

This chapter has been solely concerned with examining the techniques of information modelling described in the text so far. The method used here is not a prescribed method, nor a rigorous methodology which must be followed. We might summarise the method as follows.

- Begin with a high level process model.

- Follow this with a fairly detailed data model.

- The data model and the data processing model which may raise overlap data model or problems with the process model.

- The designer iterates around these activities, checking details with the system users, until a correct and consistent model is achieved.

During the 1990s there has been an explosion of interest in an approach to information systems design known as 'object-oriented' analysis and design. Although the object-oriented approaches have not yet proven themselves as robust as relational and E-R approaches, their impact is growing and it is now important for anyone working the information systems area to have an understanding of the basic concepts and how they related to the information model presented in this text. In this chapter we present a review of the main issues surrounding object-oriented information systems.

After studying this chapter you should be able to:

- understand the concepts of objects and messages

- understand the concepts of encapsulation and inheritance

- understand the relationship between objects and entities

- understand the likely developments in object-oriented and relational systems.

16.1   Introduction

During the 1990s there has been an explosion of interest in an approach to information systems design known as 'object-oriented' (OO) design. Although object-oriented programming languages have been available for many years, it is only recently that methods advocating OO systems analysis and design have become popular. The rise of OO analysis and design methods has coincided with the increasing power of local workstations and the ensuing demands from users to have things that they can understand rather than deal with things that the analysts and programmers can understand.

SQL has not been successful as an end-user language, as in order to use it effectively a user needs to understand the structure of the underlying database. Users may be very happy interacting with views as they package the data in a way which is appropriate to their needs. But trying to compose *ad hoc* queries in SQL is a task too distant from people's work to make it either desirable or effective. The argument runs that users want to interact with objects which mean something to them.

Another feature of the development of object-oriented systems is the perceived restrictions of relational systems. Relational systems are seen to be appropriate to highly text-based systems. With multi-media systems becoming more common — systems which use video, graphics and sound in addition to textual data — the relational model is seen to be something of an anachronism.

Although the object-oriented bandwagon is now firmly rolling, there are many problems with developing OO information systems. The concepts of OO are not as well-grounded as those of the data models presented here; particularly the relational model. There is no universally agreed definition of many of the fundamental concepts. There is no OO database architecture corresponding to the three level database architecture described in chapter 3. There are several competing methods for undertaking an OO analysis and design. In short, whilst an understanding OO concepts and their application is important for systems developers of the current era, the methods will continue to develop over the next few years. How useful they turn out to be remains to be seen.

16.2   The basic concepts

The fundamental principal underlying the object oriented approach to information systems development is that the enterprise should be represented as a number of communicating objects. OO systems employ the abstraction techniques described in chapter 5 and so it is not surprising to find that object instances are grouped together into object types, or object classes. In a typical information system one would expect to see Customer objects, Order objects, Product objects and so on. Indeed one of the fundamental premises of OO methods is that everything is an object.

The most important distinction between the data-centred methods described in this text and the OO approaches is that each object class is a *combination* of a data structure and the procedures which can act on that structure. Thus an object combines the data, processing and data processing models which go to make up the information model. An object can be seen as a miniature information system — something which provides information about a part of the enterprise which is perceived as a meaningful object (sometimes by the programmers and sometimes by the users). Because the objects have bundled the data and is a similar con... internal structure of an object can be changed w..... object being aware. It also provides a much simpler interface to both users and other objects. Users communicate with objects by sending messages to the objects. Users do not (in general) interact directly with the properties, or attributes of the objects. Such details are hidden from the users. Instead they send messages, or commands, which invoke the procedures maintained in the objects (called 'methods' in OO speak). These methods then provide a suitable response.

One further important aspect of the object concept is that objects are developed hierarchically. Lower level objects *inherit* the properties (both static attributes and dynamic behaviours) of higher level objects. This makes for a highly economical implementation and encourages the reuse of objects. For example if an organisation has a generalised object for displaying a standard window in a graphical user interface, then a programmer can define a new window as a member of that object class. The new window can then inherit the structure and processing of the standard window.

Object-oriented systems, thus provide a rather different view of information systems than that provided by the data-centred approaches of the relational model, functional dependencies between data elements and the entity-relationship approach. Most importantly, OO systems rely heavily on the two notions of inheritance and encapsulation. The interplay between these leads to a number of perceived benefits. The most notable of these is the concept of polymorphism. Polymorphism is the ability of different sub-types of objects to respond to the same message in different ways. For example, in an enterprise there may be various types of employee — some get bonus payments, some get commission, some just get a basic salary and so on. In an OO implementation the object class employee would be defined in terms of its attributes (*Name, Address, Position* and so on) and in terms of its behaviours. For example, there might be a behaviour called 'new' which enabled users to add a new employee and another called 'earns' which returns the amount which the employee earns. Since the amount which an employee earns varies with the different types of employee, the sub-types of employee will respond differently to the message; the employee object simply returns the required value, but the other types have to do additional calculations to include the bonus or commission. Thus different sub-types of employee will react differently to the message

earns, but the user will be protected from seeing this. Sometimes the
users does have to be aware of the differences, e.g. there might be a
method 'bonus' which retrieved and displayed just the employee's
bonus. Clearly this would only be appropriate for those employees who
were paid on a bonus basis.

Given this rather different way of looking at the enterprise, how does a
designer go about identifying objects and relationships and structuring
the information system?

16.3   Approaches to object-oriented design

Many extravagant (and typically unsubstantiated) claims have been
made for object-oriented techniques; most notably that the approach
leads to a more natural design. For example, Rosson and Alpert (1990)
claim that 'A particularly attractive aspect of OO design is that it seems
to support a better integration of problem and solution' (p. 361) whilst
admitting that 'very little empirical evidence exists concerning the
naturalness of objects as ways of representing problem entities' (p. 363).

In OO design analysts/designers are encouraged to identify objects in
the domain and use these as the basis for the conceptual model. Various
advice is offered on how to spot objects. For example 'identifying classes
and objects involves finding key abstractions in the problem space and
important mechanisms that offer the dynamic behaviour over several
such objects.' (Booch, 1992).

The analysts should 'develop an object model which describes the static
structure of the system with classes and relationships. The dynamic
model captures the temporal aspects, the functional model describes the
computation' (Rumbaugh *et al.* 1991).

'The designer looks for classes of objects trying out a variety of schemes
in order to discover the most natural and reasonable way to abstract the
system. ...In this phase the major tasks are to discover the classes
required to model the application and to determine what behaviour the
system is responsible for and assign these specific responsibilities to
classes' (CACM, 1990).

All this may be good advice, but it is rather vague. Unfortunately
vagueness characterises the OO world. One approach to developing OO
systems does not ask designers to identify 'objects' without help. Known
as the synthesist approach (Sully, 1993), it develops an object model
starting from a data-centred design consisting of an entity-relationship
model, dataflow diagrams and data processing model.

and delete...take directly into
application' and *fundamental activities* which are associated with the
purpose of the system, accessing and updating instances which can be
derived from a dataflow diagram.

This of course is exactly what we have advocated in this text in terms of
developing an information model. Consider the similarity between the
approach identified by Rumbaugh above and the approach described
here (and in detail in chapter 14). The data model describes a static,
structural view of the system, the process model describes the functional
view and the data processing view describes the temporal aspects. Sully
suggests that in the entity-relationship model, relationships suggest the
messages which will be needed for objects. For example, a Person is
assigned to a Schedule leads to a Person object and a Schedule object
plus a message 'assign' in both objects. A transaction/entity matrix can
be useful in identifying messages.

In Sully's approach, candidate objects are first identified from the entity-
relationship model (entities = objects). The designer then looks at the
accessing behaviour of the dataflows (i.e. how the processes read and
write to the datastores). These are attached to the objects as messages.
The designer then looks at the input and output flows on the DFD.
These can be used to create a higher level, coordinating object which
accepts inputs and produces outputs by sending suitable messages to
the coordinated objects.

16.4   An Object view of Disco Jones

In order to see this approach in operation, we will return to Disc Jones.
By looking at the final E-R model for Disco Jones (Figure 15.24) we
might identify the following possible objects: Customer, SpecialOrder,
Disc, Sale, Supplier, Label, Delivery, Order. The attributes of these
objects will be the attributes associated with the original entity
descriptions and the initial choice of messages which the objects must
respond to are identified on the transaction/entity matrix (Figure 15.37).
This provides the following basic object model (Figure 16.1).

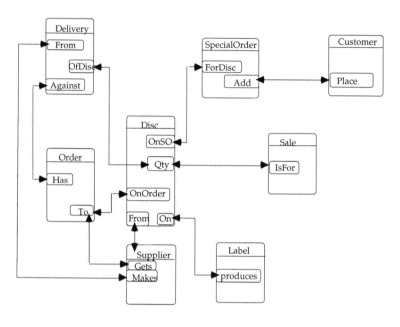

Figure 16.1   *Outline object model for Disco Jones*

The principal objects in Disco Jones will, not surprisingly, be very
similar to the entities in a data model of the application. The difference
is that the relationships and processing are bundled in with the object
definitions, with the links shown as arrows on the object diagram. By
considering the E-R model, the dataflow diagrams and the
transaction/entity matrix we can arrive at definitions of the objects. For
example, consider special orders. By examining the entities and
processing associated with special orders we can see that there is close
connection between these objects (indeed the mandatory participation of
these entities on the E-R diagram suggests this). Hence we might design
a special order object as follows:

object SpecialOrder
attributes
       SpecialOrderNo:
       SODatePlaced:
       CustomerName:
       CustomerAddress
methods
Record Sale = Delete (process 1.3.1)
Check special orders = Retrieve (process 4.3.2)
Place Special Order = Add (process 2.2) + insert link(s) to Disc objects

ordered or the Disc object will have a list of pointers to special ~~~~~ related to the discs (for a brief discussion of pointers see chapter 6). In a similar fashion, the processes associated with Disc will be grouped together into a Disc object, deliveries into a Delivery object, orders, suppliers and so on.

The final choice of objects will depend on a number of factors. Indeed the same sorts of factors which are associated with the second and third level designs of the information model (section 14.1). The conceptual information model can be mapped onto an object-oriented implementation.

16.5 Discussion

There can be little doubt that object-oriented systems are here to stay — at least for a few more years. What is in doubt is how the software will evolve to support such systems and how designers should go about developing such systems. Date (1995b) is very clear as to how relational and OO systems map onto one another. In his paper with Hugh Darwen entitled *The Third Manifesto* (Date and Darwen, 1995), he discusses which aspects of relational and which aspects of OO are worth pursuing. He comes out in favour of two main issues: 'objects as domains' and the idea of inheritance. One of the big debates about the difference between OO and relational systems is whether a relation is an object. Date makes clear that it is not, though his argument is rather esoteric. He argues that relations cannot be objects because you can do things with relations which you cannot do with objects. However, it is certainly true that in many systems an object implementation will have objects which correspond to the relations in a relational implementation of the same system.

Domains as objects are, however, more exciting and more consistent with the relational model. At present domains in the relational model are typically very simple data types — integers, strings and so on. However, there is nothing in the relational model which prevents users having very complex data types such as employees, products and so on. It is here, then, that the relational and object models can be brought together. In a similar fashion, we can see objects as being similar to views (*cf.* chapter 8). A view encapsulates certain functions and provides a tailor-made view of the underlying base relations for the users. Users can think of the system in terms of the objects which interest them and do not need to be concerned about the underlying relational design. They are protected from the complexities of having to construct their own queries if they have had appropriate views created for them. Although Date would argue that views are not objects because views are relations and relations are not objects, there is once again an intuitive understanding that they are talking about the same thing.

It would clearly be a retrograde step to throw away the benefits afforded by normalisation which ensures a database which minimises redundancy and the problems which we know that causes. It would also be a mistake to throw away the advantages which *ad hoc* queries provide and which are based on the secure relational model. People's requirements for information cannot be totally predicted before implementation and the ability to make *ad hoc* queries is central to the flexibility which was originally part of the design of relational systems.

However, it seems equally clear that we need to move information systems closer to people, to use concepts which they understand and to present things in a way in which they can access easily. Object systems also map neatly onto the graphical user interfaces (GUIs) of today where the whole structure of the system is based on sending messages (usually by selecting items from a menu) to objects. Users can have graphics to represent the objects in their systems and when they click on an object, the appropriate methods or messages which are applicable appear as menu items relevant to that object.

Over the next few years, then we can expect to see a coming together of the technologies. Relational systems will still remain as the large, corporate, centralised information structure. Hopefully these systems will provide increased support for user-defined domains (objects) which will constrain the processing which can be done and increase the amount of meaning which can be built into systems. At the 'client' end of this we can expect to see systems exploiting the idea of objects in presenting information to users in ways which are appropriate for their work.

16.6   Key points

Object-oriented systems represent an important new development in information systems and a difficult challenge for information system designers.

- Object-oriented systems employ the abstraction mechanisms of classification and aggregation.

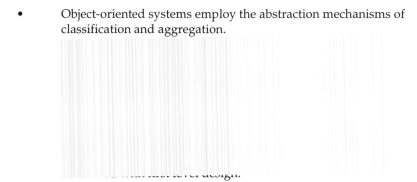

- Object-oriented systems and relational systems are likely to merge, building on the strengths of each.

Further reading

Date, C. J. (1995c) Marrying Objects and Relational. In Date, C. J. (1995b) *Relational Database Writings 1991–1994* Addison-Wesley: Reading, MA (pp 513–536)

> This is an edited version of an interview which Chris Date gave to *Data Base Newsletter* in 1994 and provides an excellent discussion of the issues facing OO systems, where they differ from relational, where there is confusion and what needs to be done. It is well worth reading in order to understand in more detail a number of the points raised in this chapter.

Sully, P. (1993) *Modelling the World with Objects* Prentice-Hall International, London

> Phil Sully presents a good overview of OO methods and includes some detail on the 'synthesist approach' described here.

Maidenhead, UK. To be published.

Benyon, D. R. (1995) A Data-Centred Approach to User Centred design In Gilmore, D. (ed.) *Proceedings of INTERACT '95* North Holland, Amsterdam

Benyon, D. R. (1996) From Tasks to Domains: Data Centred design. In Benyon, D. R. and Palanque, P. (1996) *Critical Issues in User Interface Systems Engineering,* Springer-Verlag, London

Benyon, D. R. and Green, T. R. G. (1995) Displays as Data Structures. In Nordby, K., Helmersen, P. H., Gilmore, D. J, and Arnesen, S. A. (Eds.) *Human-Computer Interaction: INTERACT-95.* Chapman and Hall, London

Bernstein, P. A. (1976) Synthesising third Normal Form Relations from Functional Dependencies *ACM Transactions on Database Systems* 1 no. 4 Dec.

Booch, G. (1992) *Object-oriented Design with Applications* Benjamin/Cummings

Bubenko, J. A. (ed.) (1983) *Information Modelling* Chartwell-Bratt, Lund, Sweden

CACM (1990) *Communications of the ACM* 33(9)

Checkland, P. B. (1981) *Systems Theory, Systems Practice* Wiley, Chichester

Chen, P. P-S. (1976) Towards a Unified View of Data *ACM Transactions on Database Systems (TODS)* vol. 1 no. 4 March pp 9 - 36

Codd, E.F. (1970) The Relational Model of Data for large shared Data Banks *Communications of the ACM* Vol 13 no.6, June

Codd, E. F. (1990) *The Relational Model for Database management Version 2* Addison-Wesley Reading, MA

Computer Journal vol. 28 no. 3 July 1985. pp 193 - 216

Date, C. J. (1995) *An Introduction to Database Systems* 6th Edition Addison-Wesley, Reading, MA

Date, C. J. (1995b) *Relational Database Writings 1991 –1994* Addison-Wesley: Reading, MA

Date, C. J. (1995c) Marrying Objects and Relational. In Date, C. J. (1995b) *Relational Database Writings 1991 - 1994* Addison-Wesley, Reading, MA (pp 513 - 536)

Date, C. J. and Darwen, H. (1992) *Relational Database Writings 1989 - 1991* Addison-Wesley, Reading, MA

Date, C. J. with Darwen, H. (1993) *A guide to the SQL standard* 3rd edition Addison-Wesley, Reading, MA

Date, C. J. and Darwen, H. (1995) The Third Manifesto. In Date, C. J. (1995b) *Relational Database Writings 1991 - 1994* Addison-Wesley, Reading, MA (pp 309 - 336)

DeMarco, T. (1981) *Structured Analysis. Structured Specification* Yourdon, Englewood Cliffs, NY

Eco, U. (1976) *A Theory of Semiotics* Indiana University Press, Bloomington

Elmasri, R. and Navathe, S. B. (1994) *Fundamentals of Database Systems* 2nd edition Benjamin/Cummings Redwood City, CA

Fagin R. (1979) Normal Forms and the Relational Database Operators. In *Proceedings of ACM and GMOD International Conference on Management of Data.* ACM Press, NY

Green, T. R. G. and Benyon, D. R. (1996) The skull beneath the skin; Entity-relationship modelling of Information Artefacts. *International Journal of Human-Computer Studies* 44 (6) 801–828

Halpin, T. (1995) *Conceptual Schema and Relational Database Design* 2nd Edition. Prentice-Hall, Sydney, Australia

Hirschheim, R., Klein, H. K. and Lyytinen, K. (1995) *Information Systems Development and Data Modelling: Conceptual and Philosophical Foundations* Cambridge University Press, Cambridge, UK

Howe, D. R. (1989) *Data Analysis for Database Design* 2nd Edition Edward Arnold, London

Kent, W. (1978) *Data and Reality* North-Holland, Amsterdam

Kent, W. (1981) Consequences of assuming a Universal Relation *ACM Transactions on Database Systems* 6, no. 4 Dec.

Kent, W. (1983a) The five normal forms *Communications of the ACM* vol 26 no. 2 Feb.

Kent, W. (1983b) The Universal Relation revisited *ACM Transactions on Database Systems* vol 8 no. 4 Dec.

Maier, D. (1983) *The Theory of Relational Databases* Pitman, London

Maier, D. , Ullman, J. D. and Varadi , M. Y. (1984) On the foundations of the Universal Relation Model *ACM Transactions on Database Systems* vol 9 no. 2 June

Martin, J. and McClure, C. (1985) *Diagramming techniques for Analysts and Programmers* Prentice-Hall, Englewood Cliffs, NJ

Modell, M. (1992) *Data Analysis, Data Modelling and Classification.* McGraw-Hill, New York

Preece, J. J., Rogers, Y. R., Sharp, H. C., Benyon, D. R., Holland, S. and Carey, T. (1994) *Human Computer Interaction* Addison-Wesley, Wokingham

Raphael, B. (1976) *The Thinking Computer* Freeman

Ross, R. (1981) *Data Administration and Data Dictionaries* AMACOM

Rosson, M. B. and Alpert, S. R. (1990) The Cognitive Consequences of Object-Oriented design in *Human Computer Interaction* vol 5 345 - 379

Rothwell, D. M. (1993) *Databases: an introduction.* McGraw-Hill International, Maidenhead

Rumbaugh, J., Blaha, M., Premerelani, W., Eddy, F. and Lorensen, W. (1991) *Object-Oriented Modelling and Design* Prentice-Hall, Englewood Cliffs, NJ

Senn, J. (1986) *Analysis and Design of Information Systems* McGraw-Hill International, Maidenhead

Shannon, C. and Weaver, W. (1949) *The Mathematical Theory of Communication* University of Illinois Press

Shlaer, S. and Mellor, S. J. (1992) *Object Life cycles.* Prentice-Hall, Englewood Cliffs, NJ

Simsion, G. (1994) *Data Modelling Essentials: analysis, design and innovation* International Thompson Publishing, Boston, MA

Smith, H. C. (1985) Database Design: Composing Fully normalised tables from a rigorous dependency diagram in *Communications of the ACM* vol 28 no. 8 Aug.

Stamper, R. (1985) *Information* B. T. Batsford Publishers, London,

Sully, P. (1993) *Modelling the world with objects* Prentice-Hall International, London

Sundgren, B. (1975) *The Theory of Database* Mason/Charter

Sundgren, B. (1979) Database Design in theory and practice In *Issues in database Management* by H. Weber and A. Wasserman (eds). North-Holland, Amsterdam

ter Bekke, J. H. (1992) *Semantic Data Modelling* Prentice-Hall International, London

Tsichritzis, D. and Lochovsky, F. (1982) *Data Models* Prentice-Hall Englewood Cliffs, NJ

Ullman, J. D. (1982) *Principles of Database Systems* Pitman, London

Ullman, J. D. (1983) On Kent's 'Consequences of assuming a Universal Relation, *ACM Transactions on Database Systems* 8 no. 4 Dec.

Van Duyn, J. (1982) *Developing a Data Dictionary System.* Prentice-Hall, Englewood Cliffs, NJ

Veryard, R. (1992) *Information Modelling: practical guidance* Prentice-Hall International, London

Weldon J - L (1981) *Data Base Administration* Plenum, NY

Wirfs-Brock, R., Wilkerson, B. and Weiner, L. (1990) *Designing Object Oriented Software.* Prentice-Hall, Englewood Cliffs, NJ

Wittgenstein, L. (1953) *Philosophical Investigations* Basil Blackwell, Oxford

Yourdon, E. (1989) *Modern Structured Analysis* Prentice-Hall, Englewood Cliffs, NJ